IN THE COMPANY OF SCHOLARS

IN THE COMPANY OF SCHOLARS

A COMMENTARY ON
AL-NAWAWI'S FORTY HADITH

BY **FURHAN ZUBAIRI**

Printed in the United States of America

First Publishing, 2020

ISBN: 9798676961732

Content input: Jawad Beg
Cover design, layout, and typesetting: Mohammad Bibi
Typeset in Lato, Nassim, and KFGQPC Uthmanic Script HAFS
Arabic Symbols: KFGQPC Arabic Symbols 01

Dedicated to my teacher, mentor, and friend
Shaykh Nomaan Baig.

CONTENTS

Transliteration & Pronunciation Key

Arabic Letter	Transliteration	Sound
ء	ʾ	A slight catch in the breath, cutting slightly short the preceding syllable.
ا	*ā*	An elongated *a* as in *cat.*
ب	*b*	As in *best.*
ت	*t*	As in *ten.*
ث	*th*	As in *thin.*
ج	*j*	As in *jewel.*
ح	*ḥ*	Tensely breathed *h* sound made by dropping tongue into back of throat, forcing the air out.
خ	*kh*	Pronounced like the *ch* in Scottish *loch*, made by touching back of tongue to roof of mouth and forcing air out.
د	*d*	As in *depth.*
ذ	*dh*	A thicker *th* sound as in *the.*
ر	*r*	A rolled *r*, similar to Spanish.
ز	*z*	As in *zest.*
س	*s*	As in *seen.*
ش	*sh*	As in *sheer.*
ص	*ṣ*	A heavy *s* pronounced far back in the mouth with the mouth hollowed to produce full sound.
ض	*ḍ*	A heavy *d/dh* pronounced far back in the mouth with the mouth hollowed to produce a full sound.
ط	*ṭ*	A heavy *t* pronounced far back in the mouth with the mouth hollowed to produce a full sound.
ظ	*ẓ*	A heavy *dh* pronounced far back in the mouth with the mouth hollowed to produce a full sound.
ع	ʿ	A guttural sound pronouned narrowing the throat.
غ	*gh*	Pronounced like a throaty French *r* with the mouth hallowed.
ف	*f*	As in *feel.*
ق	*q*	A guttural *q* sound made from the back of the throat with the mouth hallowed.
ك	*k*	As in *kit.*
ل	*l*	As in *lip.*
م	*m*	As in *melt.*
ن	*n*	As in *nest.*
ه	*h*	As in *hen.*

و	*w* (at the beg. of syllable)	As in *west*.
	ū (in the middle of syllable)	An elongated *oo* sound, as in *boo*.
ي	*y* (at beg. of syllable)	As in *yes*.
	ī (in the middle of syllable)	An elongated *ee* sound, as in *seen*.

﷿ Used following the mention of Allah, God, translated as, "Glorified and Exalted be He."

ﷺ Used following the mention of the Prophet Muḥammad, translated as, "May God honor and protect him."

﵇ Used following the mention of any other prophet or Gabriel, translated as, "May God's protection be upon him."

﵃ Used following the mention of the Prophet Muḥammad's Companions, translated as, "May God be pleased with them."

﵁ Used following the mention of a male Companion of the Prophet Muḥammad, translated as, "May God be pleased with him."

﵂ Used following the mention of a female Companion of the Prophet Muḥammad, translated as, "May God be pleased with her."

﵄ Used following the mention of two Companions of the Prophet Muḥammad, translated as, "May God be pleased with them both."

﵏ Used following the mention of the major scholars of Islam, translated as, "May God have mercy on them."

﵀ Used following the mention of a major scholar of Islam, translated as, "May God have mercy on him."

Introduction

From the Author

In the name of Allah the Most Merciful,
the Very Merciful.

All thanks and praise are due to Allah ﷻ, the Lord of the worlds, and may His blessings and protection be upon His last and final Messenger, Muḥammad ﷺ, his family, his Companions, and those who follow them until the end of times.

It truly is a great blessing of Allah ﷻ that He has given us the opportunity and the ability to read and learn the noble tradition of our Prophet ﷺ. In this short book we will be exploring the words, actions, approvals, and characteristics of the last and final Messenger, the leader of the Prophets, the most noble human being to walk on the face of this Earth, Muḥammad ﷺ. My teachers used to say that it is an honor and a privilege for a student to be given the opportunity to study anything related to the aḥādīth of the Prophet ﷺ.

Imām al-Nawawī's رحمه الله collection of forty ḥadīth, which actually consists of forty two ḥadīth, is perhaps the most widely studied ḥadīth collection across the Muslim world. It is taught and studied in Islamic schools, seminaries, universities, and ḥadīth gatherings across all academic traditions and throughout every Muslim community. The wide acceptance of this compilation and the fact that it is still being studied today is a testimony to the sincerity, hard work, and dedication of its author.

In this work, Imām al-Nawawī ﵀ selected those narrations that he felt covered the most fundamental concepts of faith and religion. Narrations that he felt captured the most important aspects of our faith and the essence of our religion. His motivation behind the compilation of this work was primarily based off of two narrations of the Prophet ﷺ that describe the virtues, rewards, and blessings of preserving and conveying the ahādīth of the Prophet ﷺ.

The first ḥadīth has been narrated from a number of different Companions and has a few different versions, but they all convey the same general meaning. The Prophet ﷺ said,

مَن حَفِظَ عَلَى أُمَّتِي أَربَعِينَ حَدِيثًا مِن أَمرِ دِينِهَا بَعَثَهُ اللهُ يَومَ
القِيَامَةِ فِي زُمرَةِ الفُقَهَاءِ وَالعُلَمَاءِ

"Whoever preserves for my nation forty ḥadīth related to its religion, Allah will then resurrect him in the company of the jurists and scholars."[1]

Imām al-Nawawī ﵀ in his introduction comments that this particular narration is weak.

The second narration is that the Prophet ﷺ said,

نَضَّرَ اللَّهُ عَبْدًا سَمِعَ مَقَالَتِي فَوَعَاهَا ثُمَّ بَلَّغَهَا عَنِّي فَرُبَّ حَامِلِ فِقْهٍ
غَيْرِ فَقِيهٍ وَرُبَّ حَامِلِ فِقْهٍ إِلَى مَنْ هُوَ أَفْقَهُ مِنْه

"May Allah cause to flourish a slave (of His) who hears my words and understands them, then he conveys them from me. There are those who have knowledge but no understanding, and there may be those who convey knowledge to those who may have more understanding of it than they do."[2]

---

1 al-ʿAsqalānī, *Sharḥ al-Arbaʿīn al-Nawawiyyah*, 72

2 Ibn Mājah, *al-muqaddimah*, 242

Through commenting on this compilation I hope Allah ﷻ includes me and whoever reads and benefits from this work within the virtues of both of these narrations as well.

This short book will try to provide a brief yet comprehensive explanation of each ḥadīth. I will approach each narration in a very structured and systematic manner highlighting the following four aspects:

1. The text of the ḥadīth along with its translation
2. A brief biography of the Companion narrator
3. Explanation of the ḥadīth
4. Lessons and Benefits

Alḥamdulillāh, through the grace and mercy of Allah ﷻ, I have been blessed with the opportunity to develop and teach a course through IOK Extension, which is now the IOK Part-Time Seminary, on the Forty Ḥadīth. While preparing for the course, I compiled a set of personal notes that I would use to teach the class. The course is also taught to the IOK Seminary students in their second year of the program. I thought that it would be beneficial for our students, as well as other students of knowledge and the community in general, to compile my notes into a short book that can serve as a brief explanation of this amazing work.

I compiled the notes primarily from five sources:

1. *A Commentary on the Forty Hadith of al-Nawawi* by Jamaal al-Din M. Zarabozo
2. *Jāmiʿ al-ʿUlūm wa al-Ḥikam* by ibn Rajab al-Ḥanbalī رحمه الله
3. *Sharḥ Matn al-Arbaʿīn al-Nawawiyyah* by Imām al-Nawawī رحمه الله himself
4. *al-Wāfī fī Sharḥ al-Arbaʿīn al-Nawawiyyah* by Dr. Muṣṭafā al-Bughā and Dr. Muḥyī al-Dīn Mistu
5. *Sharḥ al-Arbaʿīn Ḥadīthan al-Nawawiyyah* by ibn Ḥajar al-ʿAsqalānī رحمه الله.

This is not an original work; rather, it is a summary of what I found to be beneficial and important for beginning students of knowledge.

I would like to thank all of those individuals who provided suggestions, comments, improvements and took the time out of their busy schedules to edit this short work. May Allah ﷻ reward our IOK Seminary students Mudassir Mayet and Munir Eltal, continue to bless them, and increase them in knowledge. A special thanks to Sr. Sara Bokker and my wife, Fatima Rangoonwala, who provided benefcial suggestions and helped edit and review the work.

I ask Allah ﷻ to bless this small effort and make it beneficial for those who read it. I ask Allah ﷻ to bless all of us with a deep appreciation for the Sunnah of the Prophet and to increase our love for him ﷺ. May Allah ﷻ shower His blessings and mercy upon His last and final messenger, Muḥammad ﷺ.

Furhan Zubairi
Diamond Bar, CA
September 10, 2019 / Muḥarram 11, 1441

Brief Biography of Imam Al-Nawawi

His full name is al-Imām al-Ḥāfiẓ Muḥyī al-Dīn Abū Zakariyyā Yaḥyā ibn Sharaf ibn Murī ibn Ḥasan ibn Ḥasan ibn Muḥammad ibn Jumuʿah ibn Ḥizām al-Ḥizāmī al-Nawawī ﷺ. Muḥyī al-Dīn is a nickname that was given to him, which means "one who gives life to the religion". His kunyah is Abū Zakariyyā even though he never had a child by that name. As a matter of fact, he was never married. For short, he is known as Yaḥyā ibn Sharaf al-Nawawī or just al-Imām al-Nawawī, the great scholar of ḥadīth and fiqh.

He was born in the year 631 (1233) and passed away in the year 676 (1277) at the age of 45. Despite his young age, he left a legacy of written work that can fill multiple shelves in a library.

He was born in the small town of al-Nawā, just south of the famous city of Damascus, where he grew up and spent his childhood. From a very young age he was inclined towards scholarship and had a very deep love for the Quran. At the age of ten he started his initial studies and was so engrossed in them that the other kids would force him to play with them. He wasn't like the average kid. Some stories mention that he would even run away from them crying while reciting the Quran. He dedicated himself to studying religion.

At the age of 19, his father took him to Damascus to complete his studies. He enrolled at a school called Madrasah Dār al-Ḥadīth and lived in a small room at another madrasah, al-Madrasah al-Rawāḥiyyah. It is mentioned that the room was so small and full of books that if he had guests he would have to move the books to make room for them.

Imām al-Nawawī ﷺ was exceptionally bright, intelligent, and gifted. He was an extremely hard worker. The pursuit of knowledge literally consumed his entire life. He used to attend twelve daily lessons on assorted topics including the Arabic Language, Uṣūl al-Fiqh, Fiqh, Ḥadīth, and Uṣūl al-Ḥadīth. He would have approximately twelve hours a day of lessons and on top of that he would review all of these lessons daily.

He would not waste any time whatsoever. For six years straight, as a student of knowledge, he never slept until sleep overcame him. He would continue studying late into the night until he couldn't keep his eyes open and then would rest his head on his book for a short while. As soon as he woke up he would start studying again. He himself said that for two years he never slept on his bed. Even when he was walking in the streets he would be busy going over what he learned in his lessons and reviewing his notes.

In addition to his dedication to seeking knowledge, he was also known for his simplicity and modesty. Some of his biographical accounts mention that the only clothing he owned was a turban and a long robe. As mentioned earlier, he was among those famous scholars of the past who chose not to marry.

His dedication to knowledge, simplicity, modesty, and piety made him one of the leading scholars of his time. He was an expert in both Ḥadīth and Fiqh who left a legacy that is still read and studied till this day.

WORKS

Some of the biographers of Imām al-Nawawī ﷺ mention that there are three distinct aspects that stand out when going through his works:

1. Widespread acceptance and appreciation – at least two of his works are studied in every single Muslim community throughout the world and at least one of his works is found in every single masjid throughout the world.
2. How much he was able to write and produce in such a short period of time.
3. Writing style – clarity of expression, conciseness, and comprehensiveness.

He started writing and compiling works in the year 663 or 664. In a span of 12-13 years he wrote and compiled works that fill several shelves in any Islamic library. He wrote the most widely-used and accepted commentary on Ṣaḥīḥ Muslim that spans at least 9-10 volumes. It is said that he would fill an entire notebook every single day throughout his writing career. He authored over 50 works ranging in size from multi-volume collections to small booklets on a number of different topics. Some of his most famous works are:

1. *al-Minhāj fi Sharḥ Ṣaḥīḥ Muslim ibn al-Ḥajjāj* – The most widely-used commentary on *Ṣaḥīḥ Muslim.*
2. *al-Majmūʿ Sharḥ al-Muhadhdhab* – an amazing work on Shāfiʿī fiqh. It is a commentary on a standard Shāfiʿī text.
3. *Riyāḍ al-Ṣāliḥīn* – A compilation of carefully selected ḥadīth focusing on personal and moral reformation.
4. *al-Adhkār* - A beautiful compilation of daily litanies and phrases of remembrance for the morning and evening.
5. *al-Tibyān fi Ādāb Ḥamalat al-Quran* - A book that highlights the inward and outward characteristics and qualities students and teachers of the Quran should adorn themselves with.
6. *Bustān al-ʿĀrifīn* - A work on heart softeners and asceticism from words of the Prophet ﷺ, his Companions, and other righteous individuals.

DEATH

Imām al-Nawawī ﵀ passed away in his hometown of Nawā on the 24th of Rajab in the year 676 (1277) at the young age of 45. By the grace and mercy of Allah ﷻ, his accomplishments during his short life were equivalent to many who lived twice as long as he did. May Allah ﷻ reward him and elevate his rank.

ETIQUETTE WHEN MENTIONING SCHOLARS OF THE PAST

It is recommended for students of knowledge and anyone who reads and benefits from the works of the scholars of the past to pray for them and mention their names with a sense of respect, honor, and gratitude.

Imām al-Nawawī ﷺ writes in the introduction of his commentary on *Ṣaḥīḥ Muslim*, "It is recommended for every scribe (writer) of ḥadīth that when they come across the mention of Allah they should write "عز وجل" or "تعالى" or "سبحانه وتعالى" or "تبارك وتعالى" or "جل ذكره" or "تبارك اسمه" or "جلت عظمته" and whatever else resembles that. Similarly at the mention of the Prophet ﷺ, they should write "ﷺ" in its entirety and not just suffice with indicating towards it. And similarly for a Companion they should say رضى الله عنه and if it is a Companion and the son of a Companion they should say رضى الله عنهما. Similarly, they should pray and send mercy upon all the scholars and chosen people, meaning that is recommended as well... And whoever is careless of this has been deprived of great good and has lost a heavy reward."[1]

This is part of the scholarly and academic tradition; to mention those who came before with respect and honor.

1 al-Nawawī, *al-Minhāj fī Sharḥ Ṣaḥīḥ Muslim ibn al-Ḥajjāj*, 1:39

Imam Al-Nawawi's Introduction

Praise and thanks belong to Allah, Lord of the worlds, Eternal Guardian of the heavens and the earths, Disposer of all created beings, Who sent Messengers, may the blessings and protection of Allah be upon them all, to the legally responsible in order to guide them and clarify religious laws with definitive proofs and clear evidences. I praise Him for His favours and ask Him to increase His grace and generosity. I bear witness that there is no god but Allah alone, He having no associate, the One, the Subduer, the Generous, the Pardoner, and I bear witness that our master Muḥammad is His servant and His messenger, His dear one and His beloved, the best of created beings, who was honoured with the precious Quran, the enduring miracle through the passing of the years, and with the practices that illuimnate those seeking guidance; our master Muḥammad, favored with concise and comprehensive speech and tolerance in religion, may the blessings and protection of Allah ﷺ be upon him, the rest of the prophets and messengers, their families, and the righteous.

To proceed: It has been transmitted to us on the authority of ʿAlī ibn Abī Ṭālib, ʿAbdullah ibn Masʿūd, Muʿādh ibn Jabal, Abū al-Dardā'a, ibn ʿUmar, ibn ʿAbbās, Anas ibn Mālik, Abū Hurairah and Abū Saʿīd Al-Khudrī, may Allah be pleased with them all, through many chains of authorities and in various versions, that the messenger of Allah ﷺ said: "Whosoever memorizes and preserves for my people forty aḥādīth relating to their religion, Allah

ﷻ will resurrect him on the Day of Judgment in the company of jurists and religious scholars."

In another version it reads: "Allah ﷻ will resurrect him as a jurist and religious scholar." In the version of Abū al-Dardā'a it reads: "On the Day of Judgment I shall be an intercessor and a witness for him." In the version of ibn Masʿūd it reads: "It will be said to him: Enter by whichever of the doors of Paradise you wish." In the version of ibn ʿUmar it reads: "He will be written down in the company of the religious scholars and will be resurrected in the company of the martyrs." Scholars of ḥadīth agree that it is a weak ḥadīth despite its many chains of transmission.

The religious scholars, may Allah be pleased with them, have composed innumerable works in this field. The first one I know of who did so was ʿAbdullah ibn al-Mubārak,[1] followed by Muḥammad ibn Aslam al-Ṭūsī,[2] the godly scholar, then al-Ḥasan ibn Sufyān al-Nasawī,[3] Abū Bakr al-Ājurrī,[4] Abū Bakr Muḥammad ibn Ibrāhīm al-Aṣfahānī,[5] al-Dāraquṭnī,[6] al-Ḥākim,[7] Abū Nuʿaim,[8] Abū ʿAbd al-Raḥmān al-Sulamī,[9] Abū Saʿīd al-Mālīnī,[10] Abū

---

1 ʿAbdullah ibn al-Mubārak ibn Wāḍiḥ al-Ḥandhalī Abū ʿAbd al-Raḥmān. He is a Tabʿ al-Tābiʿī and one of the great scholars and imams of Islam. He passed away in the year 181.

2 Muḥammad ibn Aslam al-Ṭūsī Abū al-Ḥasan. He is among the scholars of ḥadīth and authored a book entitled A Refutation of the Jahmiyyah. He passed away in the year 242.

3 al-Ḥasan ibn Sufyān ibn ʿĀmir al-Nasawī al-Shaybānī. He was the ḥadīth scholar of Khurāsān during his time and passed away in the year 303.

4 Muḥammad ibn al-Ḥusayn ibn ʿAbd Allah al-Ājurrī. He was a Shāfiʿī jurist as well as a ḥadīth scholar and passed away in the year 360.

5 Abū Bakr Muḥammad ibn Ibrāhīm ibn ʿAlī al-Aṣfahānī. He was a scholar of ḥadīth and the author of al-Fawā'id and al-Muʿjam al-Kabīr. He passed away in the year 381.

6 Abū al-Ḥasan ʿAlī ibn ʿUmar ibn Aḥmad al-Dāraquṭnī. He is the author of the famous Sunan and the imam of ḥadīth during his time. He passed away in the year 385.

7 Abū ʿAbd Allah Muḥammad ibn ʿAbd Allah ibn Ḥamdawayh more well-known as al-Ḥākim. He is a very well-known scholar of ḥadīth, the author of al-Mustadrak ʿalā al-Ṣaḥīḥayn. He passed away in the year 405.

8 Abū Nuʿaym Aḥmad ibn ʿAbd Allah ibn Aḥmad al-Aṣfahānī. He is the author of Hilyah al-Awliyā'a and other works. He is a scholar of ḥadīth and a historian. He passed away in the year 430.

9 Abū ʿAbd al-Raḥmān Muḥammad ibn al-Ḥusayn ibn Muḥammad al-Sulamī. He was a sūfī shaykh who passed away in the year 412.

10 Abū Saʿīd Aḥmad ibn Muḥammad ibn ʿAbd Allah al-Mālīnī. He is the author of a 40 aḥādīth collection and *ʿAqīdah al-Salaf*. He was from the scholars of ḥadīth of Khurāsān and passed away in the year 481.

ʿUthmān al-Ṣābūnī,[11] ʿAbdullah ibn Muḥammad al-Anṣārī,[12] Abū Bakr al-Baihaqī,[13] and countless others, both ancient and modern.

I have asked Allah Almighty for guidance in bringing together forty aḥādīth in emulation of those eminent religious leaders and guardians of Islam. Religious scholars have agreed that it is permissible to act upon a weak ḥadīth related to virtuous deeds; despite this, I do not rely on this ḥadīth but on his having said the [following] sound ḥadīth: "Let him who was a witness among you inform him who was absent", and on his having said: "May Allah make radiant [the face of] someone who has heard what I have said, has learnt it by heart and has transmitted it as he heard it."

Furthermore, there were some religious scholars who brought together forty aḥādīth on the basic rules of religion, on subsidiary matters, or on jihād, while others did so on asceticism, on rules of conduct, or on sermons. All these are godly aims, may Allah be pleased with those who pursued them. I, however, considered it best to bring together forty aḥādīth more important than all of these, being forty aḥādīth which would incorporate all of these, each ḥadīth being one of the great precepts of religion, described by religious scholars as being "the axis of Islam " or "half of Islam" or "third of it ", or the like, and to make it a rule that these forty aḥādīth be [classified as] sound and that the majority of them be in the ṣaḥīḥ collections of al-Bukhārī and Muslim. I narrate them without the chain of narrators so as to make it easier to memorise them and to make them of wider benefit if Allah Almighty wills, and I append to them a section explaining obscure expressions.

Every person wishing to attain the Hereafter should know these aḥādīth because of the important matters they contain and the directions they give in respect of all forms of obedience, this being obvious to anyone who has reflected upon it. On Allah ﷻ do I rely and depend and to Him do I entrust myself; to Him be praise and grace, and with Him is success and immunity [to errors].[14]

---

11 Abū ʿUthmān Ismāʿīl ibn ʿAbd al-Raḥmān ibn Aḥmad al-Ṣābūnī. He was a ḥadīth scholar from Khurāsān and passed away in the year 481.

12 Abū Ismāʿīl ʿAbd Allah ibn Muḥammad al-Harawī al-Anṣārī. He was among the scholars of Khurāsān known for his expertise in the Arabic Language and ḥadīth. He passed away in the year 481.

13 Abū Bakr Aḥmad ibn al-Ḥusayn ibn ʿAlī al-Bayhaqī. He was a Shāfiʿī jurist and a leading scholar of ḥadīth. He passed away in the year 458.

14 The translation of the introduction is taken mosty from Ibrahim's and Johnson-Davies's translation of the Forty Hadith. Ibrahim, Ezzedin and Johnson-Davies, Denys. *An-Nawawi's Forty*

EXPLANATION

Imām al-Nawawī ؒ starts his introduction by first praising Allah ﷻ and then sending blessings and protection upon the Prophet ﷺ. This is the standard of how every single author, both past and present, start their works. Every single book within the realm of Islamic Studies, whether it is a book of tafsīr, ḥadīth, fiqh, or even Arabic grammar, will start with ḥamd and salām. The wording differs from being very short and concise to being very long and poetic. However, the purpose is the same, which is to start by praising Allah ﷻ and sending blessings and protection upon the Prophet ﷺ.

This is done for several reasons including following the style of the Quran as well as the style of the Prophet ﷺ when he used to speak. Another reason is the well-known ḥadīth narrated by Abū Hurairah ؓ that the Prophet ﷺ said,

كُلُّ أَمْرٍ ذِى بَالٍ لاَ يُبْدَأُ فِيهِ بِالْحَمْدِ أَقْطَعُ

"Every affair of significance that doesn't begin with praising Allah is severed."[15]

Similarly, there's another version of the ḥadīth in which the Prophet ﷺ said, "Every important affair that doesn't begin with praise of Allah and blessing upon me is devoid of any blessings." In order to avoid the warning mentioned in these narrations and to ensure that their works are blessed Imām al-Nawawi ؒ and others started with ḥamd and salām.

REASON BEHIND THE COMPILATION

After praising Allah ﷻ and sending protection and blessings upon the Prophet ﷺ, Imām al-Nawawī ؒ discusses why he compiled this collection of aḥādīth. He starts by mentioning the different chains and narrations of a particular ḥadīth that mentions the virtues and rewards for preserving forty aḥādīth. He mentions nine different companions that have narrated that the Messenger of Allah ﷺ said, "Whoever preserves for my ummah forty aḥādīth

Hadith. Dar Al Taqwa Ltd, 2010.

15 Ibn Mājah, *k. al-nikāḥ*, 1969.

related to the religion, Allah will then resurrect him in the company of the jurists and the scholars." Another narration states: "Allah will raise him as a jurist and a scholar." In the narration from Abū al-Dardā'a ﵁, it is stated: "On the Day of Resurrection, I will be an intercessor and witness for him." In the narration from ibn Masʿūd ﵁ it is stated that the Prophet ﷺ said, "It will be said to him 'Enter Paradise through any door you wish.'" In the narration from ibn ʿUmar ﵄, one finds the words, "He will be recorded among the company of the scholars and will be resurrected in the company of the martyrs."

After mentioning all these different chains and versions of the ḥadīth Imām al-Nawawī ﵀ himself states, "However, the scholars of ḥadīth agree that although this ḥadīth has numerous chains, it is weak." Despite the fact that the ḥadīth is weak, scholars throughout the past have compiled collections of forty aḥādīth in hopes of receiving the blessings and rewards mentioned in this narration.

Imām al-Nawawī ﵀ then lists a number of scholars from the past who compiled collections of forty aḥādīth such as ʿAbdullah ibn al-Mubārak, al-Dāraquṭnī, and al-Baihaqī. He then mentions that he sought Allah's guidance and counsel in gathering forty aḥādīth following the example of these great scholars of the past and how the scholars have agreed that it is permissible to act upon weak aḥādīth that deal with virtues.

Basically, he's clarifying that the basis for compiling this work wasn't simply a weak ḥadīth. Rather, he's following in the footsteps of these great scholars that came before him as well as the fact that the scholars have agreed that it's permissible to act upon weak aḥādīth that deal with virtues.

Perhaps that's why he then also clarifies that the basis for compiling this work wasn't simply this one weak ḥadīth but other authentic narrations from the Prophet ﷺ that encourage preserving and transmitting aḥādīth. For example, the Prophet ﷺ said, "Let him who was present amongst you inform those who are absent". Similarly the Prophet ﷺ said, "May Allah make radiant the slave who has heard what I said, preserved it in his memory and conveyed it in the way that he heard it."

After mentioning his motivation behind compiling this work, Imām al-Nawawī ﵀ discusses the nature of forty aḥādīth collections and mentions what distinguishes his collection and makes it unique. He mentions that in the past scholars compiled forty aḥādīth collections on various topics. There are collections that focus on faith and belief (uṣūl), practical matters (furūʿ), jihād, asceticism (zuhd), and manners (adab). He praises these works and makes duʿā for their authors.

He then mentions that his aim was to collect forty aḥādīth that not only incorporated these topics but also deal with more important and significant issues. Particularly those aḥādīth that dealt with the fundamentals of faith and practice. He wanted each ḥadīth in the collection to be one of those that is considered to be a great general precept from the foundations of religion. Those narrations that have been described as being the axis around which Islam revolves, or that are considered to be half of Islam or a third of Islam. He also mentions that he restricted himself to those aḥādīth that are authentic and that the majority of them are found in Bukhārī and Muslim.

He concludes by saying, "Everyone who desires and looks forward to the Hereafter must be familiar with these aḥādīth because they cover the most important aspects of the religion and offer direction to all forms of obedience of Allah. This is clear to anyone who ponders these aḥādīth. I rely only upon Allah and I entrust my affair only to Him. To Him is all Praise and Grace, from Him is Guidance and protection from error."

Since Imām al-Nawawī ﵀ mentioned that the Scholars have said that it's permissible to use weak ḥadīth when it comes to virtues, it's important to understand what he meant by that.

ACTING ON WEAK HADĪTH

Now a question that does arise is can weak aḥādīth be used? What is their legal value? Can they be used to derive or establish legal rulings? Can they be acted upon? Is it even permissible to narrate them?

The scholars of ḥadīth, uṣūl, and the jurists maintain that it is permissible to narrate weak aḥādīth with two conditions:

1. The ḥadīth should not be related to the field of belief or creed and
2. The ḥadīth should not be associated with legal rulings.

Based on the above two conditions, the majority of scholars are of the opinion that it is permissible to narrate weak aḥādīth that are related to virtuous deeds, encouraging good, discouraging evil, character, and stories.

However, when narrating a weak ḥadīth it should not be attributed directly to the Prophet ﷺ using definitive terms. Instead of using the expression "the Prophet ﷺ said such and such", one should say that "such and such was narrated about him" or "it has been narrated from him". The scholars use language that is in the passive voice.

When it comes to acting upon weak aḥādīth or using them as legal proofs there is unanimous agreement that it is not permissible to use weak aḥādīth for issues related to belief or creed. The vast majority also agree that it is not permissible to use weak aḥādīth to establish legal rulings. There is a disagreement amongst the scholars regarding the usage of weak aḥādīth related to the virtues or rewards of deeds, faḍāʾil al-aʿmāl.

There are basically three major opinions when it comes to using weak aḥādīth for faḍāʾil al-aʿmāl.

1. Weak aḥādīth should not be acted upon without exception, regardless of whether they are in beliefs, legal rulings, encouraging and warning, or righteous deeds. This was the opinion of great ḥadīth scholars such as, Yaḥyā ibn Maʿīn, al-Bukhārī, Muslim, ibn al-ʿArabī the scholar of the Mālikīs, Abū Shama al-Muqaddasī from the scholars of the Shafiʿī's, and ibn Ḥazm.
2. It is permissible to act upon weak aḥādīth without exception if there is nothing else related in that area of discussion. This was the opinion of Abū Ḥanīfah, al-Shāfiʿī, Mālik, and Aḥmad ibn Ḥanbal.
3. It is permissible to act upon weak aḥādīth that are related to fadāʾil al-aʿmāl, encouraging and warning (targhīb and tarhīb), and not those that are related to beliefs and legal rulings.

It is important to note that the scholars who permitted the use of weak aḥādīth for virtues and to promote good and warn against evil did not leave the door wide open to allow citing every single weak ḥadīth. Rather, they placed three conditions that regulate the use of weak ḥadīth:

1. That the ḥadīth not be very weak. Basically, it should not be a fabricated ḥadīth.
2. That the ḥadīth be within the scope of an authentic legal principle that is applied and accepted in either the Quran or Sunnah.
3. That its weakness, not authenticity, be realized when applying it.

> What that means is that when acting upon it a person should not believe with full certainty that the Prophet ﷺ himself actually said it or did it. Rather, there is a possibility that he did so and it is being acted upon in the hope of receiving reward.

No scholar permitted the narration and use of weak aḥādīth indiscriminately, but rather, stipulated the conditions mentioned above.

HADITH 1

Intentions and Sincerity

عَنْ أَمِيرِ الْمُؤْمِنِينَ أَبِي حَفْصٍ عُمَرَ بْنِ الْخَطَّابِ رَضِيَ اللهُ عَنْهُ قَالَ: سَمِعْتُ رَسُولَ اللَّهِ صلى الله عليه وسلم يَقُولُ: "إنَّمَا الْأَعْمَالُ بِالنِّيَّاتِ، وَإِنَّمَا لِكُلِّ امْرِئٍ مَا نَوَى، فَمَنْ كَانَتْ هِجْرَتُهُ إلَى اللَّهِ وَرَسُولِهِ فَهِجْرَتُهُ إلَى اللَّهِ وَرَسُولِهِ، وَمَنْ كَانَتْ هِجْرَتُهُ لِدُنْيَا يُصِيبُهَا أَوْ امْرَأَةٍ يَنْكِحُهَا فَهِجْرَتُهُ إلَى مَا هَاجَرَ إلَيْهِ".

رَوَاهُ إِمَامَا الْمُحَدِّثِينَ أَبُو عَبْدِ اللهِ مُحَمَّدُ بنُ إِسْمَاعِيل بن إِبْرَاهِيم بن الْمُغِيرَة بن بَرْدِزبَه الْبُخَارِيُّ الْجُعْفِيُّ، وَأَبُو الْحُسَيْنِ مُسْلِمُ بنُ الْحَجَّاج بن مُسْلِم الْقُشَيْرِيُّ النَّيْسَابُورِيُّ رَضِيَ اللهُ عَنْهُمَا فِي "صَحِيحَيْهِمَا" اللذَينِ هُمَا أَصَحُّ الْكُتُبِ الْمُصَنَّفَةِ.

From the Leader of the Faithful, Abū Ḥafṣ ʿUmar ibn al-Khaṭṭāb ﷺ who said I heard the Messenger of Allah ﷺ saying, "Actions are only by their intentions, and every person will only get what they intended. He whose migration was for Allah and His Messenger, his migration is for Allah and His Messenger, and he whose migration was to achieve some worldly benefit or to marry a woman, then his migration is for what he migrated for."

The two leaders of the scholars of ḥadīth, Abū ʿAbdillah Muḥammad ibn Ismāʿīl ibn Ibrāhīm ibn al-Mughīrah ibn Bardizbah al-Bukhārī and Abū al-Ḥusain Muslim ibn al-Ḥajjāj ibn Muslim al-Qushairī an-Naisābūrī narrated it in their two Ṣaḥīḥ collections, which are the most authentic compiled works.

THE NARRATOR

The narrator of this ḥadīth is the well-known Companion of the Prophet ﷺ ʿUmar ibn al-Khaṭṭāb ؓ. He is known as Amīr al-Muʾminīn Abū Ḥafṣ ʿUmar ibn al-Khaṭṭāb al-Qurashī al-ʿAdawī. He is the second of the four rightly guided Caliphs. He was the first person to be given the title of Amīr al-Muʾminīn, the leader of the faithful, which is the honorific title given to the Caliph.

He was a very well-respected member of Quraish and during the days of ignorance he was one of their assigned delegates. He was known for his strength, courage, bravery, and intelligence. He held a high position in their tribal society. Initially, he was a very staunch enemy of Islam and at one point intended to go and kill the Prophet ﷺ. The story of how he accepted Islam is widely known.

He accepted Islam in the sixth year of Prophethood after forty men and eleven women while the Muslim community was still very small. His acceptance of Islam was a huge encouragement for the small, but rapidly growing, early believing community. It was also a source of strength for the Muslims. Ibn Masʿūd ؓ mentions that the Muslims weren't able to pray at the Kaʿbah until ʿUmar ؓ accepted Islam. He migrated openly in defiance to the leaders of the Quraish and participated in every single battle with the Prophet ﷺ.

He was selected as the Khalīfah the day Abū Bakr ؓ passed away in the 13th year after Hijrah. During his time as Khalīfah the borders of Islam expanded to the East and West. He liberated Shām, Iraq, al-Quds, and Egypt. It is said that 12,000 pulpits were established during his time as Khalīfah.

He was martyred in the year 23 after being stabbed by a person named Abū Luʾluʾ al-Majūsī while he was praying fajr. He lived for three days after being stabbed and then left this world, may Allah ﷻ be pleased with him.

IMPORTANCE AND BACKGROUND

This ḥadīth has been described as the axis around which Islam revolves because it highlights the value, importance, and significance of sincerity. Islam, in its most technical sense, is external submission to Allah ﷻ through acts of worship, which include ritual acts such as prayer and fasting, and general acts such as being kind to one's neighbor. In order for these acts to be accepted and serve as a means for earning reward, mercy, and forgiveness, they have to be coupled with sincerity.

Imām Abū Dāwūd ﷺ said this ḥadīth is half of Islam. Imām al-Shāfiʿī ﷺ said this ḥadīth encompasses half of knowledge. A person's actions and knowledge can be classified into two broad categories of internal and external. This ḥadīth deals with sincerity, which is an internal action of the heart. In another narration, Imām al-Shāfiʿī ﷺ said it is a third of knowledge and can be applied to seventy chapters of fiqh. Imām Aḥmed ﷺ wrote that this ḥadīth covers one-third of knowledge. The rationale behind the description of a third is that a person's actions emanate from three places; the heart, tongue, and limbs. Sincerity is found in the heart.

Imām Aḥmed ﷺ also said that the foundation of Islam revolves around three aḥādīth:

1. "Actions are only by their intentions..."[1]
2. "Whoever introduces a new matter into this affair of ours..."[2] and,
3. "The permissible is clear..."[3]

Imām Abū Dāwūd ﷺ said, "I have written 500,000 aḥādīth from the Prophet ﷺ and I chose 4800 aḥādīth for my collection (Sunan). Out of those, four aḥādīth are enough for a person's practice of Islam:

1. "Actions are only by their intentions..."
2. "From the perfection of one's Islam is to leave that which doesn't concern him..."[4]
3. "None of you truly believes until you love for your brother what you love for yourself",[5] and
4. "The permissible is clear..."[6]

Imām al-Bukhārī ﷺ started his collection with this ḥadīth instead of a

1 Ḥadīth #1 in this collection
2 Ḥadīth #5 in this collection
3 Ḥadīth #6 in this collection
4 Ḥadīth #12 in this collection
5 Ḥadīth #13 in this collection
6 Ḥadīth #6 in this collection

formal introduction to highlight and emphasize the importance of sincerity; to remind the student or reader that an action that is not done sincerely for the sake of Allah 🕌 has no benefit in this life or the next. Ibn Mahdī 🕸 said, "It is a must for everyone who is to write a book to begin with this ḥadīth in order to instill within the student the need for a proper intention."[7]

As for the background of this particular ḥadīth, some scholars mention what is known as the story of "the migrant of Umm Qais", which is recorded in al-Ṭabarānī on the authority of ibn Masʿūd 🕸. He mentions that there was a Companion among them who had proposed to a woman known as Umm Qais, who used to live in Madinah. She refused to marry him unless he migrated to Madinah. So he migrated in order to marry her and was then known as Muhājir Umm Qais.[8]

EXPLANATION

The narration can be divided into three sections:
1.   Actions are only by their intentions
2.   Every every person will only get what they intended
3.   He whose migration was for Allah and His Messenger...

1. "ACTIONS ARE ONLY BY THEIR INTENTIONS..."

The word "innamā" in the Arabic Language is known as kalimah ḥaṣr, or the word of exclusivity. It gives the meaning of exclusivity and is usually translated as "only". Exclusiveness means that the ruling in the sentence applies to what is stated and is denied for anything else.

al-Aʿmāl is the plural of ʿamal, which means action or deed. The word in this context is general, referring to all types of actions including those of the body, speech, obligatory or voluntary, small or large. It is important to note that the actions being referred to here are those that are done consciously, voluntarily, or intentionally, not those that are done unintentionally or involuntarily. The reason for this specification is because an intention can only be coupled with a voluntary action. Within the scope of the Sharīʿah, human conduct or behavior with respect to its legal ruling falls into three

---

7   All of the statemetns regarding the importance of this ḥadīth are taken from ibn Rajab's *Jāmiʿ al-ʿUlūm wa al-Ḥikam*

8   al-ʿAsqalānī, *Sharḥ al-Arbaʿīn al-Nawawiyyah*, 82

broad categories:

1. Acts of obedience: These would include acts that are classified as obligatory (farḍ), mandatory (wājib), and recommended (mustaḥab[9]).
2. Acts of disobedience: These would include acts that are impermissible (ḥarām) and disliked (makrūh).
3. Permissible acts: These would include everyday acts the are considered to be permissible (mubāḥ).

A sincere intention is recognized and rewarded in acts of obedience and permissible acts. A person's intention will not be given any consideration when voluntarily engaging in an act of disobedience. Meaning, a person cannot engage in an act of disobedience with a noble intention expecting to receive reward.

al-Niyyāt is the plural of niyyah, which is translated as intention. Linguistically it is defined as intention, purpose, goal, aim, resolve, endeavor, and resolution. Technically, scholars define it is a determination, want, and aspiration to do something. It is the intent in the heart that accompanies and precedes any act of worship. Ibn al-Qayyim 🙵 defined it as the knowledge of a doer of what he's doing and the purpose behind the action.[10] The niyyah is an internal action of the heart.

The general meaning of this first portion of the ḥadīth is that actions will be weighed, judged, accepted, and rewarded according to their intentions. If the intention behind an act is pure and sincere then it will be accepted and rewarded. On the other hand, if the intention behind an act is corrupt and insincere, then the act will not be accepted or rewarded.

The scholars of ḥadīth have mentioned that there is an implied meaning in this statement, something that is understood but not explicitly mentioned. However, they offered different explanations of what that implied meaning is. Some scholars said that the implied meaning is "valid", meaning actions are only valid with intentions. The validity, acceptance or rejection, of an action depends upon the intention. If the intention is pure the act will be accepted and if it is corrupt then the act will be rejected. Others mention

---

9   This includes those acts that are broadly classified as Sunnah.

10   al-Jawziyyah, *Ighāthah al-Lahafān*, 1:137

that the implied meaning is "completeness" meaning an act is not complete except with intention. Others mention reward, that an act is rewarded only by its intention.

The simplest way to describe the meaning of the first part of the ḥadīth is what is mentioned above: actions will be weighed, judged, accepted, and rewarded according to their intentions. The purpose of this sentence is to encourage sincerity in one's actions.

However, if the meaning of the word "al-ʿamāl" is restricted to every conscious, voluntary act that a person performs and excludes those that are done unintentionally or involuntarily, there is no need for this implied meaning. Every act that a person does consciously or voluntarily is accompanied by an intention. The meaning of the statement is that every conscious act has an intention behind it as a driving force that brought it about. The Prophet ﷺ was stating a fact. This is the opinion of ibn Rajab al-Ḥanbalī. He writes, "Deeds occur or come about due to intention. So this is an informative statement indicating that conscious-voluntary acts don't occur except with an intention from the doer."[11]

2. *"EVERY PERSON WILL ONLY GET WHAT THEY INTENDED"*

This part of the ḥadīth starts with the word "innamā", which was discussed earlier. It conveys the meaning of exclusivity. In this statement the predicate (khabr) precedes the subject (mubtada'). In Arabic, the general structure of a sentence is for the subject to come first followed by the predicate. Switching the order also conveys the meaning of exclusiveness; meaning every person will get only what they intended.

Some scholars mention that this statement simply emphasizes the first. It has been emphasized to show the importance of sincerity and avoiding ostentation (riyā') and showing off. However, there is a principle in the Arabic language that a new statement adds meaning not just emphasis. The first statement clarified that every conscious deed has an intention behind it. This statement is explaining the consequences of that intention. If the intention is good and pure, then the deed will be accepted and rewarded. If the intention is evil and corrupt, then the deed will be rejected and a person may be deserving of sin.

An act performed by two individuals may be exactly the same; however

---

11 ibn Rajab, *Jāmiʿ al-ʿUlūm wa al-Ḥikam*, 23

the intentions behind it are completely different. One of them may have the loftiest intention, to earn the pleasure and approval of Allah, while the other's intention is to show-off and be praised by people.

This statement also conveys the meaning that a person will be rewarded for having multiple intentions for a single deed. A person can do one deed with several good intentions and they will be rewarded for each of those noble intentions. For example, if a person goes to the masjid they can have the intention of praying in congregation, reciting Quran, remembering Allah, supplication, charity, remaining in the masjid (iʿtikāf), and meeting the community.

This portion of the ḥadīth also indicates towards the power of a sincere intention. An everyday act can be transformed into an act of worship through a pure and sincere intention. For example, simple everyday tasks such as eating, sleeping, drinking, brushing one's teeth, washing the dishes, doing the laundry, and helping one's neighbors can be transformed into amazing acts of worship that will bring reward and blessings simply by having a pure and sincere intention. This is a very powerful concept. A person can transform their entire life into an act of worship through their intentions. That is the purpose of a person's existence; to worship Allah ﷻ. As Allah ﷻ says in Surah al-Dhāriyāt, "I created jinn and mankind only to worship Me."[12]

The Prophet ﷺ then gives a practical example of the principle highlighted in this ḥadīth in order to clarify the concept of actions and intentions.

3. "HE WHOSE MIGRATION WAS FOR ALLAH AND HIS MESSENGER"

Linguistically the word "hijrah" means to leave or avoid something, or to move from one place to another. Technically, the scholars define hijrah in two different ways. One of them is referring to a physical migration and the other is referring to a spiritual migration. The physical migration is to move from a land of disbelief to a land of belief in order to freely practice one's faith. Spiritual hijrah is to leave off sins and what is prohibited and return to Allah ﷻ in obedience and submission.

During the life of the Prophet ﷺ, migrating from Makkah to Madinah was an extremely difficult act of worship. Migrating to Madinah usually meant leaving one's home, wealth, family, and other material possessions.

12 وَمَا خَلَقْتُ الْجِنَّ وَالْإِنسَ إِلَّا لِيَعْبُدُونِ - 51:56

They would often migrate under the fear of persecution and harassment. It meant starting one's life over again. That is perhaps one of the reasons why the Prophet ﷺ chose migration as an example to illustrate the importance of sincerity and pure intentions.

Grammatically speaking, this is a conditional sentence and a general rule in the Arabic Language is that the condition has to be different than the result (consequence). However, here they are both the same. That is why there is an implied meaning that is understood. The meaning of the statement is, "Whoever migrates with the intention to please Allah and His Messenger, then his reward for his migration will be with Allah and His Messenger. And whoever migrates with the intention to achieve some worldly benefit or to marry a woman, then their migration is for that which they migrated."

Again, through the last portion of this ḥadīth, the Prophet ﷺ illustrates the principle of sincerity. He first mentions an example of a very difficult act of worship done with a pure intention. Then he mentions an example of the same difficult act of worship with a worldly intention.

LESSONS AND BENEFITS

1. THE MEANING OF SINCERITY

The word used for sincerity in Arabic is الإخلاص, the verbal noun from the verb يُخلِص / أَخلَصَ, which literally means to dedicate, be loyal, devoted, or faithful. It comes from the root letters خ ل ص that convey the meaning of purifying or cleaning something. When a person is sincere they have purified their intention and cleansed it from anything else besides Allah ﷻ. Sincerity means to worship Allah ﷻ with the sole objective or goal of attaining His nearness. Whenever a person performs an act of worship or a good deed the intention behind it is pure; it is being done solely to seek the pleasure of Allah ﷻ. They are not looking for any type of material benefit, praise, fame, and recognition from people. Rather it is being done out of submission and obedience to Allah ﷻ; out of love for Him and to earn His mercy and forgiveness.

As Allah ﷻ says, "And they were not commanded except to worship Allah, [being] sincere to Him in religion, inclining to truth, and to establish prayer and to give zakah. And that is the correct religion."[13] Similarly, Al-

13 وَمَا أُمِرُوا إِلَّا لِيَعْبُدُوا اللَّـهَ مُخْلِصِينَ لَهُ الدِّينَ حُنَفَاءَ وَيُقِيمُوا الصَّلَاةَ وَيُؤْتُوا الزَّكَاةَ ۚ وَذَٰلِكَ دِينُ الْقَيِّمَةِ - 98:5

lah ﷻ tells the Prophet ﷺ, "Say, 'My prayers and sacrifice, my life and death, are all for Allah, Lord of all the worlds; He has no partner. This is what I have been commanded, and I am the first to submit myself to Him."[14]

2. *THE IMPORTANCE, CENTRALITY, AND SIGNIFICANCE OF PURE INTENTIONS AND SINCERITY*

Ikhlāṣ is a precondition for the acceptance of anything a person does. Allah ﷻ only accepts those deeds that are done solely for His sake. For example, most books of fiqh mention the intention first while discussing the preconditions for prayer, fasting, zakāh, ḥajj, and all other acts of worship. Imām al-Bayḍāwī رحمه الله said, "Actions are not valid without an intention for an intention without action is rewarded, but an action without intention is useless. The example of the intention in an action is like that of the soul in the body. There is no existence for a body without a soul, and a soul can't exist in this world without a body."

3. *THE POWER OF A SINCERE INTENTION*

The intention is something that is very powerful. A sincere intention can transform a normal everyday activity such as sleeping and eating into a beautiful, meaningful, and powerful act of worship. A person can also be rewarded simply for intending to do something even though they may not be able to do it later on because of some type of excuse. ʿAbdullah ibn al-Mubārak رحمه الله used to say, "Many small actions are exalted by an intention and many great actions are diminished by an intention."

4. *SPIRITUAL MIGRATION*

Hijrah, or migration from Makkah to Madinah, was an extremely difficult, yet highly rewarding, act of worship. It was a sign of a person's faith, dedication, steadfastness, sincerity, and willingness to sacrifice one's wealth and safety for Allah ﷻ. After the conquest of Makkah, migrating from Makkah to Madinah was no longer considered to be an act of immense sacrifice and worship. The Prophet ﷺ said, "There is no migration after the conquest of Makkah."[15] Although the opportunity to migrate from Makkah to Madinah no longer exists, the opportunity to abandon sins and disobedience and

---

14 قُلْ إِنَّ صَلَاتِي وَنُسُكِي وَمَحْيَايَ وَمَمَاتِي لِلَّهِ رَبِّ الْعَالَمِينَ لَا شَرِيكَ لَهُ ۖ وَبِذَٰلِكَ أُمِرْتُ وَأَنَا أَوَّلُ الْمُسْلِمِينَ - 6 :162-163

15 Bukhārī, *k. Al-jihād wa al-siyar, b. Wujūb al-nafīr wa mā yajibu min al-jihād wa al-niyyah*, 2825

migrate to the obedience of Allah ﷻ does. The Prophet ﷺ said, "The true migrant is one who abandons disobedience and sins."[16]

5. LOVE OF THIS WORLD

One of the most consuming and powerful diseases of the heart is love of the world. The great scholar Ḥasan al-Baṣrī said, "Love of the world is the origin of every sin."[17] The root cause of every single sin or act of disobedience a person commits is love of this world. The reason for that one glance, the reason for cheating that one time, the reason for speaking ill of so and so that one time, or the reason why a person missed prayer is love for the life of this world.

The word "dunyā" literally translates as the world. It shares the same root letters as the verb danā/yadnū, which means to be near or to be close. It can also mean to be low or lowly. This world is called the dunya because of its nearness or because of its lowliness. The word signifies the enjoyments, blessings, or good of the present world or life; worldly blessings or prosperity. The term refers to temporal things or possessions; earthly things or concerns. It is not just the world and everything it contains. Rather, it is everything that pleases the self and does not lead to merit in the life to come. This can include wealth, property, material possessions, clothes, shoes, jewelry, tv's, cell phones, tablets, watches, cars, homes, food and drink, women, sports, and anything else that takes one away from remembrance of the life to come. Anything in this world that distracts a person from their true purpose in life can be classified as dunya.

One of the most powerful and constant reminders throughout the Quran is that the life of this world is temporary. It is not going to last forever. In several places throughout the Quran, Allah ﷻ reminds humanity about the reality of the life of this world. This world is temporary and fleeting and will eventually come to an end. The life to come, the life of the hereafter, is a life of eternity.

6. THE PROPHETIC METHOD OF CORRECTING PEOPLE'S MISTAKES

The Prophet ﷺ is the perfect example of a kind, caring, concerned, sin-

16 Ibn Mājah, *k. Al-fitan, b. Ḥurmah dam al-mu'min wa mālihi*, 3934

17 al-Suyūṭī, *Tadrīb al-Rāwī*, 1: 486

cere, and genuine teacher. When people would make mistakes he wouldn't call them out in public, embarrass them, scold them, reprimand them, or yell at them. He would correct their mistakes in such a way that would help them change and increase their love, appreciation, and respect for him. Muʿāwiyah ibn al-Ḥakam said, "I have not seen a better teacher than the the Prophet ."[18] This ḥadīth is an example of the Prophetic method for correcting people's mistakes. The Prophet didn't single out this individual by name and embarrass him in front of the other Companions. He turned the incident into a teaching moment and used it to explain a general and important principle.

---

18   Muslim, k. Al-masājid wa mawāḍiʿ al-ṣalāh, b. Taḥrīm al-kalām fī al-ṣalāh wa naskh mā kāna min ibāḥatihi, 537

HADITH 2

Islam, Iman, and Ihsan

عَنْ عُمَرَ رَضِيَ اللَّه عَنْهُ أَيْضًا قَالَ: "بَيْنَمَا نَحْنُ جُلُوسٌ عِنْدَ رَسُولِ اللَّهِ صلى الله عليه و سلم ذَاتَ يَوْمٍ، إذْ طَلَعَ عَلَيْنَا رَجُلٌ شَدِيدُ بَيَاضِ الثِّيَابِ، شَدِيدُ سَوَادِ الشَّعْرِ، لَا يُرَى عَلَيْهِ أَثَرُ السَّفَرِ، وَلَا يَعْرِفُهُ مِنَّا أَحَدٌ. حَتَّى جَلَسَ إلَى النَّبِيِّ صلى الله عليه و سلم . فَأَسْنَدَ رُكْبَتَيْهِ إلَى رُكْبَتَيْهِ، وَوَضَعَ كَفَّيْهِ عَلَى فَخِذَيْهِ، وَقَالَ: يَا مُحَمَّدُ أَخْبِرْنِي عَنْ الْإِسْلَامِ. فَقَالَ رَسُولُ اللَّهِ صلى الله عليه و سلم الْإِسْلَامُ أَنْ تَشْهَدَ أَنْ لَا إلَهَ إلَّا اللَّهُ وَأَنَّ مُحَمَّدًا رَسُولُ اللَّهِ، وَتُقِيمَ الصَّلَاةَ، وَتُؤْتِيَ الزَّكَاةَ، وَتَصُومَ رَمَضَانَ، وَتَحُجَّ الْبَيْتَ إنْ اسْتَطَعْت إلَيْهِ سَبِيلًا. قَالَ: صَدَقْت . فَعَجِبْنَا لَهُ يَسْأَلُهُ وَيُصَدِّقُهُ! قَالَ: فَأَخْبِرْنِي عَنْ الْإِيمَانِ. قَالَ: أَنْ تُؤْمِنَ بِاَللَّهِ وَمَلَائِكَتِهِ وَكُتُبِهِ وَرُسُلِهِ وَالْيَوْمِ الْآخِرِ، وَتُؤْمِنَ بِالْقَدَرِ خَيْرِهِ وَشَرِّهِ .قَالَ: صَدَقْت. قَالَ: فَأَخْبِرْنِي عَنْ الْإِحْسَانِ. قَالَ: أَنْ تَعْبُدَ اللَّهَ كَأَنَّك تَرَاهُ، فَإِنْ لَمْ تَكُنْ تَرَاهُ فَإِنَّهُ يَرَاك. قَالَ: فَأَخْبِرْنِي عَنْ السَّاعَةِ. قَالَ: مَا الْمَسْئُولُ عَنْهَا بِأَعْلَمَ مِنْ السَّائِلِ. قَالَ: فَأَخْبِرْنِي عَنْ أَمَارَاتِهَا؟ قَالَ: أَنْ تَلِدَ الْأَمَةُ رَبَّتَهَا، وَأَنْ تَرَى الْحُفَاةَ الْعُرَاةَ الْعَالَةَ رِعَاءَ الشَّاءِ يَتَطَاوَلُونَ فِي الْبُنْيَانِ. ثُمَّ انْطَلَقَ، فَلَبِثْتُ مَلِيًّا، ثُمَّ قَالَ: يَا عُمَرُ أَتَدْرِي مَنْ السَّائِلُ؟ قُلْتُ: اللَّهُ وَرَسُولُهُ أَعْلَمُ. قَالَ: فَإِنَّهُ جِبْرِيلُ أَتَاكُمْ يُعَلِّمُكُمْ دِينَكُمْ".

رَوَاهُ مُسْلِمٌ.

From ʿUmar ibn al-Khaṭṭāb ﵁ who said: One day while we were sitting with the Messenger of Allah ﷺ a man appeared before us whose clothes were extremely white and whose hair was extremely black. No signs of travel could be seen on him and none of us knew him. He walked up and sat down in front of the Prophet ﷺ, with his knees touching against the Prophet's ﷺ and placing the palms of his hands on his thighs he said, "O Muḥammad, tell me about Islam." The Messenger of Allah ﷺ said, "Islam is to bear witness that there is no deity worthy of worship but Allah and that Muḥammad is the Messenger of Allah, to perform prayer, to pay zakāh, to fast in Ramaḍān, and to make the pilgrimage to the House if you are able to do so." He said, "You have spoken the truth"; and we were amazed at him asking him and saying that he had spoken the truth. He [the man] then said, "Tell me about īmān." The Prophet ﷺ said, "It is to believe in Allah, His Angels, His Books, His Messengers, and the Last Day, and to believe in divine pre-knowledge (qadr), both the good and the evil of it." He said, "You have spoken the truth." He [the man] said, "Then tell me about iḥsān." The Prophet ﷺ said, "It is to worship Allah as though you see Him, and if you do not see Him, then He truly sees you." He said, "Then tell me about the Hour." The Prophet ﷺ said, "The one questioned about it knows no better than the questioner." He said, "Then tell me about its signs." The Prophet ﷺ said, "That the slave-girl will give birth to her mistress, and that you will see barefoot naked destitute shepherds competing in constructing lofty buildings." Then he [the man] left, and I stayed for a time. Then he [the Prophet ﷺ] said, "O 'Umar, do you know who the questioner was?" I said, "Allah and His Messenger know best." He said, "It was Jibrīl, who came to teach you your religion."

Muslim narrated it.

IMPORTANCE

This ḥadīth is considered to be one of the most important and comprehensive sayings of the Prophet ﷺ. It is in essence a summary of the entire mission and message of the Prophet ﷺ. It is a summary of what has been explained in detail throughout the life of the Prophet ﷺ through his sunnah; his sayings, actions, and approvals. The vast majority of aḥādīth discuss three major subjects: beliefs, actions, and manners and this narration addresses all three. It touches upon almost every deed of Islam; both external and internal.

Some scholars have said that all of the various branches of the Sharīʿah return to this ḥadīth and are derived from it. Just like Sūrah al-Fātiḥah is a summary of the Quran, similarly this ḥadīth is a summary of the entire corpus of aḥādīth. That is why it is known as Umm al-Ḥadīth, or "the foundation of ḥadīth". It is also known as the Ḥadīth of Jibrīl.

Ibn Ḥajar ؒ mentions that this incident took place near the end of the life of the Prophet ﷺ. Others mention it took place a little before the Farewell Pilgrimage. It is as if the Prophet ﷺ was summarizing his mission and message for his Companions ﷞.

EXPLANATION

The narration starts by describing how the Angel Jibrīl ؑ came to the Prophet ﷺ and asked a series of questions. He came in such a manner that would attract the attention of the Companions ﷞ towards him and his questions. That is why he did many things that seem contradictory. His appearance was immaculate; deep, dark black hair, and extremely white clothes. His appearance made it seem that he was a local from the city. Yet, he was unknown to the people, meaning that he must have been a traveler.

He entered the gathering saying salām, showing that he was aware of the manners and etiquettes of a gathering. Yet, he climbed over the necks of people to reach the Prophet ﷺ, showing that he was ill-mannered. Once he reached the Prophet ﷺ, he sat in front of him with his hands on his thighs like one sits in prayer. Then he placed his hands on the thighs of the Prophet ﷺ showing that he was unaware of the proper etiquettes.

He then asks the Prophet ﷺ a question, implying that he was unaware of the answer, but then he would verify the response showing that he was actually aware of the answer. Again, he did all these seemingly contradictory things to attract the attention of the gathering towards himself, so that they would pay close attention to what he was saying.

Jibrīl (عليه السلام) then asked the Prophet ﷺ a series of four important and fundamental questions:

1. What is Islam?
2. What is īmān?
3. What is iḥsān? and
4. When is the Day of Judgment?

ISLAM

The Prophet ﷺ responded to the first question saying, "Islam is to bear witness that there is no deity worthy of worship but Allah and that Muḥammad is the Messenger of Allah, to perform prayers, to pay zakāh, to fast in Ramadan, and to make the pilgrimage to the House if you are able to do so." That is how the Prophet ﷺ explained the concept of Islam.

It is important to have a holistic understanding of the word Islam. Oftentimes people translate Islam as peace or they say Islam means peace. Islam does not mean peace. Linguistically, the word Islam is a verbal noun from the verb أَسلَمَ/يُسلِمُ, which means to submit or to obey. Islam literally means submission or obedience; submission through devotion, servitude, and obedience whether that's with the heart, tongue, or limbs. Technically speaking, Islam has two definitions. The first definition is that Islam is the proper noun for the entire way of life or religion (dīn) revealed by Allah ﷻ. As Allah ﷻ says, "Today I have perfected your religion for you, completed My blessing upon you, and chosen as your religion Islam."[19] Allah ﷻ also says, "True Religion, in God's eyes, is Islam."[20]

The second definition is external submission (الاِنْقِياد الظاهِرى) through the tongue and limbs. Islam consists of external acts of submission, obedience, devotion, and servitude to Allah ﷻ. That is why the Prophet ﷺ defined Islam as to bear witness that there is no God but Allah and that Muḥammad ﷺ is His Messenger, to establish prayer, to give zakāh, to fast

19 5:3 - الْيَوْمَ أَكْمَلْتُ لَكُمْ دِينَكُمْ وَأَتْمَمْتُ عَلَيْكُمْ نِعْمَتِي وَرَضِيتُ لَكُمُ الْإِسْلَامَ دِينًا
20 3:19 - إِنَّ الدِّينَ عِندَ اللَّهِ الْإِسْلَامُ

Ramadan, and to perform ḥajj if one is able to do so. All five of these are external acts of submission, obedience, and devotion and they are the fundamental pillars of Islam. The Prophet's ﷺ intent is not to limit Islam to these five specific acts, rather he is indicating to five different categories of actions that are expressions of external submission. The testimony of faith represents verbal acts of submission, prayer represents physical acts of submission, fasting represents refraininnment as an act of submission, zakāh represents financial acts of submission, and ḥajj represents those acts of submission that have both a physical and financial component.

The questioner then affirms the answer of the Prophet ﷺ saying, "You have spoken the truth". This shocked ʿUmar رضي الله عنه along with the other companions who were present. Why would this individual ask a question and then affirm the answer? As mentioned earlier, one of the reasons was to grab the attention of the audience to make sure that they were paying close attention.

ĪMĀN

The questioner then asks the Prophet ﷺ about īmān. The Prophet ﷺ responds by saying, "It is to believe in Allah, His Angels, His Books, His Messengers, and the Last Day, and to believe in divine pre-knowledge (qadr), both the good and the evil of it." The Prophet ﷺ defined īmān with what are known as the six articles of faith:

1. Belief in Allah,
2. His Angels,
3. His books,
4. His Messengers,
5. The Last Day, and
6. Divine Pre-Knowledge

Belief in Allah ﷻ includes believing in His existence, oneness, might, power, glory, and omnipotence. Tawḥīd, belief in the oneness of Allah ﷻ, is the cornerstone of Islamic creed. This concept is so important that the primary purpose of all Prophets and Messengers was to explain it to their people. It is the belief that Allah ﷻ is One without partners in His dominion, One without similitude in His essence and attributes, and One without rival in His Divinity in worship. It is the belief that Allah ﷻ alone is the Creator of the Heavens and the Earth and everything they contain without partner. He alone is the Nourisher, the Sustainer, the One who gives life and death, the Almighty, the All-Powerful, the All-Hearing, the All-Seeing, the All-Knowing, and the Controller of all affairs. He alone has the right to be worshipped and He is completely unique. Nothing in this universe resembles Him in any way, shape, or form.

Belief in His Angels includes believing in their existence, their descriptions as mentioned in various verses of the Quran and aḥādīth of the Prophet ﷺ, and the tasks that have been assigned to them. Angels are a unique creation of Allah ﷻ that are honored and noble. They are made of a unique light and have been created to worship, obey, and serve Allah ﷻ. They do not disobey the orders of Allah and do as they are commanded.

Belief in His books means to believe in all of the scriptures that were divinely revealed to the Prophets and Messengers throughout history including the Ṣuḥuf of Ibrāhīm, the Psalms of David, the Towrah, the Injīl, and the Quran. The Quran is the last and final revelation sent for the guidance of humanity until the end of times.

Belief in His Messengers is considered to be the second most fundamental principle of faith after belief in Allah ﷻ. It entails believing in and accepting all the Prophets and Messengers Allah ﷻ has sent for the guidance of humanity. Starting from Adam ﷺ until the last and final Messenger, the Seal of Prophethood, Muḥammad ﷺ. One must believe in all of them and accept the message they came with as the truth.

Belief in the Last Day, or belief in the ākhirah, is referring to the fundamental concept of life after death. It is considered to be the third most important article of faith after belief in Allah and His Prophets and Messengers. One must have firm conviction that the life of this world is temporary and that the life to come is for eternity, and one must believe in resurrection and judgment. One must believe that every single human will be held accountable for what they used to do in the life of this world. It includes belief in the concepts of accountability, reward and punishment, forgiveness and repentance, Paradise and Hell.

The last article of faith, and perhaps the most complex and complicated, is belief in Divine Pre-Knowledge, which is known as al-qaḍā'a wa al-qadr. Belief in al-Qadr means to believe that Allah ﷻ has eternal knowledge regarding all things; whatever has happened, whatever is happening, and what will happen, regardless of whether that thing is good or bad, big or small, apparent or hidden, physical or metaphysical. All of this has been recorded in al-Lawḥ al-Maḥfūẓ, the Preserved Tablet. Allah ﷻ knows, with His ultimate and infinite knowledge, what all His creation will do, even before the creation took place. Allah ﷻ recorded all this knowledge in the Preserved Tablet. It is the will of Allah that these things will take place, whether they are good or bad. Belief in al-qaḍā'a means to believe that everything that has happened in this universe, everything that is happening, and everything that will happen in the future, whether it's good or bad, physical or metaphysical, is created by Allah ﷻ. Nothing happens in this universe without the will and decree of Allah ﷻ. So much so that all of the actions of human beings, both good and bad, intentions and thoughts, are also brought into existence by Allah.

Linguistically the word إيمان is derived from the verb أمن/يأمن, which means to be safe or feel safe. Later the word إيمان started being used to convey the meaning of تَصدِيق, which means belief or faith. The reason or the relationship between the two meanings is that a person who is believed is now safe or protected from being rejected or called a liar. The primary linguistic meaning given for īmān is belief or faith, which is submission specifically through the heart.

Technically, throughout history scholars have defined īmān according to their own personal theological and religious context. Although the wording of the definitions may differ, they are describing the same reality. Some scholars, specifically the scholastic theologians, define īmān as believing everything that is necessarily known from the teachings of the Prophet ﷺ.[21] A simpler version of this definition is to believe everything that is necessarily known to be a part of the religion.[22]

Another more comprehensive definition developed a little later on. It describes īmān as a complex reality made up of three primary components:

1. Belief in the heart,
2. Declaration with the tongue, and
3. Actions with the limb

---

21 التَّصْدِيْقُ بِمَا عُلِمَ مَجِيءُ النَّبِي ﷺ بِهِ ضَرُوْرَةً، تَفْصِيْلاً فِيْمَا عُلِمَ تَفْصِيْلاً وَإِجْمَالاً فِيْمَا عُلِمَ إِجْمَالاً

22 تَصْدِيْقُ مَا عُلِمَ مِنَ الدِّيْنِ بِالضَّرُوْرَةِ

According to this definition, the root of īmān is the firm unshakeable belief in one's heart in the existence and oneness of Allah ﷻ and all of the articles of faith. A person then declares this faith with the tongue through the testimony of faith, by saying, "I bear witness that there is no deity worthy of worship except for Allah, and I bear witness that Muḥammad ﷺ is His servant and messenger." This faith then expresses itself through a person's behavior and speech.

Both Islam and īmān have been described and compared in different ways. Ibn Kathīr رحمه الله writes that īmān is more specific than Islam; it is a higher level of faith and practice. This is also shown in the Ḥadīth of Jibrīl عليه السلام when he questioned the Prophet ﷺ about Islam, then īmān, and then iḥsān. Moving the general matter to one more specific, then even more specific. Another way of understanding it is that Islam refers to outward submission and īmān refers to internal submission. Īmān refers to affirmation in one's heart, firm and unshakeable belief in the oneness of Allah ﷻ and in His last and final Messenger ﷺ. Islam refers to complete surrender and obedience to Allah ﷻ and His Messenger ﷺ; they complement one another. Belief in the heart has to express itself through statements and actions and at the same time statements and actions don't mean anything without īmān. Īmān is an inner quality of the heart and manifests itself outwardly while Islam starts outward and culminates in the heart. They are necessities of one another. Īmān without Islam is impossible and Islam without īmān is impossible. Basically, it is not possible to be a Muslim but not a Mu'min or be a Mu'min without being a Muslim.

The questioner then affirms the answer of the Prophet ﷺ saying, "You have spoken the truth". This second affirmation was just as shocking and surprising as the first. Why would this individual ask a question and then affirm the answer? As mentioned above, one of the reasons was to grab the attention of the audience to make sure that they were paying close attention.

IḤSĀN

The questioner then asks the Prophet ﷺ about iḥsān. The Prophet ﷺ responds, "It is to worship Allah as though you see Him, and if you do not see Him, then He truly sees you." Linguistically, iḥsān is a verbal noun from the verb أَحسَنَ/يُحسِنُ, which means to do something well, to master something, be proficient, to do good, or be charitable. The word iḥsān literally means perfection or goodness. Iḥsān is the concept of doing things in the best way possible; it is the hallmark of an upright, moral, and God-conscious believer. A believer should strive for excellence and perfection in everything they do. In another ḥadīth the Prophet ﷺ said, "Truly Allah has prescribed iḥsān upon everything."[23] Iḥsān is considered to be the highest level or station a person can reach when performing an act of worship. It is worship or any other deed accompanied with God-consciousness, which leads to humility, concentration, and sincerity in one's actions. This state of iḥsān is achieved by recognizing that Allah ﷻ is watching and is aware of a person's innermost thoughts and feelings.

SIGNS OF THE DAY OF JUDGMENT

The questioner then asks when is the Day of Judgment. The Prophet ﷺ responds with a statement that is full of wisdom and humility. He says, "The one questioned about it knows no better than the questioner." The Prophet ﷺ is clarifying that knowledge of the unseen, which includes knowing when the Day of Judgment will take place, is known only to Allah ﷻ. The ghayb, or the unseen, refers to what is invisible in the sense of belonging to another order of reality; things that lie beyond human faculties of perception. It can refer to those things that have not yet come into existence, or have come into existence but Allah ﷻ has not informed anyone regarding it. al-Ghayb includes information such as when and where a person will be born, what they are going to do, how many breaths they are going to take, and where they are going to die. All of this information is known only to Allah ﷻ. It also includes when Resurrection and the Day of Judgment will occur. al-Ghayb is the realm of Allah ﷻ, only He alone has knowledge of it. Allah ﷻ says in Sūrah al-Naml, "Say: None in the heavens or on the earth know the unseen, except Allah."[24] Allah ﷻ explains in Sūrah al-Anʿām, "He has the keys to the unseen: no one knows them but Him. He knows all that is in the land and sea. No leaf falls without His knowledge, nor is there a single grain in the darkness of the earth, or anything, fresh or withered, that is not written in a clear Record."[25] In Sūrah Luqmān Allah ﷻ says, "Knowledge of the Hour [of

23 Muslim, *k. al-ṣayd wa al-dhabā'iḥ wa mā yu'kalu min al-ḥaywān, b. Al-amr bi iḥsān al-dhabḥ wa al-qatl wa taḥdīd al-shafrah*, 1955

24 27:65 - قُل لَّا يَعْلَمُ مَن فِي السَّمَاوَاتِ وَالْأَرْضِ الْغَيْبَ إِلَّا اللَّـهُ

25 6:59 - وَعِندَهُ مَفَاتِحُ الْغَيْبِ لَا يَعْلَمُهَا إِلَّا هُوَ ۚ وَيَعْلَمُ مَا فِي الْبَرِّ وَالْبَحْرِ ۚ وَمَا تَسْقُطُ مِن وَرَقَةٍ إِلَّا يَعْلَمُهَا وَلَا حَبَّةٍ فِي ظُلُمَاتِ الْأَرْضِ وَلَا رَطْبٍ وَلَا يَابِسٍ إِلَّا فِي كِتَابٍ مُّبِينٍ

Resurrection] belongs to God; it is He who sends down the relieving rain and He who knows what is hidden in the womb. No soul knows what it will reap tomorrow, and no soul knows in what land it will die; it is God who is all knowing and all aware."[26]

The questioner then asks the Prophet ﷺ to tell him about some of the signs of the Day of Judgment. The Prophet ﷺ responds by describing two distinct signs of the Day of Judgment. The first is that "the slave-girl will give birth to her mistress". This has been interpreted in a few different ways. Some scholars mention that this is a reference to widespread ignorance of the Sharīʿah. According to Islamic Law, a slave-woman who has a child from her owner is entitled to freedom at the time of his death and therefore can't be sold. Due to ignorance of the law she will be sold and eventually end up in the ownership of her own daughter. Another more common interpretation is that this is referring to the fact that disrespect for mothers will become common and widespread; it will become the norm. Children will treat their mothers as if they were their servants and slaves, ordering them around while insulting and humiliating them. This is something that has unfortunately become prevalent in society.

The second sign is that barefoot, naked, and destitute shepherds will compete in constructing tall buildings. This is also seen in today's world where we have nations that earlier in this century were considered to be bedouins and are now competing with each other to build the tallest buildings in the world. Some commentators mention that this statement is an allusion to the affairs of this world being turned upside down. The weakest and poorest people will become rich, and unqualified and undeserving individuals will assume positions of power and authority. Ignorance will spread and knowledge will slowly disappear. Falsehood will seem like the truth and injustice will seem like justice.

After asking these four questions, the individual leaves. After a while the Prophet ﷺ asks ʿUmar رضي الله عنه if he knew who this person was. ʿUmar رضي الله عنه responded with humility saying, "Allah and His Messenger know best." The Prophet ﷺ responded, "It was Jibrīl, who came to teach you your religion." Meaning, the Angel Jibrīl عليه السلام came in the form of a human being and asked these particular questions as a means of summarizing the mission and

26 31:34 - إِنَّ اللَّـهَ عِندَهُ عِلْمُ السَّاعَةِ وَيُنَزِّلُ الْغَيْثَ وَيَعْلَمُ مَا فِي الْأَرْحَامِ ۖ وَمَا تَدْرِي نَفْسٌ مَّاذَا تَكْسِبُ غَدًا ۖ وَمَا تَدْرِي نَفْسٌ بِأَيِّ أَرْضٍ تَمُوتُ ۚ إِنَّ اللَّـهَ عَلِيمٌ خَبِيرٌ

teachings of the Prophet ﷺ.

LESSONS AND BENEFITS

1. AWARENESS OF ONE'S COMMUNITY

Islam is not an individualistic religion. As a matter of fact, a great deal of importance is placed on social interactions, maintaining relationships, and community life. A person should be aware of who their community is and should be familiar with the people they interact with on a regular and daily basis. This leads towards mutual love, respect, and unity. They should notice if someone new comes to the masjid, as is seen in this particular incident. The companions noticed this person who seemed like he was a local but none of them knew or recognized him. Communal life in Islam is built upon brotherhood, sisterhood, concern for each other, and love for the sake of Allah ﷻ. That requires being aware of one's community.

2. IMPORTANCE OF APPEARANCE AND LOOKS

It is recommended to dress and look in a way that is common, clean, and presentable. A person's clothes should be neat, clean, and ironed. A person's hair should be neat and combed. This is especially true when participating in public spaces such as a masjid, class, lecture, or gathering of knowledge. Jibrīl ﷺ came to the gathering as a teacher through his words, actions, and appearance. The Prophet ﷺ said, "A person who has a particle's weight of pride in the heart will not enter Paradise." A Companion responded, "Truly a man likes for his clothes and shoes to be nice." The Prophet ﷺ responded, "Truly Allah is beautiful and loves beauty. Arrogance is to deny the truth and belittle others."[27]

3. ASKING GOOD QUESTIONS

Asking good questions is extremely important for a person's pursuit of knowledge, understanding, clarity, and practice.

4. ISLAM, ĪMĀN, AND IḤSĀN

Islam, Īmān, and Iḥsān are three extremely important and foundational

27 Muslim, *k.al-īmān, b. Taḥrīm al-kibr wa bayānihī*, 91

concepts within the way of life of Islam. That is one of the reasons why the Prophet ﷺ concluded by saying, "It was Jibrīl, who came to teach you your Dīn (religion)." They are also considered to be three stages in the journey towards Allah ﷻ, or three different stations or levels of practice and commitment. The first level is Islam; surrendering to Allah ﷻ through obedience, devotion, and servitude; trying one's best to obey the commands of Allah ﷻ and stay away from His prohibitions. As a person carries out these external acts of worship and obedience, their relationship with Allah ﷻ, their īmān slowly starts becoming stronger and stronger. Eventually a person's īmān reaches such a level that they experience a unique type of enjoyment and sweetness known as the sweetness of faith (ḥalāwah al-īmān). They enjoy praying, fasting, giving charity, and serving others and don't see it as an obligation or task that simply needs to be done. The last stage on the journey to Allah ﷻ is iḥsān, excellence and perfection, worshipping Allah ﷻ as if one can see him, and since He can't been, worshipping Him with the knowledge that He is the All-Seeing.

5. SIGNS OF THE DAY OF JUDGMENT

There are several verses of the Quran and aḥādīth of the Prophet ﷺ that mention various signs of the Day of Judgment. The purpose of these signs is to remind us that the Day of Judgment is a reality that is near and that it is something a believer should be conscious of and prepare for. Eschatological realties are a part of the belief system of Islam. However, there are some individuals and groups who become overly obsessed with signs of the end of times and prophecies associated with them adopting a fatalistic attitude. This leads towards a skewed perception of the world and is not the attitude one should adopt. Rather one should work hard and struggle in this world as if they are going to live forever and prepare for the hereafter as if they are going to die tomorrow.

HADITH 3

The Five Pillars of Islam

عَنْ أَبِي عَبْدِ الرَّحْمَنِ عَبْدِ اللَّهِ بْنِ عُمَرَ بْنِ الْخَطَّابِ رَضِيَ اللَّهُ عَنْهُمَا قَالَ: سَمِعْت رَسُولَ اللَّهِ صلى الله عليه و سلم يَقُولُ: " بُنِيَ الْإِسْلَامُ عَلَى خَمْسٍ: شَهَادَةِ أَنْ لَا إلَهَ إلَّا اللَّهُ وَأَنَّ مُحَمَّدًا رَسُولُ اللَّهِ، وَإِقَامِ الصَّلَاةِ، وَإِيتَاءِ الزَّكَاةِ، وَحَجِّ الْبَيْتِ، وَصَوْمِ رَمَضَانَ".

رَوَاهُ الْبُخَارِيُّ، وَمُسْلِمٌ.

From Abū ʿAbd al-Raḥmān ʿAbdullāh ibn ʿUmar ibn al-Khaṭṭāb ﷺ, who said that I heard the Messenger of Allah ﷺ say, "Islam is built upon *five* [pillars]: testifying that there is no deity worthy of worship except Allah and that Muḥammad ﷺ is the Messenger of Allah, establishing prayer, paying zakāh, performing ḥajj to the House, and fasting in Ramaḍān."

Narrated by al-Bukhārī and Muslim.

THE NARRATOR

ʿAbdullāh ibn ʿUmar ibn al-Khaṭṭāb ﷺ is the son of Amīr al-Mu'minīn ʿUmar ibn al-Khaṭṭāb ﷺ, who was from the most honorable families of Quraish. He was born two years after Muḥammad ﷺ was commissioned as a Prophet and Messenger. He accepted Islam with his father as a child. When he accepted Islam he had not yet reached the age of puberty. He migrated to Madinah with his parents at the age of 11 and he was turned away from both the battle of Badr and Uḥud because of his young age. He was not allowed to participate in any of the battles until he turned 15. The first battle he took part in was the battle of Khandaq.

He is considered to be among the most knowledgeable companions regarding the Sunnah of the Prophet ﷺ. He is considered an expert in ḥadīth and is also one of the Companions that would give fatwā. He followed the Sunnah in every single aspect of his life and is known for his piety and God-consciousness. He passed away in the year 73. He narrated 2,630 aḥādīth, may Allah ﷻ be pleased with him.

IMPORTANCE

Scholars of Ḥadīth refer to this narration as "The Pillars of Islam", because in it the Prophet ﷺ explains that Islam is built upon five foundational acts. This ḥadīth is extremely important because it explains the fundamental aspects of outward submission to Allah ﷻ; it outlines the five pillars of Islam. External acts of submission and obedience to Allah ﷻ are built upon these five pillars. The other acts of Islam are completions and finishing touches.

EXPLANATION

In this ḥadīth the Prophet ﷺ is comparing Islam to a strong building that is built upon a firm and solid foundation. Just as a building is constructed upon a solid foundation without which it will crumble; similarly, Islam is built upon pillars without which it would be useless. In order for a building to be strong and firm, to be able to withstand the natural elements, the passage of time, and natural disasters such as earthquakes, storms, and tornados, it has to be built upon a solid foundation. Similarly, in order for a person's

Islam to be strong and firm, it has to be built upon a rock-solid foundation.

The example of a tent makes the comparison clearer. When erecting a tent, there is a central pillar (pole) without which the tent can't stand at all. That central pillar is the Shahādah, or the testimony of faith. Then it has four pillars (poles) in each corner, without which the tent can't stand properly. These are the other four pillars of Islam. However, it is important to know that Islam is not limited to these five pillars. That is why the Prophet ﷺ did not say, "Islam is five pillars," he said, "Islam is built upon five pillars." Obeying all the commands of Allah ﷻ and staying away from all His prohibitions are included in Islam. All of these things are necessary for one's Islam to be complete. Just like a building standing on its foundations is incomplete without walls, a roof, doors, windows and furniture, similarly, Islam is incomplete without acts of obedience.

The first pillar that the Prophet ﷺ mentioned is the testimony of faith, to testify or to bear witness that there's no deity worthy of worship except Allah ﷻ and that Muhammad ﷺ is His Messenger. This is the absolute most important and central pillar of Islam because this is what enters a person into the fold of Islam. It is a verbal expression of the faith that lies in one's heart. When a person verbalizes the shahādah they are testifying, bearing witness, that they firmly believe in and affirm the existence and oneness of Allah ﷻ and firmly believe that the Prophet ﷺ is His last and final Messenger. They affirm all of his teachings. This expression is so powerful that it brings a person into the fold of Islam. It wipes away anything that a person may have done before Islam. It is so powerful that whoever says it with sincerity and true belief will enter Paradise. As the Prophet ﷺ said, "Whoever says 'lā ilāha illa Allah' will enter Paradise."[28]

The second pillar mentioned by the Prophet ﷺ is establishing prayer. That is why it has been called عماد الدين or the pillar of religion. It is called غرة الطاعات, the finest or highest form of worship. It is one of the most comprehensive forms of worship and remembrance. It is an act that is supposed to involve tongues, hearts, minds, and bodies. It engages the entire being.

The importance of prayer is something that can't be over-emphasized. There are several verses of the Quran and several aḥādīth that talk about the importance, virtues, rewards, and blessings of ṣalāh. Throughout the Quran, in over thirty places, Allah ﷻ commands believers to "establish prayer." This

28 ibn Ḥibbān, *Ṣaḥīḥ*, 169

is a very important point. Nowhere in the Quran does Allah ﷻ simply give the command to pray. The command is always to "establish prayer". The command comes from the verb aqāmah/yuqīmu, which means to make something straight and upright without any crookedness or deficiencies. Iqāmah al-Ṣalāh means to establish prayer; to pray it properly, at its time, fulfilling all of its pre-conditions, performing all of its integrals, and sunan. More importantly it means to pray with purpose, meaning, and understanding. Praying with humility and khushūʿ; to contemplate, reflect, think, and ponder over the words and phrases being recited.

Iqāmah al-Ṣalāh has two main aspects:

1. Outward (external) and
2. Inward (internal)

The outward aspect is praying properly according to the Sunnah of the Prophet ﷺ; the form of prayer itself. It includes making sure every aspect of prayer is being performed properly. The inward aspect refers to praying with the presence of heart and mind, consciousness and awareness, and with ikhlāṣ and iḥsān. This is what some would refer to as the substance or spirit of prayer.

Ibn ʿAbbās ؓ described iqāmah al-ṣalāh as, "Establishing the prayer is to perform its bowing, prostrations, and recitation in a complete manner as well as having fear of Allah and complete attention to it." It means praying with the quality of the Prophet ﷺ so that it becomes the coolness of one's eyes as well. The Prophet ﷺ said, "The coolness of my eyes was placed in prayer."[29] The Prophet ﷺ found peace, happiness, tranquility, serenity, and contentment in prayer.

Most Muslims recognize the importance and value of prayer. Although they may know it, the reality of how important it is may not hit home. This is the one commandment that instead of sending the Angel Jibrīl ؑ from the heavens to the Prophet ﷺ, the Prophet ﷺ himself was called up to the heavens to receive it directly from Allah ﷻ. It is the first thing that will be asked about on the Day of Judgment. The Prophet ﷺ said, "The first of man's deeds for which he will be called to account on the Day of Resurrection will be ṣalāh. If it is sound, he will be saved and successful; but if it is corrupt, he will be

29 al-Nasāʾī, k. *ʿashrah al-nisāʾa*, b. *ḥubb al-nisāʾa*, 3940

unfortunate and a loser."[30] The Day of Judgment is a reality; it is an absolute certainty. One day every single human being will stand before Allah ﷻ and be judged for whatever they said or did in the life of this world. Out of every single thing that a person has done throughout their lives, the first thing they will be asked about is prayer. Success in the hereafter is dependent on the soundness of prayer.

Ṣalāh also has a direct relationship with faith. As a matter of fact, some scholars are of the opinion that if a person intentionally leaves prayer they might as well leave Islam. That may sound severe and harsh, but that is the level of emphasis that has been placed on ṣalāh. The Prophet ﷺ said, "Between a man and disbelief is leaving prayer."[31] In another narration the Prophet ﷺ said, "The treaty I have with my followers is prayer, whoever leaves it, it is as if he has disbelieved."[32] According to these narrations, prayer is not something that should be taken lightly. They highlight that there is a direct relationship between faith and prayer.

The main catalyst behind prayers is īmān. If a person's īmān is strong and firm then prayer is something that they will do naturally. It will not be seen as some sort of burden or chore. It will be something that they would look forward to and actually enjoy. That is the sweetness of faith. Recognizing the importance of prayer leads to an appreciation of prayer. One of the great scholars of the past, ibn Qudāmah ؒ, writes that the stronger a person's faith in the hereafter the more importance they will give to prayer. He says, "When you see that your heart is not present in prayer, then know that the cause of that is a weakness of īmān. Therefore strive hard and struggle in strengthening it."[33]

The Prophet ﷺ mentions paying zakāh as the third pillar. When looking towards the Quran and Sunnah the two acts of worship that are most commonly mentioned together are ṣalāḥ and zakāh. It is considered to be the greatest and most important act of worship after ṣalāh. That is why when Allah ﷻ describes the believers in the Quran, one of the descriptions He gives is that they are individuals who pay their zakāh. It is an act of worship

30 Tirmidhī, *k. al-ṣalāh, b. mā jā'a anna awwala mā yuḥasabu bihī al-ʿabd yawm al-qiyāmah al-ṣalāh*, 413

31 Muslim, *k. al-īmān, b. Bayān iṭlāq ism al-kufr ʿalā man taraka al-ṣalāh*, 82

32 Tirmidhī, *k. al-īmān, b. mā jā'a fī tark al-ṣalāh*

33 Ibn Qudāmah, *Mukhtaṣar Minhāj al-Qāṣidīn*

that is related to wealth. Zakāh is a specific amount of wealth that is given to the poor when a person owns the niṣāb (minimum amount of wealth that makes zakāh obligatory) for an entire year. It is an act of worship that serves to purify wealth and to purify hearts. It serves to remove greed, stinginess, and love for wealth and material possessions.

The fourth pillar mentioned in the hadīth is performing ḥajj. Ḥajj is an act of worship that involves both a person's body and wealth (عبادة مالية وبدنية). It is obligatory to perform ḥajj once in a lifetime as soon as one is able to (physically and financially).

Ḥajj is one of the most powerful, awe-inspiring, humbling, and beautiful acts of worship in Islam. Muslims from every single part of the world, with different types of backgrounds, races, colors, languages, old and young, rich and poor gather together in the same place for the same purpose. They all gather together to show their love, devotion, obedience, and submission to Allah ﷻ. It is the most amazing display of unity seen in the entire world. No other religion, no other way of life can claim to have something even similar to ḥajj. It is one amazing collective act of worship.

Just as it has this collective benefit, ḥajj is also a very personal act. It is an opportunity for a person to completely change their lives and start over. It is one of the greatest acts of worship a person can do. The Prophet ﷺ said, "Whoever performs ḥajj for the sake of Allah and is not obscene and does not sin will return like the day his mother gave birth to him."[34] Meaning, just like a newborn is sinless, similarly a person who performs ḥajj will also be sinless. In another narration the Prophet ﷺ said, "An accepted ḥajj has no reward other than Jannah."[35] An accepted ḥajj has been called one of the best acts of worship by the Prophet ﷺ.

The last pillar mentioned by the Prophet ﷺ is fasting the month of Ramaḍān. Fasting the month of Ramaḍān is one of the greatest acts of worship we can perform, specifically in terms of sincerity and reward. Abū Hurairah رضي الله عنه narrated that the Prophet ﷺ said: "Allah ﷻ said, 'Every single act of the son of Adam is for himself except for fasting. For it is for me and I give the reward for it.'"[36] It is an act that cleanses one's mind, body, and soul from the spiritual and physical impurities of this world.

---

34 Bukhārī, *k. al-hajj, b. faḍl al-ḥajj al-mabrūr*, 1521

35 Bukhārī, *k. al-'umrah, b. wujūb al-'umrah wa faḍliha*, 1773

36 Muslim, *k. al-ṣiyām, b. faḍl al-ṣiyām*, 1151

It is an act that develops God-consciousness. Allah ﷻ says in the Quran, "O you who believe! Fasting is prescribed for you as it was prescribed for those before you, so that you may be God conscious."[37] The Prophet ﷺ told us, "Whoever fasts the month of Ramadan with true faith and expecting reward, then all his previous sins will be forgiven."[38]

LESSONS AND BENEFITS

1. FORM AND SUBSTANCE

When it comes to ritual acts of worship and devotion in Islam, it is important that they be performed correctly according to the teachings of the Prophet ﷺ, the form, and at the same time they be done with meaning and purpose. For example, one should pray according to the Sunnah of the Prophet ﷺ. The Prophet ﷺ said, "Pray as you have seen me praying."[39] At the same time one should pray with humility, focus, and concentration trying their best to understand what they are reciting in prayer.

The acts of worship in Islam, specifically those mentioned in this ḥadīth, are not meant simply to be rituals that a person goes through in life. They have higher objectives and aims behind them. They are meant to be transformative; to change a person's life and strengthen their relationship with Allah ﷻ.

2. FOUNDATIONS AND FINISHINGS

As mentioned earlier, the acts of worship mentioned in this narration are known as the five pillars of Islam. It is important to recognize that they are the foundation of one's Islam, but they are not the entirety of Islam. The Prophet ﷺ mentioned them specifically because of their importance. There are many other aspects of Islam; voluntary acts of worship, charity, reciting Quran, engaging in the remembrance of Allah, supplication, being kind to one's neighbors, honoring and serving guests, respecting and obeying parents, teaching, encouraging good, forbidding evil, tazkiyah, adab, and the list can go on and on.

37 2:183 - يَا أَيُّهَا الَّذِينَ آمَنُوا كُتِبَ عَلَيْكُمُ الصِّيَامُ كَمَا كُتِبَ عَلَى الَّذِينَ مِن قَبْلِكُمْ لَعَلَّكُمْ تَتَّقُونَ

38 Bukhārī, *k. al-īmān, b. ṣawm ramaḍān īmān wa iḥtisāb min al-īmān*, 38

39 Bukhārī, *k. al-adab, b. raḥmah al-nās wa al-bahā'im*, 6008

3. PRIORITIES

In terms of priorities and focus, the five pillars are the most important acts of worship to focus on, strengthen, develop consistency in, and perfect.

4. FAITH AND ACTION

It is understood from this ḥadīth that Islam is both faith and practice; there is no benefit to actions without faith, and there is no faith without action. A person's īmān has to express itself through speech and behavior.

HADITH 4

Human Development and Al-Qadr

عَنْ أَبِي عَبْدِ الرَّحْمَنِ عَبْدِ اللَّهِ بْنِ مَسْعُودٍ رَضِيَ اللَّهُ عَنْهُ قَالَ: حَدَّثَنَا رَسُولُ اللَّهِ صلى الله عليه و سلم -وَهُوَ الصَّادِقُ الْمَصْدُوقُ-: "إنَّ أَحَدَكُمْ يُجْمَعُ خَلْقُهُ فِي بَطْنِ أُمِّهِ أَرْبَعِينَ يَوْمًا نُطْفَةً، ثُمَّ يَكُونُ عَلَقَةً مِثْلَ ذَلِكَ، ثُمَّ يَكُونُ مُضْغَةً مِثْلَ ذَلِكَ، ثُمَّ يُرْسَلُ إلَيْهِ الْمَلَكُ فَيَنْفُخُ فِيهِ الرُّوحَ، وَيُؤْمَرُ بِأَرْبَعِ كَلِمَاتٍ: بِكَتْبِ رِزْقِهِ، وَأَجَلِهِ، وَعَمَلِهِ، وَشَقِيٍّ أَمْ سَعِيدٍ؛ فَوَاَللَّهِ الَّذِي لَا إلَهَ غَيْرُهُ إنَّ أَحَدَكُمْ لَيَعْمَلُ بِعَمَلِ أَهْلِ الْجَنَّةِ حَتَّى مَا يَكُونُ بَيْنَهُ وَبَيْنَهَا إلَّا ذِرَاعٌ فَيَسْبِقُ عَلَيْهِ الْكِتَابُ فَيَعْمَلُ بِعَمَلِ أَهْلِ النَّارِ فَيَدْخُلُهَا. وَإِنَّ أَحَدَكُمْ لَيَعْمَلُ بِعَمَلِ أَهْلِ النَّارِ حَتَّى مَا يَكُونُ بَيْنَهُ وَبَيْنَهَا إلَّا ذِرَاعٌ فَيَسْبِقُ عَلَيْهِ الْكِتَابُ فَيَعْمَلُ بِعَمَلِ أَهْلِ الْجَنَّةِ فَيَدْخُلُهَا".

رَوَاهُ الْبُخَارِيُّ، وَمُسْلِمٌ.

From ʿAbdullah ibn Masʿūd ﵁, who said that the Messenger of Allah ﷺ - and he is the truthful, the believed - narrated to us, "Verily the creation of an individual is brought together in their mother's womb for forty days in the form of a nuṭfah (drop), then an ʿalaqah (clot of blood) for a similar period of time, and then a muḍghah (morsel of *flesh*) for a similar period of time. Then the Angel is sent to them and blows their soul into them. The Angel is commanded with four matters: to record their rizq (sustenance), their life span, their actions, and whether they will be unhappy or happy. By the One besides Whom there is no other deity, verily one of you performs the actions of the people of Paradise until there is nothing but an arms-length between them and it, and then the Divine decree overtakes them. So they perform the actions of the people of the Fire and then enter it. Truly one of you performs the actions of the people of the Fire, until there is nothing but an arms-length between them and it, and then the Divine decree overtakes them. So they perform the actions of the people of Paradise and then they enter it."

Narrated by al-Bukhārī and Muslim.

THE NARRATOR

Abū ʿAbd al-Raḥmān ʿAbdullah ibn Masʿūd رضي الله عنه is among one of the more well-known Companions of the Prophet ﷺ. He was one of the first people to accept the call of the Prophet ﷺ during the early days of Islam. The Prophet ﷺ took him as a very close companion, similar to an assistant. He would enter the house of the Prophet ﷺ, carry his shoes, walk in front of him, cover him when he bathed, and wake him up when he slept. Because of his proximity to the Prophet ﷺ he became one of the best reciters of the Quran. The Prophet ﷺ said, "Learn the Quran from four people: ʿAbdullah ibn Masʿūd, Sālim mawlā Abū Ḥudhaifah, Ubayy ibn Kaʿb, and Muʿādh ibn Jabal."[40] The Prophet ﷺ also listened to him reciting the Quran. Ibn Masʿūd رضي الله عنه narrates that the Prophet ﷺ said, "Recite the Quran to me." I said, "Shall I recite to you while the Quran was revealed to you?" He ﷺ said, "Yes." I recited Sūrah al-Nisā until I reached the verse "What will they do when We bring a witness from each community, with you [Muḥammad] as a witness against these people?" He ﷺ said, "That is enough for now." I looked at him and his eyes were flowing with tears.[41]

He was considered to be closest in manners to the Prophet ﷺ as well as one of the most knowledgeable companions. He undertook both migrations, prayed towards both Qiblahs, participated in Badr, Uḥud, Khandaq, and all other battles with the Prophet ﷺ. He is the one who dealt Abū Jahl, the sworn enemy of Islam, the fatal blow.

He was sent to Kūfah during the time of ʿUmar رضي الله عنه to teach. He passed away in the year 32 at the age of 69 and is buried in the famous graveyard of Madinah, al-Baqīʿ. He narrated 848 aḥādīth, may Allah be pleased with him.

IMPORTANCE

This ḥadīth is important and meaningful covering two separate subjects:

1. It describes the gradual creation of human beings while in the wombs of their mothers through the various stages of embryonic development; and

---

40 Bukhārī, *k. manāqib al-anṣār, b. manāqib Muʿādh ibn Jabal*, 3806

41 Bukhārī, *k. faḍā'il al-Quran, b. qawl al-muqri' li al-qārī hasbuk*, 5050

2. It describes the concept of belief in al-Qadr.

Both of these subjects highlight the might, power, glory, magnificence, wisdom, and infinite knowledge of Allah ﷻ. It provides human beings a clear understanding of who their Lord and Creator is and how the concept of al-Qadr functions. It also provides a complete timeline of human life: from the moment of conception until the final destination in the life of the hereafter.

EXPLANATION

In this ḥadīth the Prophet ﷺ tells us that a fetus passes through three distinct stages during a period of 120 days. During the first forty days the unborn child is described as a nuṭfah, which is a mixture of male and female fluid in the womb of a woman. The word nuṭfah is usually translated as a drop. It is referring to a drop of semen, which in Arabic is called manyy. Some commentators mention that the word nuṭfah is referring to both the male and female reproductive cells. The male reproductive cell or gamete is the sperm and the female reproductive cell is the egg. When the sperm fertilizes the egg it forms what is known as the zygote. So it is possible that the word nuṭfah is referring to the zygote. The fact that the Quran and the Prophet ﷺ discussed this more than 1400 years ago, before the advent of modern science is amazing.

After forty days the nuṭfah develops into an ʿalaqah, which is translated as a leech-like clot, suspended thing, or blood clot. As the fertilized egg is implanted into the wall of the uterus, it clings to it. That is why the word ʿalaqah is used to describe this stage.

Then after another forty days the ʿalaqah develops into a muḍghah, which is translated as a lump of flesh or a chewed substance. This word is used to describe the embryo because in its initial stages it looks like a lump of chewed flesh. These three stages are also mentioned in the Quran in Sūrah al-Ḥajj and al-M'uminūn. In Sūrah al-Ḥajj Allah ﷻ says, "People, [remember,] if you doubt the Resurrection, that We created you from dust, then a drop of fluid, then a clinging form, then a lump of flesh, both shaped and unshaped: We mean to make Our power clear to you. Whatever We choose We cause to remain in the womb for an appointed time, then We bring you forth as infants and then you grow and reach maturity. Some die young and some are left to live on to such an age that they forget all they once knew. You sometimes see the earth lifeless, yet when We send down water it stirs and swells and produces every kind of joyous growth."[42] In Sūrah al-Mu'minūn Allah ﷻ says, "We created man from an essence of clay, then We placed him as a drop of fluid in a safe place, then We made that drop into a clinging form, and We made that form into a lump of flesh, and We made that lump into bones, and We clothed those bones with flesh, and later We made him into other forms—glory be to God, the best of creators!"[43]

The embryo passes through these three stages. Each stage takes 40 days, for a total of 120 days. After the completion of 120 days, which is 4 months, the soul (rūḥ) is breathed into the fetus and is given life. This moment is considered to be the beginning of life. The rūḥ is the spirit, soul, or life of an individual. It is defined as what gives life to a human being. Imām al-Nawawī رحمه الله defines it as "a delicate substance interwoven in the human body similar to sap interwoven in a green branch."[44] Imām al-Ghazālī رحمه الله defines it as an independent substance that traverses through the body.[45]

The nature or reality of the rūḥ itself is something that is unknown. Human beings have been given very little knowledge regarding it. Allah ﷻ says, "[Prophet], they ask you about the Spirit. Say, 'The Spirit is part of my Lord's domain. You have only been given a little knowledge.'"[46]

After the soul or spirit is blown into the fetus giving it life the Angel is commanded to write or record four things:

1. Sustenance - how much wealth, food, water, shelter, clothes, and provisions the individual will receive. A person's provision has been recorded for them; they will not get any more or any less than what has already been decided by Allah ﷻ. The Prophet ﷺ said, "No soul

---

42 22:5 - يَا أَيُّهَا النَّاسُ إِن كُنتُمْ فِي رَيْبٍ مِّنَ الْبَعْثِ فَإِنَّا خَلَقْنَاكُم مِّن تُرَابٍ ثُمَّ مِن نُّطْفَةٍ ثُمَّ مِنْ عَلَقَةٍ ثُمَّ مِن مُّضْغَةٍ مُّخَلَّقَةٍ وَغَيْرِ مُخَلَّقَةٍ لِّنُبَيِّنَ لَكُمْ ۚ وَنُقِرُّ فِي الْأَرْحَامِ مَا نَشَاءُ إِلَىٰ أَجَلٍ مُّسَمًّى ثُمَّ نُخْرِجُكُمْ طِفْلًا ثُمَّ لِتَبْلُغُوا أَشُدَّكُمْ ۖ وَمِنكُم مَّن يُتَوَفَّىٰ وَمِنكُم مَّن يُرَدُّ إِلَىٰ أَرْذَلِ الْعُمُرِ لِكَيْلَا يَعْلَمَ مِن بَعْدِ عِلْمٍ شَيْئًا ۚ وَتَرَى الْأَرْضَ هَامِدَةً فَإِذَا أَنزَلْنَا عَلَيْهَا الْمَاءَ اهْتَزَّتْ وَرَبَتْ وَأَنبَتَتْ مِن كُلِّ زَوْجٍ بَهِيجٍ

43 12:23-14 - وَلَقَدْ خَلَقْنَا الْإِنسَانَ مِن سُلَالَةٍ مِّن طِينٍ ثُمَّ جَعَلْنَاهُ نُطْفَةً فِي قَرَارٍ مَّكِينٍ ثُمَّ خَلَقْنَا النُّطْفَةَ عَلَقَةً فَخَلَقْنَا الْعَلَقَةَ مُضْغَةً فَخَلَقْنَا الْمُضْغَةَ عِظَامًا فَكَسَوْنَا الْعِظَامَ لَحْمًا ثُمَّ أَنشَأْنَاهُ خَلْقًا آخَرَ ۚ فَتَبَارَكَ اللَّهُ أَحْسَنُ الْخَالِقِينَ

44 جسم لطيف سار فى البدن مشتبك به اشتباك الماء بالعود الأخضر

45 جوهر مجرد متصرف فى البدن

46 17:85 - وَيَسْأَلُونَكَ عَنِ الرُّوحِ ۖ قُلِ الرُّوحُ مِنْ أَمْرِ رَبِّي وَمَا أُوتِيتُم مِّنَ الْعِلْمِ إِلَّا قَلِيلًا

will die until it receives its sustenance in full."[47]

2. Lifespan - how long a person will live for in the life of this world is determined and set by Allah ﷻ. A person will not leave this world a moment earlier or a moment later. Allah ﷻ says, "There is a time set for every people: they cannot hasten it, nor, when it comes, will they be able to delay it for a single moment."[48]
3. Deeds - everything a person does in the life of this world, good or bad, big or small, public or private, has all been recorded by Allah ﷻ.
4. Whether he will be unhappy or happy, unfortunate or fortunate - where a human being will end up in the hereafter is also recorded by Allah ﷻ. He knows who is going to Paradise and who is going to the fire of Hell.

The Prophet ﷺ ends the statement by providing a real-world example of the divine decree and will of Allah ﷻ. He first describes a person who spends their entire life as a believer engaged in acts of worship, obedience, and righteousness. They are so close to gaining entry into Paradise, the Prophet ﷺ describes them as being an arms-length away, but then what has been decreed for them comes to pass. They do something near the end of their life that causes them to be among the people of Hell. He ﷺ then describes the opposite; a person who spends their entire life in disbelief engaged in all types of sins, disobedience, and immoral behavior. They are so close to going to the fire of Hell, the Prophet ﷺ describes it as being only an arms-length away, but then what has been decreed for them comes to pass. They do something near the end of their life that causes them to be among the people of Paradise.

This part of the ḥadīth is supposed to create a sense of fear or uneasiness in a person's heart; specifically fear of the unknown. A person does not know what is going to happen in the future. They should never feel a sense of complacency; rather, there is always room to improve, increase one's faith, and get closer to Allah ﷻ. A person should seek Allah's help for a good ending and fear a bad ending. They should seek refuge with Allah ﷻ from a bad ending.

---

47 al-Haythamī, *Majmaʿ al-Zawā'id*, 74

48 7:34

It is important to note that the first scenario described by the Prophet ﷺ is very rare. It is not often that a person spends their entire life engaged in righteousness and then all of a sudden changes near the end of their lives. Similarly, the second scenario is very common. It is very common that a person ends up changing their ways before they leave this world. This is one of the expressions of Allah's ﷻ infinite mercy in this world.

LESSONS AND BENEFITS

1. PROOF OF PROPHETHOOD

The stages of embryonic development mentioned in this ḥadīth and the Quran are explicit proof that the Prophet ﷺ was receiving revelation from Allah ﷻ. This is knowledge that was unknown to anyone in the world at that time. It is a proof of his prophethood and that his claim of being assigned as a prophet and messenger is true.

2. CERTAINTY IN RESURRECTION AND LIFE AFTER DEATH

The entire process of procreation, embryonic development, and birth is a physical and observable proof that Allah ﷻ has the power to resurrect human beings after their bodies and bones have decomposed and turned to dust.

3. PLANNING AND CARE

Through the process of human development and passing from stage to stage, Allah ﷻ is teaching human beings to be careful, deliberate, and to take their time when doing something important. There is no need to rush through something and be hasty. Rush and haste can lead towards unintentional mistakes that could have extremely negative consequences. The Prophet ﷺ said, "Patient deliberation is from Allah and haste is from Shayṭān."[49]

4. ABORTION

Based off this ḥadīth, the majority of scholars consider the beginning of life to be at 120 days after conception. This plays an important role in determining the Islamic ruling regarding abortions. The following is a fairly comprehensive fatwā regarding the issue written by Mufti Muhammad ibn

49 Tirmidhī, *k. al-birr wa al-ṣilah ʿan rasūlillah ﷺ, b. Mā jā'a fī al-ta'annī wa al-ʿajalah*, 2012

Adam:

Abortion and the termination of pregnancy is the expulsion of a fetus from the womb of a woman. This may be carried out either by consuming of certain drugs or by emptying the womb through the process of suction.

Life is sacred:

Islam regards human life to be sacred. Allah Most High says: "And verily we have honoured the children of Adam." (Surah al-Isra, V.70) It does not matter where the life exists. Whether the life is extra-uterine or intra-uterine, its location has no significance on its sanctity. This sanctity applies not only to human life, but to the human body as well. Hence, according to [the] Shariah, the physical body of a human after death is just as sacred as it was before death. The degree of sanctity of life is greater than that of the body. This is one of the reasons why it is unlawful (haram) to consume the meat of a human, dead or alive.

The Shariah ruling on abortion:

Abortion can be divided into two stages:

1. Abortion after the soul (rūḥ) enters the fetus,
2. Abortion prior to the entry of the soul into the fetus

Before mentioning the ruling on abortion with regards to these two stages, it must be remembered here, that according to Shariah, the soul (rūḥ) enters the fetus at 120 days (4 months) from conception.

The Jurists (fuqahā') have based this duration upon a Qur'anic verse and a statement of the beloved of Allah (Allah bless him & give him peace). In the verse, Allah Almighty states the stages of development of the embryo in the womb of the mother. Allah Almighty says: "And verily we did create man from a quintessence (of clay). Then we placed him (as a drop of sperm) in a place of rest, firmly fixed. Then we made the sperm into a clot of congealed blood. Then of that clot we made a (fetus) lump. Then we made out of that lump bones and clothed the bones with flesh. Then we developed out of it another creature (by breathing life into it). So blessed be Allah, the most marvellous creator." (Surah al-Mu'minun, 12-14)

In the Hadith recorded by the two most authentic authorities, Imam al-Bukhari and Imam Muslim, in their respective Sahih collections, the Messenger of Allah (Allah bless him & give him peace) discussed in detail the periods elapsing between these stages, mentioned by the Qur'an. Sayyiduna Abd Allah ibn Mas'ud (Allah be pleased with him) narrates that the Messenger of Allah (Allah bless him & give him peace) said: "The seed of one of you remains in the womb of the mother for forty days in the form of a Nutfa (sperm). Then it remains like a clot for another forty days, and then for a same number of days like a lump of flesh (when the formation of the limbs and the growth of the bones begin)." (Sahih al-Bukhari & Sahih Muslim)

The great Hanafi Faqih, Imam Ibn Abidin states in his Radd al-Muhtar: "The soul enters the fetus at one hundred and twenty days (4 months), as established by the Hadith." (Radd al-Muhtar, 1/202)

The ruling on abortion in stage (a) i.e. after the entry of the soul into the fetus which is (as explained) 120 days, is that, it is totally unlawful and tantamount to murder, as it results in the taking out of an innocent life. All the scholars have unanimously condemned such a ghastly act.

Imam Ibn Taymiyyah states in his Fatawa collection: "Aborting a fetus has been declared unlawful (haram) with the consensus of all the Muslim scholars. It is similar to burying an infant alive as referred to by Allah Almighty in the verse of the Qur'an: "And when the female infant, buried alive, will be asked as to what crime she was killed for". (Surah al-Takwir, 8)" (Fatawa Ibn Taymiyya, 4/217)

Allama Ibn Abidin (Allah have Mercy on him) also states the prohibition of this gruesome act in his treatise 'Radd al-Muhtar': "If a woman intends to abort her pregnancy, then the Fuqaha have said: If the period of the soul being blown into the fetus has elapsed, it will be impermissible." (Radd al-Muhtar, 5/276)

However, some Fuqaha and contemporary scholars have given a dispensation to abort the pregnancy after 120 days, in the situation where the life of the mother is in certain and absolute danger.[50] This is based on the Juristic principle stated in the books of Usul al-Fiqh and Qawa'id (juristic principles): "If one is overtaken by two evils, one should choose the lesser of the two." (al-Ashbah wa al-Naza'ir, P.98) They state that the mother's life should be saved and the fetus aborted, as the mother is established in life, with duties and responsibilities, whereas the unborn child is still in the mother's womb. But it should be remembered, that the mother's life must be in certain danger, and that this should be advised by a qualified and experienced Muslim doctor.

With regards to stage (b) i.e. prior to the entry of the soul into the fetus (120 days), the ruling on aborting the pregnancy is that, even in this case it will be unlawful (haram) to abort it.

The reason why abortion prior to the soul entering the body will not be permitted is that, although there may not be life in the fetus, but the fetus is considered to be part and parcel of the mother's body as long as it remains in the womb. Thus, just as one's very own life and also all the limbs and organs of the human body are trust given by the Almighty Creator, so too is the fetus also a trust given to the mother by Allah, and she will not have a right to abort it.

The only difference here is that the sin of aborting the fetus will be of a lesser degree than aborting it after 120

50 Suleiman, Omar. "Islam and the Abortion Debate." *Yaqeen*, Yaqeen Institute, 20 March 2017, https://yaqeeninstitute.org/en/omar-suleiman/islam-and-the-abortion-debate/

days. It would not be regarded as murder, rather violating the rights of a human organ entrusted to the mother by Allah Almighty.

It is stated in Radd al-Muhtar: "It is not permissible to abort the pregnancy before and after the entry of the soul into the fetus." (Radd al-Muhtar, 5/279)

However, in certain extreme circumstances, it would be permitted to abort the pregnancy before the entry of the soul (120 days), such as: when the woman conceives after being raped, the mother's life or health is in danger, or repeated pregnancies severely damages her health, etc...

Imam al-Haskafi writes in Durr al-Mukhtar: "Aborting the pregnancy will be permissible due to a valid reason, provided the soul has not yet entered the fetus."

It should be remarked here that pregnancy due to unlawful and illegal sex is no reason and excuse for abortion. The embryonic life farm in the mother's womb is honoured and sacred even though it is a result of adultery. (Hidaya, 2/292)

In conclusion, abortion after 120 days is totally unlawful and tantamount to murder. Some Fuqaha, however, have given a dispensation only in the situation where the mother's life is in certain danger. As far as abortion before the 120 days have elapsed is concerned, it will still be unlawful, though the sin will be of a lesser degree, and it will become permissible if there is a genuine and valid reason. And Allah Knows Best."[51]

5. QAḌĀ'A AND QADR

Having faith in the decree of Allah ﷻ and His pre-knowledge is one of the most fundamental aspects of faith; it is an integral part of īmān. Muslims believe that everything in their lives has already been decreed. All matters and affairs in the entire history and future of the universe are known to Allah ﷻ, and are a direct result of His willing them, decreeing them, and, through

51 Ibn Adam, Muhammad. "Islamic Ruling on Abortion." *daruliftaa*. Daruliftaa, 6/3/2004, http://www.daruliftaa.com/node/5925?txt_QuestionID=

His power and ability, bringing them into existence. Allah ﷻ has determined the measure of everything: lifespans, financial provisions, and destinations in the next life. All of this has been written and recorded in the Preserved Tablet.

Qadr is defined linguistically as a specified measure or amount, or to measure the quantity of something. Īmān bī al-Qadr means to believe that Allah ﷻ has eternal knowledge regarding all things; whatever has happened, whatever is happening, and what will happen, regardless of whether that thing is good or bad, big or small, apparent or hidden, physical or metaphysical. All of this has been recorded in the Preserved Tablet. Muslims believe that Allah ﷻ knows, with His ultimate knowledge, what all His creation will do, even before the creation took place. It is the will of Allah that these things will take place, whether they are good or bad.

Īmān bī al-Qaḍā'a means to believe that everything that has happened in this universe, everything that is happening, and everything that will happen in the future, whether it is good or bad, physical or metaphysical, is created by Allah ﷻ. Nothing happens in this universe without the will and decree of Allah ﷻ; so much so that all of the actions of human beings, both good and bad, intentions and thoughts, are also brought into existence by Allah ﷻ.

Although Allah ﷻ brings everything into existence according to His pre-eternal knowledge, will and decree, human beings have been given some sort of free will. They have the choice to do something or not do it. This "choice" or type of "free will" has been called kasb. At the end of Sūrah al-Aḥzāb it is referred to as amānah. Allah ﷻ says, "We offered the Trust to the heavens, the earth, and the mountains, yet they refused to undertake it and were afraid of it; mankind undertook it- they have always been inept and foolish."[52] Based on this kasb, human beings are legally responsible (mukallaf) and are deserving of reward or punishment. Allah is the creator (al-Khāliq) of human actions and humans are kāsib. Reward and punishment is not based upon khalq, it is based upon kasb.

It becomes apparent from both rational and textual proofs that kasb (acquisition) is some sort of intermediary between coercion and creation. It is something that is used in order to make a choice between doing something or not. It plays a role in bringing actions into existence but it is not enough to do so. All voluntary actions are a result of two things: khalq and kasb. An

52 33;72

understanding of the true reality of kasb is outside of human comprehension and that is why in a few narrations the Prophet ﷺ prohibits his companions from delving too deep into it.

However, in order to have somewhat of an understanding of how it works it can be said that initially a thought comes to a person's mind. Then they give consideration to this thought; should they do it or not. After weighing the pros and cons they incline towards doing it. After that inclination, they make an intention and that intention results in giving movement to their limbs in order to perform that act until it is performed. This entire process, from the thought till the existence of the act, is a creation of Allah. As a matter of fact, till now, human beings don't have a complete picture of how this entire process works. But everyone knows, both rationally and experientially, that somewhere along this process a person made a conscious decision to do the action. This choice or decision is called kasb, on whose basis a person receives reward or punishment. If they acquire a good thing, they get rewarded, and if they acquire a bad thing, they are deserving of punishment.

Say for example that someone gives Bakr a loaded gun. He squeezed the trigger and as a result a bullet comes flying out and kills the person in front of him. All of the processes that were involved in the firing of the bullet, both before and after, Bakr had no role whatsoever in its creation. But Bakr will still be called a murderer because in this entire process he moved his finger to squeeze the trigger. If it weren't for this slight movement of his finger the gun wouldn't fire and the man wouldn't have died. The one who made the gun or the manufacturer won't be called the killer. Similarly, since kasb plays a role in the production of a person's action, they will be subject to reward and punishment.

Muslim creed lies somewhere in between absolute free will and coercion; humans don't create their own actions nor are they compelled or forced to do anything.

6. DON'T BE COMPLACENT

The final portion of the ḥadīth highlights that no human being knows what is going to happen in the future. That is one of the reasons why the Prophet ﷺ encourages believers to be vigilant and constantly work to improve themselves. The Prophet ﷺ said, "Actions are by their endings."[53]

53 Bukhārī, *k. al-Qadr, b. al-ʿaml bī al-khawātīm*, 6607

HADITH 5

Sunnah and Bid'ah

عَنْ أُمِّ الْمُؤْمِنِينَ أُمِّ عَبْدِ اللَّهِ عَائِشَةَ رَضِيَ اللَّهُ عَنْهَا، قَالَتْ: قَالَ: رَسُولُ اللَّهِ صلى الله عليه وسلم "مَنْ أَحْدَثَ فِي أَمْرِنَا هَذَا مَا لَيْسَ مِنْهُ فَهُوَ رَدٌّ".

رَوَاهُ الْبُخَارِيُّ، وَمُسْلِمٌ. وَفِي رِوَايَةٍ لِمُسْلِمٍ: "مَنْ عَمِلَ عَمَلًا لَيْسَ عَلَيْهِ أَمْرُنَا فَهُوَ رَدٌّ".

From the Mother of the Believers, 'Ā'ishah ﵂, who said that the Messenger of Allah ﷺ said, "He who introduces something new into this matter of ours that is not from it, then it is rejected."

Narrated by al-Bukhārī and Muslim. In another version narrated by Muslim, "Whoever performs an act that our affair is not upon, then it is rejected."

THE NARRATOR

Umm al-Mu'minīn Umm ʿAbd Allah ʿĀ'ishah ﵂ is the wife of the Prophet ﷺ, the Mother of the believers. She was given the nickname Umm ʿAbd Allah by the Prophet ﷺ. ʿAbdullah is the name of her nephew, the son of her sister Asmā'a ﵂.

The Prophet ﷺ married her while in Makkah and she moved in with him in the second year after hijrah. When the Prophet ﷺ left this world she was only 18 years old. She lived for 40 years after the Prophet ﷺ left this world and passed away in the year 57. Abū Hurairah ﵁ performed her funeral prayer.

She was one of the most knowledgeable among the Companions. The senior Companions would come to her to ask questions. 2,210 aḥādīth have been narrated from her, and 174 of those appear in both Bukhārī and Muslim. May Allah ﷻ be pleased with her.

IMPORTANCE

This ḥadīth is considered to be an explanation of one of the foundational teachings of Islam. As covered earlier, Imam Aḥmad ibn Ḥanbal ﵀ said that three aḥādīth form the foundation of Islam:

1. "Actions are only by their intentions",
2. "Whoever introduces...", and
3. "The permissible is clear..."

This ḥadīth provides a scale with which external acts are to be weighed, just as the ḥadīth of intention provides the scale with which internal acts are to be weighed. Just as every deed that is not done for the sake of Allah ﷻ will not be rewarded, similarly every deed that is not upon the guidance of the Quran and Sunnah will be rejected.

Imām al-Nawawī ﵀ said that all Muslims should memorize this ḥadīth. It is given so much importance because it deals with the concept of bidʿah or innovation.

EXPLANATION

This ḥadīth is considered to be among the concise and comprehensive sayings of the Prophet ﷺ. The Prophet ﷺ said, "I have been given concise comprehensive speech."[53] Meaning, the Prophet ﷺ may have only spoken a few words, but the meanings they convey are extremely profound and deep.

In this particular statement, the Prophet ﷺ is clarifying the concept and consequence of adding anything "new" to the religion of Islam. He says that whoever introduces anything new to the religion and practice of Islam that is not a part of it, that new or innovated belief or practice will be rejected. The word the Prophet ﷺ used is aḥdatha, which literally means to invent, bring forth, produce, create, or originate. The verbal noun from this verb, iḥdāth, means an invention, or innovation, which is the linguistic meaning of the word bidʿah. Anything that is considered to be a reprehensible innovation within beliefs or practices, or a bidʿah, will be rejected.

Linguistically the word bidʿah is defined as something new or an innovation, regardless of whether it is related to religious affairs or worldly affairs. Technically, scholars define it as a religious innovation; something new related to religious affairs that was not done in the time of the Messenger of Allah ﷺ, the Rightly Guided Caliphs ﷺ, and the early generations with the intention of gaining more reward, and despite being a need for it in the time of the Messenger of Allah ﷺ and his Companions, it was not implemented verbally, practically, explicitly or implicitly. It has also been defined as any innovation, specifically any new act or form of worship, that does not have a basis in the Quran, Sunnah, or Consensus. In summary, it is any new ritual act that was not around during the time of the Prophet ﷺ, the Companions ﷺ, or the Successors that goes against the Quran, Sunnah, and Ijmāʿ.

Based upon this definition, scholars mention that in order for an act to be classified as a bidʿah it must fulfill two conditions. First, it has to be an act that has no basis, proof, or evidence for it; it is not part of the dīn. Secondly, a person believes that it is part of the dīn.

LESSONS AND BENEFITS

1. ISLAM IS SUBMISSION AND FOLLOWING, NOT INNOVATING

53 Muslim, k. *al-masājid wa mawāḍʿ al-ṣalāh*, 523

Through this warning and teaching, the Prophet ﷺ has protected Islam from any distortions, changes, alterations, additions, and deletions. He has ensured that it remains unchanged by people. Islam came to change people, not to be changed by the people. That is one of the reasons why there are numerous verses in the Quran explaining that success and salvation are in following the guidance of the Prophet ﷺ without adding or deleting anything. Allah ﷻ addressing the Prophet ﷺ says, "Say, 'If you love God, follow me, and God will love you and forgive you your sins; God is most forgiving, most merciful.'"[54] Allah ﷻ also says, "This is My path, leading straight, so follow it, and do not follow other ways: they will lead you away from it- 'This is what He commands you to do, so that you may refrain from wrongdoing.'"[55]

Highlighting the dangers of innovations in religion, the Prophet ﷺ would say the following in his sermons, "The best speech is the Book of Allah and the best guidance is the guidance of Muhammad ﷺ. The worst practice is the introduction of new practices in Islam, and every bid'ah is a misguidance."[56] Another version adds, "And every misguidance is in the fire."

2. GOOD INTENTIONS ALONE ARE NOT ENOUGH

This ḥadīth encompasses the second crucial aspect of the practice of Islam, which is ensuring that the outward performance of actions is correct. The first is sincerity. Sometimes people may think that it is enough to be sincere, without making the effort to ensure that what they are doing is also correct. In addition to having a sincere intention, the action must also be performed properly in accordance with the example of the Prophet ﷺ and the guidelines of Islam. In order for an act to be accepted it has to fulfill two primary conditions:

1. a sincere intention and
2. it has to be performed according to the guidelines of the Sharīʿah.

3. BLAMEWORTHY INNOVATION AS OPPOSED TO GOOD INNOVATION

Every blameworthy innovation will be rejected especially when it comes

54 3:31 - قُلْ إِن كُنتُمْ تُحِبُّونَ اللَّهَ فَاتَّبِعُونِي يُحْبِبْكُمُ اللَّهُ وَيَغْفِرْ لَكُمْ ذُنُوبَكُمْ ۗ وَاللَّهُ غَفُورٌ رَّحِيمٌ

55 6:153 - وَأَنَّ هَٰذَا صِرَاطِي مُسْتَقِيمًا فَاتَّبِعُوهُ ۖ وَلَا تَتَّبِعُوا السُّبُلَ فَتَفَرَّقَ بِكُمْ عَن سَبِيلِهِ ۚ ذَٰلِكُمْ وَصَّاكُم بِهِ لَعَلَّكُمْ تَتَّقُونَ

56 Muslim, *k. al-jumuʿah, b. takhfīf al-ṣalāh wa al-jumuʿah*, 867

to acts of worship. At the same time, there are new things that don't go against the teachings, evidences, proofs and principles of the Sharī'ah and are in fact supported by them and will not be rejected. For example, the compilation of the Quran during the time of Abū Bakr 🙏, the codification of ḥadīth, the development and codification of all branches of Islamic Studies including the Arabic Language, Fiqh, Uṣūl al-Fiqh, Tafsīr, and 'Aqīdah.

That is why scholars clarify and explain that there are two types of "new" actions; those that go against the teachings of the Sharī'ah and are considered to be innovations, and those that do not go against the Sharī'ah and are considered to be useful and helpful. Imām al-Shāfi'ī 🙏 said, "What has been innovated that goes against the Quran or Sunnah or consensus or a narration then it is a misguided innovation, and whatever has been invented and doesn't go against any of these things then it is a praiseworthy innovation."[57]

4. THE RELIGION OF ISLAM IS COMPLETE AS IS

When a person says they are Muslim, it means that they have completely submitted to God with sincerity through devotion, worship, obedience, and servitude. It also means they have accepted Islam as a complete way of life. Islam is a perfect and complete religion. It does not need to be altered, changed, or reformed. As Allah 🙏 says, "Today I have perfected your religion for you, completed My blessing upon you, and chosen Islam as your religion."[58] Islam is complete and perfect as is and it has its own theology, practices, rituals, morals, principles, ethics, and values.

---

57   ما أحدث و خالف كتابا أو سنة أو إجماعا أو أثرا فهو البدعة الضالة، و ما أحدث من الخير و لم يخالف شيئا من ذلك فهو البدعة المحمودة

58   5:3 - الْيَوْمَ أَكْمَلْتُ لَكُمْ دِينَكُمْ وَأَتْمَمْتُ عَلَيْكُمْ نِعْمَتِي وَرَضِيتُ لَكُمُ الْإِسْلَامَ دِينًا

HADITH 6

The Lawful and the Unlawful Are Clear

عَنْ أَبِي عَبْدِ اللَّهِ النُّعْمَانِ بْنِ بَشِيرٍ رَضِيَ اللَّهُ عَنْهُمَا، قَالَ: سَمِعْت رَسُولَ اللَّهِ صلى الله عليه و سلم يَقُولُ: "إِنَّ الْحَلَالَ بَيِّنٌ، وَإِنَّ الْحَرَامَ بَيِّنٌ، وَبَيْنَهُمَا أُمُورٌ مُشْتَبِهَاتٌ لَا يَعْلَمُهُنَّ كَثِيرٌ مِنْ النَّاسِ، فَمَنْ اتَّقَى الشُّبُهَاتِ فَقْد اسْتَبْرَأَ لِدِينِهِ وَعِرْضِهِ، وَمَنْ وَقَعَ فِي الشُّبُهَاتِ وَقَعَ فِي الْحَرَامِ، كَالرَّاعِي يَرْعَى حَوْلَ الْحِمَى يُوشِكُ أَنْ يَرْتَعَ فِيهِ، أَلَا وَإِنَّ لِكُلِّ مَلِكٍ حِمًى، أَلَا وَإِنَّ حِمَى اللَّهِ مَحَارِمُهُ، أَلَا وَإِنَّ فِي الْجَسَدِ مُضْغَةً إِذَا صَلَحَتْ صَلَحَ الْجَسَدُ كُلُّهُ، وَإِذَا فَسَدَتْ فَسَدَ الْجَسَدُ كُلُّهُ، أَلَا وَهِيَ الْقَلْبُ".

رَوَاهُ الْبُخَارِيُّ، وَمُسْلِمٌ.

From Abū ʿAbd Allah al-Nuʿmān ibn Bashīr ☙ who said that I heard the Messenger of Allah ☙ say, "Truly the lawful is clear and truly the unlawful is clear, and between them are doubtful matters that many people do not know about. Whoever avoids doubtful matters clears themselves with respect to their religion and honor. The one who falls into doubtful matters falls into the unlawful, similar to the shepherd who pastures around a sanctuary, all but grazing therein. Truly every king has a sanctuary, and truly Allah's sanctuary is His prohibitions. Truly in the body there is a morsel of flesh, if it is sound then the entire body will be sound, and if it is diseased then the entire body will be diseased. Truly it is the heart."

Narrated by Bukhārī and Muslim.

THE NARRATOR

His full name is Abū ʿAbd Allah al-Nuʿmān ibn Bashīr ibn Kaʿb al-Khazrajī al-Anṣārī ﷺ. He was born 14 months after the migration of the Prophet ﷺ from Makkah to Madinah and he was the first child born to the Anṣār. Both his father and mother were also Companions of the Prophet ﷺ. He is among the younger companions. When the Prophet ﷺ left this world he was only 8 years old. He was known to be extremely generous and he was also known to be good at poetry. He was killed in the year 56. 114 aḥādīth have been narrated from him, may Allah ﷻ be pleased with him.

IMPORTANCE

This ḥadīth is also among those narrations that are considered to be a part of the foundational or most important teachings of Islam. It is described as one of those narrations around which all of Islam revolves. It is one of the three that Imam Aḥmad ﷺ mentioned:

1. "Actions are only by their intentions...",[59]
2. "Whoever introduces...",[60] and
3. "The permissible is clear...".

According to some scholars, whoever reflects over the lessons of this ḥadīth will realize that it encompasses all of the teachings of Islam; both external and internal. It mentions all of the possible external acts that a person can do: the lawful, unlawful, and doubtful, as well as the importance of purifying one's heart.

EXPLANATION

In this ḥadīth the Prophet ﷺ divided actions into three broad categories:

1. Clearly lawful,
2. Clearly unlawful, and

59 Ḥadīth #1 in this collection

60 Ḥadīth #5 in this collection

3. Doubtful

The Prophet ﷺ described those things that are clearly lawful by saying, "Truly the lawful is clear." These are actions or affairs that the Sharīʿah has explicitly made permissible through the Quran or Sunnah. Meaning, their permissibility is absolutely clear, unequivocal, unambiguous, and there are no doubts about it. For example, eating bread, speaking, sleeping, or walking.

The Prophet ﷺ describes those things that are clearly unlawful by saying, "And truly the unlawful is clear." These are actions or affairs that the Sharīʿah, through the Quran and Sunnah, has clearly and unequivocally forbidden. Their impermissibility or unlawful nature is absolutely clear; there is no doubt about their impermissibility whatsoever. For example, stealing, cheating, lying, theft, drinking, and interest.

Doubtful matters are described by the Prophet ﷺ as "and between the two of them are doubtful matters about which many people do not know." Doubtful matters or actions are those in which there is doubt regarding their permissibility or impermissibility. It is important to note that the act or matter is not doubtful in and of itself. It is doubtful with respect to the knowledge of the individual; meaning, the person does not know the legal ruling. They are unaware if it is permissible or impermissible. For example, if a person doesn't know the ruling of a particular thing, then it is necessary for that person to avoid it until asking a scholar or person of knowledge.

In the next part of the ḥadīth the Prophet ﷺ is explaining that it is much better and safer to avoid those matters, affairs, or issues that are doubtful. He ﷺ explains that by avoiding doubtful matters, a person is protecting both their religion and honor. They are protecting their religion because they are avoiding something that could potentially be unlawful or something that could cause them harm. They are protecting their honor because no one will be able to criticize them for doing something that could potentially be wrong. That is one of the reasons why there are narrations cautioning against being in situations or places that would lead to suspicions.

The Prophet ﷺ then says that whoever falls into doubtful matters will eventually fall into something that is unlawful. A person who continues to delve into doubtful acts and matters will eventually fall into something impermissible. "The disliked acts are like a check post between a person and unlawful matters. Whoever indulges frequently in disliked things will become a victim of unlawful matters. Similarly, the permissible acts are a checkpoint between a person and disliked matters. Whoever crosses the checkpoint often will commit disliked acts as well." When a person continuously does something that is doubtful they will start becoming careless, let their guard down, and eventually fall into something that is clearly forbidden.

That is why there are multiple sayings from the scholars of the past regarding staying away from doubtful matters. Abū Dardā'a ﷺ said, "Complete taqwā is that the servant is conscious of Allah ﷻ, to such an extent that he fears Him with respect to the weight of an atom, and when he leaves something that he believes to be permissible out of fear that it may be unlawful as a veil between him and what is unlawful."[61] al-Ḥasan al-Baṣrī said, "God-consciousness remains with the God-conscious as long as they leave many lawful things out of fear of the unlawful."[62] al-Thawrī said, "They have been called the God-conscious because they avoid that which isn't normally avoided."[63] Ibn ʿUmar said, "Indeed I love to leave a veil (curtain) between me and the unlawful of the lawful that I won't tear."[64]

The Prophet ﷺ then gives an example to deepen the understanding and reality of this particular concept. He compares a person that constantly indulges in doubtful matters and affairs to a shepherd who continuously grazes around the boundary of someone else's property. If he continues to allow his animals to graze along the boundary of someone else's property, eventually they will end up grazing inside.

The Prophet ﷺ then said, "Truly every king has a sanctuary, and truly Allah's sanctuary is His prohibitions." Meaning the boundary that has been set up by Allah ﷻ is His prohibitions. That is the line that Muslims are not supposed to cross or even come close to. Constantly engaging in doubtful matters and affairs brings one very close to crossing that boundary.

The Prophet ﷺ finished this ḥadīth with a very profound, powerful, deep, and important statement. He said that there is a single piece of flesh in the body, if it is sound, healthy, wholesome, and pure then the entire body will be sound, healthy, wholesome, and pure. If it is corrupt, sick, and dam-

61 تمام التقوى أن يتقي الله العبد، حتى يتقيه من مثقال ذرة، وحين يترك بعض ما يرى أنه حلال، خشية أن يكون حراما، حجابا بينه و بين الحرام

62 ما زالت التقوى بالمتقين حتى تركوا كثيرا من الحلال مخافة الحرام

63 إنما سموا المتقين لأنهم اتقوا ما لا يتقى

64 Ibn Rajab, *Jāmiʿ al-ʿUlūm wa al-Ḥikam*, v. 2 p. 161-2

aged then the entire body will be corrupt, sick, and damaged. And that is the heart. The heart being referred to in this ḥadīth is not the physical heart, the organ in the human body. Rather, what is being referred to here is the spiritual heart.

The spiritual heart is the single most important part of the human body. That is where the seed of faith is planted, nurtured, and allowed to grow. The heart is the center of faith, īmān, understanding, thought, reflection, and contemplation. The heart is the engine that drives human behavior; both actions and statements. The heart is the general or the commander and the limbs are its soldiers. If the heart is pure then the eyes, ears, and tongue will also be pure. That is why there is so much importance placed on the concepts of spirituality and purification.

Tazkiyah, which is understood as spirituality and purification of the heart, is an integral part of one's practice of Islam. Allah ﷻ describes it as one of the primary responsibilities of the Prophet ﷺ. Allah ﷻ says, "God has been truly gracious to the believers in sending them a Messenger from among their own, to recite His revelations to them, to make them grow in purity, and to teach them the Scripture and wisdom- before that they were clearly astray."[65] Human beings have both praiseworthy and blameworthy characteristics and qualities. Their responsibility is to cleanse their hearts from blameworthy qualities and adorn their hearts and character with praiseworthy qualities. A person should work on purifying their heart from spiritual ailments and diseases such as hypocrisy, jealousy, greed, hatred, pride, arrogance, doubt, cowardice, miserliness, ostentation, and love of this world. They should be replaced with truthfulness, love, selflessness, humility, certainty, bravery, generosity, sincerity, and simplicity.

LESSONS AND BENEFITS

1. THE PERMISSIBLE, IMPERMISSIBLE, AND DOUBTFUL

Knowing what is permissible and what is impermissible is essential for a person's practice of Islam. There is a base level of knowledge and literacy that every single Muslim should have that allows them to practice their faith and religion properly in a manner that is pleasing to Allah ﷻ. Seeking this base

65 3:164 - لَقَدْ مَنَّ اللَّهُ عَلَى الْمُؤْمِنِينَ إِذْ بَعَثَ فِيهِمْ رَسُولًا مِّنْ أَنفُسِهِمْ يَتْلُو عَلَيْهِمْ آيَاتِهِ وَيُزَكِّيهِمْ وَيُعَلِّمُهُمُ الْكِتَابَ وَالْحِكْمَةَ وَإِن كَانُوا مِن قَبْلُ لَفِي ضَلَالٍ مُّبِينٍ

level of literacy is an obligation upon each and every single Muslim. As the Prophet ﷺ said, "Seeking knowledge is an obligation upon every single Muslim."[66] This does not mean that everyone has to become a scholar; rather, everyone has to learn enough knowledge that will allow them to worship their Creator properly with understanding.

2. *PERSONAL PIETY*

Taqwā, God-consciousness, is one of the defining qualities of a believer. There are several verses throughout the Quran where Allah ﷻ addresses the believers commanding them to have taqwā. Oftentimes when the Prophet ﷺ was asked for advice, he would start by reminding the person to be conscious of Allah ﷻ. Taqwā, in practical terms, is described by the scholars as obeying the commandments of Allah ﷻ and staying away from His prohibitions. There is a higher level of consciousness or awareness of Allah ﷻ that leads one to staying away from doubtful matters as well, which is described as warʿ. This is a personal level of piety where a person chooses to avoid things that are doubtful, or even things that may be permissible, in order to stay far away from those things that are impermissible. By doing so they are striving to protect their religion and their honor, as described by the Prophet ﷺ. Sufyān ibn ʿUyaynah رحمه الله said, "A servant does not achieve the reality of īmān until they place between themselves and the impermissible a barrier of the permissible, and until they leave sins and what comes close to them."[67]

3. *IMPORTANCE OF GIVING EXAMPLES*

This ḥadīth provides insight into the teaching methods of the Prophet ﷺ. The Prophet ﷺ is the most perfect example of a teacher to walk on the face of this Earth. He employed different methods, styles, and strategies to teach his companions important concepts depending on the context, situation, scenario, circumstance, environment, and audience. One of those methods was to provide clear examples and analogies in order to simplify a concept.

4. *ASK QUESTIONS*

If a person has doubt regarding a specific issue or if they don't know the

---

66 Ibn Mājah, *k. al-muqaddimah*, 229

67 Ibn Rajab, *Jāmiʿ al-ʿUlūm wa al-Ḥikam*, v. 2 p. 161-2

ruling regarding a particular matter it is their responsibility to ask those who know; the scholars. Allah ﷻ says, "Ask those who have knowledge if you do not know."[68] The Prophet ﷺ said, "Good questions are half of knowledge."[69]

5. TAZKIYAH

As mentioned earlier, tazkiyah, or purification of the heart, is an essential part of Islam. Oftentimes Islam, and religion in general, is limited to ritual acts of worship and rules and regulations; a list of do's and don'ts. Islam is a comprehensive way of life that contains guidance for every single aspect of a person's life; individual, family, community, economics, and politics. The teachings of Islam can be organized into five broad categories:

1. Creed - This covers the articles of faith and the system of belief. Specifically, it covers the beliefs that make one a Muslim. What do Muslims believe about Allah? Angels? Prophets? Scripture? Life after death? Divine Decree?
2. Ritual Acts of Worship - This covers ritual acts of worship and devotion such as prayer, fasting, charity, and ḥajj.
3. Financial Transactions - This covers the rules and regulations related to business, trade, investing, partnerships, transactions that are permissible, and transactions that are impermissible.
4. Social Dealings - Every single human being plays different roles in life; people are fathers, brothers, sons, uncles, mothers, daughters, aunts, friends, neighbors, colleagues, and classmates. In each of these roles they have a certain set of rights and responsibilities.
5. Tazkiyah and Good Character - Adorning one's character with praiseworthy qualities such as sincerity, patience, forbearance, taqwā, simplicity, humility and generosity while also purifying one's heart from spiritual diseases such as hypocrisy, pride, envy, and jealousy.

---

68 16:43 - فَاسْأَلُوا أَهْلَ الذِّكْرِ إِن كُنتُمْ لَا تَعْلَمُونَ

69 al-Bayhaqī, *Shuʿab al-Īmān*, 5:2239

HADITH 7

Sincere Advice

عَنْ أَبِي رُقَيَّةَ تَمِيمِ بْنِ أَوْسٍ الدَّارِيِّ رَضِيَ اللَّه عَنْهُ أَنَّ النَّبِيَّ صلى الله عليه وسلم قَالَ: "الدِّينُ النَّصِيحَةُ." قُلْنَا: لِمَنْ؟ قَالَ: "لِلَّهِ، وَلِكِتَابِهِ، وَلِرَسُولِهِ، وَلِأَئِمَّةِ الْمُسْلِمِينَ وَعَامَّتِهِمْ."
رَوَاهُ مُسْلِمٌ.

From Abū Ruqayyah Tamīm ibn Aws al-Dārī ﵁: The Prophet ﷺ said, "The dīn (religion) is naṣīḥah (advice, sincerity)." We said "To whom?" He ﷺ said "To Allah, His Book, His Messenger, and to the leaders of the Muslims, and their common folk."

Narrated by Muslim.

THE NARRATOR

His full name is Abū Ruqayyah Tamīm ibn Aws al-Dārī ﷺ. He used to be Christian and accepted Islam in the 9th year after migration. He lived in Madinah and then moved to Shām after ʿUthmān ﷺ was martyred. He settled in Palestine and was known for his night prayers, piety, and worship. He passed away in the year 40 in Palestine. Eighteen aḥādīth have been narrated from him.

IMPORTANCE

As mentioned earlier, the Prophet ﷺ was given a special gift known as jawāmiʿ al-kalim, concise yet comprehensive speech. In a few words he was able to convey extremely deep and profound meanings. This narration is considered to be among his jawāmiʿ al-kalim. The scholars of ḥadīth write that despite its brevity and conciseness it brings together the benefits of both this world and the next. Others have written that this ḥadīth contains the entirety of Islam; meaning all of the teachings of Islam in its totality. Some scholars of hadith have said that if 1000's of aḥādīth were to be lost, this brief ḥadīth would be sufficient to guide Muslims. Imam Abū Dāwūd ﷺ said that this is one of the aḥādīth around which all of fiqh revolves. This is because in these few words, the Prophet ﷺ has captured the entire religion of Islam.

EXPLANATION

This narration starts with the Prophet ﷺ telling his Companions that, "Religion is sincere advice." Meaning that the essence, cornerstone, core, and foundation of Islam is naṣīḥah. Naṣīḥah is often translated as sincerity or sincere advice. However, this translation only captures a part of the meaning. It is a comprehensive word that embodies every type of virtue and the desire for all forms of goodness. Ibn Ḥajar ﷺ states that there is no other word in the Arabic Language that is so comprehensive. "Naṣīḥah is the seeking of an action or statement that contains goodness and improvement for the other person." It is a desire for what is good for the person who is the subject.

The Companions then ask the Prophet ﷺ, "For whom?" The Prophet ﷺ responded, "To Allah, His Book, His Messenger, and to the leaders of the

Muslims, and their common folk." The Prophet ﷺ highlighted five different avenues or aspects of naṣīḥah, the first being Allah ﷻ, the Lord of the heavens and the earth and everything they contain.

What exactly does it mean that nāṣīḥah is for Allah ﷻ? It means believing in Him, His existence, oneness, might, power, glory, and magnificence. It means denying any partners, affirming all of His divine names and attributes, obeying Him, fulfilling His commands, staying away from His prohibitions, to remember Him in all circumstances, to love for His sake, to hate for His sake, recognizing His blessings, and showing gratitude for those blessings. It also means to be sincere in our worship. Naṣīḥah for Allah includes recognizing that Allah ﷻ is absolutely unique, that nothing in this universe resembles Him in any way, shape, or form, and that He alone is deserving and worthy of worship.

Naṣīḥah to His Book means first and foremost to believe that the Quran is from Allah ﷻ; that it is His divine uncreated speech, the words of Allah ﷻ revealed to the Prophet ﷺ for the guidance of all of humanity until the end of times. It means to believe that the Quran is a miracle, the greatest miracle given to any Prophet, a miracle that can be experienced, witnessed, and felt till this day. To believe that the Quran is inimitable and that nothing similar to it can ever be produced. Being sincere to the Quran also means having an active relationship with it that includes recitation, memorization, study, reflection, and most importantly acting upon its guidance. The recitation of the Quran in and of itself is an act of worship that carries a lot of virtues, rewards, and blessings. It also means to handle the Quran with respect and manners.

Naṣīḥah to His Messenger involves first and foremost believing in his messengership; that he is the last and final Messenger sent for the guidance of mankind, the Seal of Prophethood after whom no other Prophet or Messenger will come. It includes having faith in all that he came with, obeying him in all that he ordered and forbade, helping him both in his life and after his death, having enmity with all those who have enmity with him, and having allegiance to all those who have allegiance with him. It includes fulfilling his rights, loving and honoring him, reviving his manner and Sunnah, responding to his daʿwah, spreading his Sunnah, understanding its meanings and sciences, calling towards it, and being eager in studying it, showing respect when it is mentioned, and refraining from speaking about it without knowledge. It also includes mixing among the people of the Sunnah, and behaving with the character taught by the Sunnah, and showing love towards the members of the Prophet's ﷺ Household, and his Companions. It means having this deep, unshakeable love and attachment to the Messenger of Allah ﷺ. The Prophet ﷺ said, "None of you truly believes until I am more beloved to them than their father, son, and all of mankind."[70] Naṣīḥah to the Messenger also means to take him as one's role model in every single aspect of one's life, reading and learning about him, and trying to follow his example in everything a person does.

Naṣīḥah to the leaders of the Muslims involves helping them in the truth, obeying them, ordering them with the Truth, reminding them of it with kindness and gentle words, notifying and advising them of that which they have neglected, informing them of the rights of the Muslims, not rebelling against them with the sword, gathering the hearts of the people upon obeying them, praying behind them, and making supplication for their correction. This advice can include both the leaders and scholars.

Naṣīḥah to the common folk involves guiding them towards that which will correct their affairs of both this life and the next, and helping them in that. It involves protecting them from harm, helping them in times of need, acquiring what is beneficial for them, ordering them with al-maʿrūf (good) and forbidding them from al-munkar (evil) with kindness and sincerity, and showing mercy towards them. It involves honoring and respecting their elders, showing kindness to their youngsters, and supporting them with good advice. It also includes not cheating them or having jealousy of them, that one loves for them what one loves for oneself of goodness, that one hates for them what one hates for oneself of evil, protecting their wealth and honor, and other than that from speech and action.

LESSONS AND BENEFITS

1. *RELATIONSHIPS*

In this ḥadīth the Prophet ﷺ has highlighted five different relationships that a person has:

---

70 Muslim, *k. al-īmān, b. wujūb maḥabbah al-rasūl* ﷺ *akthara min al-ahl wa al-walad wa al-wālid wa al-nās ajmaʿīn wa iṭlāq ʿadam al-īmān ʿalā man lam yuḥibbahu hādhihi al-maḥabbah*, 44

1. With Allah ﷻ
2. With the Quran
3. With the Messenger ﷺ
4. With leaders
5. With other human beings

Maintaining relationships and giving them their due rights is extremely important. That is why it is essential to understand the nature of the relationship and the foundations upon which it is built. Every single relationship consists of rights and responsibilities. Rather than focusing on one's rights within a relationship, more emphasis should be placed on fulfilling one's responsibilities. By doing so a person is working towards nurturing the relationship and becomes a means for it to grow and become stronger.

1. Relationship with Allah ﷻ - A person's relationship with Allah ﷻ is one of submission, servitude, obedience, sincerity, and devotion. Allah ﷻ is the Lord and humans are His servants. The foundation of the relationship is love, which expresses itself through hope and fear. Hoping in the mercy, forgiveness, grace, and bounties of Allah ﷻ while at the same time fearing His anger, punishment, and displeasure. This relationship is nurtured by learning about Allah ﷻ through His Divine Names and Attributes, by reflecting over His countless blessings and favors, and expressing gratitude for them.
2. Relationship with the Quran - The relationship between a believer and the Quran is that of a student and a teacher, a follower and a guide. The Quran teaches human beings about certain absolute truths and realities that form part of the system of belief of Islam. Basically, it explains the relationship between man and his Creator. The second objective is to detail the rules and regulations that govern everyday life. It provides guidance for life as an individual, as a member of a family, and as a member of society. It provides guidance with respect to individual, social, economic, and political life. That is why it is essential to build a relationship with the Quran by reading it regularly, reflecting and pondering over its meanings, and implementing its teachings and guidance into one's daily life.
3. Relationship with the Messenger ﷺ - The relationship between a

believer and the Messenger ﷺ is also that of a student and a teacher. The Messenger of Allah ﷺ is the most perfect example of a human being to walk on the face of this earth. Allah ﷻ says, "Indeed in the Messenger of Allah you have a good example to follow for him who hopes in Allah and the Last Day and remembers Allah much."[71] The Prophet ﷺ is the ideal role model for believers to follow in every single aspect of their lives; personal, social, communal, economic, and political. The Prophet ﷺ was a physical manifestation of the teachings of the Quran; his life was built upon the beliefs, morals, values, and principles mentioned in the Quran. That is why when his wife ʿĀ'ishah رضي الله عنها was asked regarding his character she replied, "His character was the Quran."[72] The Prophet ﷺ had the most noble character and manners; he was extremely kind, gentle, caring, friendly, affable, generous, compassionate, patient, forbearing, forgiving, brave, humble, and simple. He dealt with people in the most beautiful way possible. Allah ﷻ praises him in the Quran saying, "And you are surely on an excellent standard of character."[73]

The foundation of the relationship with the Messenger of Allah ﷺ is love, honor, respect, and reverence. The way to build and develop that is by learning about his life through studying his sīrah (biography), character, and physical appearance. It is also nurtured by following his Sunnah and sending abundant salutations upon him ﷺ.

4. Relationship with those in Positions of Authority - The relationship between believers and their leaders is very interesting and unique. Allah ﷻ says, "You who believe, obey God and the Messenger, and those in authority among you. If you are in dispute over any matter, refer it to God and the Messenger, if you truly believe in God and the Last Day: that is better and more fair in the end."[74] In this verse, Allah ﷻ not only commands people of faith to obey God and His Messenger, He also commands them to obey those in authority among

71 33:21 - لَّقَدْ كَانَ لَكُمْ فِي رَسُولِ اللَّـهِ أُسْوَةٌ حَسَنَةٌ لِّمَن كَانَ يَرْجُو اللَّـهَ وَالْيَوْمَ الْآخِرَ وَذَكَرَ اللَّـهَ كَثِيرًا

72 *al-Adab al-Mufrad*

73 68:4 - وَإِنَّكَ لَعَلَىٰ خُلُقٍ عَظِيمٍ

74 4:59 - يَا أَيُّهَا الَّذِينَ آمَنُوا أَطِيعُوا اللَّـهَ وَأَطِيعُوا الرَّسُولَ وَأُولِي الْأَمْرِ مِنكُمْ ۖ فَإِن تَنَازَعْتُمْ فِي شَيْءٍ فَرُدُّوهُ إِلَى اللَّـهِ وَالرَّسُولِ إِن كُنتُمْ تُؤْمِنُونَ بِاللَّـهِ وَالْيَوْمِ الْآخِرِ ۚ ذَٰلِكَ خَيْرٌ وَأَحْسَنُ تَأْوِيلًا

you. It is important to recognize that this obedience is not absolute and unrestricted. Rather, it has certain limits, boundaries, and guidelines. One of the most important principles in dealing with authority is highlighted in the words of the Prophet ﷺ, "There is no obedience for the creation in the disobedience of the Creator."[75]

Islam places a lot of importance on order, peace, security, and safety within society. Part of that is having a clear structure of governance, leadership, and law. Without these things any society or community would quickly devolve into chaos. Muslims as citizens or residents of a polity or state are required to follow the law of the land and respect the hierarchy of governance. However, as mentioned above, this is not absolute. They are required to do so as long as it doesn't infringe upon their personal rights and religious freedoms.

5. Relationships with Others - One of the major components of Islamic teachings is social behavior and interaction. There is a lot of emphasis placed on family, community, and community building. Islam is not an individualistic or self-centered religion; rather, it is communal and selfless. Muslims are taught to treat others with respect, kindness, care, sympathy, compassion, generosity, love, mercy, and forgiveness. There is guidance on how to live as parents, children, spouses, in-laws, relatives, neighbors, co-workers, classmates, and any other relationship one can think of. The goal of these teachings is to produce healthy, productive, and vibrant families and communities that live their lives in a manner that is pleasing to Allah ﷻ.

2. ISLAM GUIDES ALL ASPECTS OF LIFE

Islam is not limited to ritual and devotional acts of worship. Islam is not simply a creed or a theology. Islam is a complete way of life.

---

75 Haythamī, *majmaʿ al-zawā'id*, 9:189

HADITH 8

Sanctity of Muslim Life

عَنْ ابْنِ عُمَرَ رَضِيَ اللَّهُ عَنْهُمَا، أَنَّ رَسُولَ اللَّهِ صلى الله عليه و سلم قَالَ: "أُمِرْتُ أَنْ أُقَاتِلَ النَّاسَ حَتَّى يَشْهَدُوا أَنْ لَا إلَهَ إلَّا اللَّهُ وَأَنَّ مُحَمَّدًا رَسُولُ اللَّهِ، وَيُقِيمُوا الصَّلَاةَ، وَيُؤْتُوا الزَّكَاةَ؛ فَإِذَا فَعَلُوا ذَلِكَ عَصَمُوا مِنِّي دِمَاءَهُمْ وَأَمْوَالَهُمْ إلَّا بِحَقِّ الْإِسْلَامِ، وَحِسَابُهُمْ عَلَى اللَّهِ تَعَالَى".

رَوَاهُ الْبُخَارِيُّ، وَمُسْلِمٌ.

From ibn ʿUmar ﷺ that the Messenger of Allah ﷺ said: "I have been commanded to fight the people until they bear witness that there is no deity worthy of worship except Allah and that Muḥammad is the Messenger of Allah, and until they establish ṣalāh and pay zakāh. If they do that then their lives and property will be protected from me except through the right of Islam, and their accounting will be with Allah."

Narrated by al-Bukhārī and Muslim.

IMPORTANCE

This ḥadīth is considered to be important for several reasons:

1. It highlights the primary purpose and objective of jihād in Islam
2. It emphasizes the importance of faith coupled with action
3. It underlines two of the most fundamental objectives of Islamic Law:
    a. Protection of life
    b. Protection of wealth
4. Absolute judgment and justice based on what is in a person's heart is the right of Allah ﷻ, not human beings.

EXPLANATION

The wording of this ḥadīth is fairly clear, explicit, and unambiguous. The Prophet ﷺ is saying that he has been commanded by Allah ﷻ to fight "the people" until they enter the fold of Islam by declaring the testimony of faith and following its teachings, specifically establishing prayer and paying zakāh. Once they accept Islam, their lives and property will be protected and considered sacred, unless they commit a crime that is so egregious, such as intentional homicide, that it removes the sanctity of their lives. What is meant by "except in accordance with the right of Islam" is any crime or offence that will remove that protection such as murder or unjust rebellion.

The Prophet ﷺ concludes the ḥadīth by highlighting that what lies inside of a person's heart in terms of truthfulness and sincerity in known only to Allah ﷻ. When it comes to a person's practice of religion, they are to be taken at face value and what is apparent. If they claim to be Muslim, pray, pay zakāh, and practice to the best of their ability, then they will be treated as Muslims. Judging whether they were truthful and sincere in their claim and practice is the realm of Allah ﷻ. Their sincerity and truthfulness is between them and Allah ﷻ; only Allah can judge them.

As soon as a person declares the testimony of faith with sincerity and truthfulness, they enter into the fold of Islam. By simply testifying, one is entitled to the rights of a Muslim and also carries responsibilities towards other Muslims. Meaning as soon as a person declares the testimony of faith, they are entitled to everything that a Muslim is entitled to, and at the same time they also bear the same responsibilities. However, this testimony does not carry any weight without action. That is why the Prophet ﷺ highlighted the importance of establishing prayer and paying zakāh. Faith has to be coupled with action.

In order to have a holistic and proper understanding of this ḥadīth, it is extremely important to note who exactly is meant by "the people". Is this a general statement referring to all non-Muslims or is it referring to a specific group of people? The vast majority of ḥadīth scholars are of the opinion that "the people" is referring to the Arab Polytheists of that time, because other evidence excludes Jews and Christians. One of the versions of this ḥadīth actually mentions the Polytheists by name.[76] For those who are familiar with the Sīrah of the Prophet ﷺ and early Islamic History, the Polytheists were sworn and open enemies of the Prophet ﷺ and his followers. They persecuted, harassed, and tortured them, eventually driving them out of their homes forcing them to migrate to Madinah.

The Prophet ﷺ was commanded by Allah ﷻ to fight them until they accepted the rule of Allah ﷻ and ceased their opposition. This objective can be met through several means that are referenced in the Quran and Sunnah. For example, this objective can be met through a peace treaty or mutual agreement (ṣulḥ), or through them accepting to live under the rule of God. The command mentioned here is not a license to force people to accept Islam. The aḥādīth of the Prophet ﷺ must be contextualized and understood within the complete framework of Islam. A ruling or judgment is never made by simply looking at one report from the Prophet ﷺ. Scholars research and examine all the reports, relevant verses and teachings concerning that topic, and then formulate an answer. An explicit principle of the Quran is that there is no compulsion in religion. Allah ﷻ says, "Let there be no compulsion in religion, for the truth stands out clearly from falsehood."[77]

LESSONS AND BENEFITS

1. *ISLAM DID NOT SPREAD BY THE SWORD*

Orientalist scholars, Islamophobes, and others who have prejudice or bias towards Islam use this ḥadīth and other similar texts to raise objections,

76 al-Nasā'ī, *k. taḥrīm al-dam*, 3966

77 2:256 - لَا إِكْرَاهَ فِي الدِّينِ ۖ قَد تَّبَيَّنَ الرُّشْدُ مِنَ الْغَيِّ

create doubts and uncertainties, and critique Islam. Based on these texts, they argue that Islam is inherently violent, intolerant, and that it was spread by the sword.

The Orientalists are scholars who take an interest in what is known as "Eastern" studies. A part of these Oriental studies is the study of Islam, and the primary purpose associated with it is not necessarily to seek the truth or gain knowledge, rather it is to deconstruct Islam. Dr. Brown writes in *Hadith: Muhammad's Legacy in the Medieval and Modern World*, "Western criticism of the hadīth tradition can be viewed as an act of domination in which one world-view asserts its power over another by dictating the terms by which 'knowledge' and 'truth' are established. From this perspective, one could ask why the 'light' that Western scholars shed on hadiths is necessarily more valuable to 'the advancement of human understanding' than what the Muslim hadīth tradition has already offered. As the likes of Edward Said have shown, knowledge is power, and studying an object is an act of establishing control over it. It is thus no coincidence that two of the three main avenues through which the Western study of the Islamic world progressed, that of Ottoman studies and the study of Persianate culture in South Asia, were originally tied to the European pursuit of diplomatic and colonial agendas in the Ottoman Empire and India. Western discussions about the reliability of the hadith tradition are thus not neutral, and their influence extends beyond the lofty hall of academia. The Authenticity Question is part of a broader debate over the power dynamic between 'Religion' and 'Modernity', and between 'Islam' and the 'West'."[78]

Interestingly, many of these scholars are experts in research and may actually know a lot more about Islam than the average Muslim. One of the many objections they raise is that the concept of jihād in Islam exists as a mechanism to force people to accept Islam. They argue that the only way for Islam to have spread so rapidly across the world is through forced conversion under the threat of the sword. Therefore, Islam was spread by the sword and is by nature an intolerant religion.

This particular narrative of Islam being spread by the sword has been, and continues to be, used to paint Islam and Muslims in a very negative light. However, there are now a growing number of historians that challenge

---

78 Brown, Jonathan. *Hadith: Muhammad's Legacy in the Medieval and Modern World*. Oneworld Academic, 2018.

this narrative. They recognize that Islam spread through other means such as daʿwah, trade, intermarriage, migration, influencers, Islam's emphasis on justice and unity, and the universality of Islam.[79] For example, Hassam Munir in his paper "Did Islam Spread by the Sword? A Critical Look at Forced Conversions" cites De Lacy O'Leary who wrote in 1923 that "the legend of fanatical Muslims sweeping through the world and forcing Islam at the point of the sword upon conquered races is one of the most fantastically absurd myths that historians have ever repeated."[80] Based on historical facts, observations, research, and Islamic texts the claim that Islam spread by the sword is based either in intellectual dishonesty, ignorance, or blind prejudice. There may have been some cases of forced conversions, "but they were rare, exceptional, occured in particular contexts, and in violation of the Quranic prohibition of this practice."

2. *THERE IS NO COMPULSION IN RELIGION*

Allah ﷻ says, "Let there be no compulsion in religion, for the truth stands out clearly from falsehood."[81] Ibn Kathīr رحمه الله writes that this verse means, "Do not force anyone to become Muslim, for Islam is plain and clear, and its proofs and evidences are plain and clear. Therefore, there is no need to force anyone to embrace Islam."

3. *FAITH IS COUPLED WITH ACTION*

In most places throughout the Quran, when īmān is mentioned it is coupled with righteous deeds; action. Allah ﷻ says in Sūrah al-ʿAṣr, "By time, truly mankind is in loss. Except for those who have believed and done righteous deeds and advised each other with the truth and advised each other with patience."[82] A person's faith expresses itself through their speech, actions, behavior, and the way they carry themselves.

79 Munir, Hassam. "How Islam Spread throughout the World" Yaqeen, Yaqeen Institute, 14 December 2018, https://yaqeeninstitute.org/en/hassam-munir/how-islam-spread-throughout-the-world/

80 Munir, Hassam. "Did Islam Spread by the Sword? A Critical Look at Forced Conversions" Yaqeen, Yaqeen Institute, 12 May 2018, https://yaqeeninstitute.org/en/hassam-munir/did-islam-spread-by-the-sword-a-critical-look-at-forced-conversions/

81 لَا إِكْرَاهَ فِي الدِّينِ ۖ قَد تَّبَيَّنَ الرُّشْدُ مِنَ الْغَيِّ - 2:256

82 وَالْعَصْرِ إِنَّ الْإِنسَانَ لَفِي خُسْرٍ إِلَّا الَّذِينَ آمَنُوا وَعَمِلُوا الصَّالِحَاتِ وَتَوَاصَوْا بِالْحَقِّ وَتَوَاصَوْا بِالصَّبْرِ - 103 :1-3

4. OBJECTIVES OF THE SHARĪʿAH

The detailed laws, rules, and regulations of the Sharīʿah have higher aims and objectives, which are termed Maqāṣid al-Sharīʿah. The laws of Islam are designed to promote peace, prosperity, security, and freedom by establishing a healthy and vibrant society that is built upon faith and morality. The Scholars identify five main objectives:

1. Protection of Faith
2. Protection of Life
3. Protection of Lineage
4. Protection of Intellect, and
5. Protection of Property

This ḥadīth highlights the Protection of Life and Property.

5. CRIME AND PUNISHMENT

Every single society, whether big or small, rural or urban, tribal or otherwise, is in need of a system of governance. In order for a society to be healthy, productive and flourish, in order for a society to function properly, there needs to be a working system of governance that regulates behavior. Without these laws and regulations a society will quickly devolve into absolute chaos. That is why throughout history societies have developed and refined various forms of governance and law.

Usually speaking, at least in the modern world, there are two primary realms of law:

1. Civil Law, and
2. Criminal Law

Civil law deals with people's rights over and obligations to each other. This includes contract, marriage, divorce and property. It regulates disputes between parties. Criminal law regulates wrongs done to the public, society or state. Civil wrongs are punished by compensation. Criminal wrongs are punishable by incarceration, corporal, or even capital punishment.

Just like any other system of law that exists or has existed, one aspect of the Sharīʿah is criminal law. Criminal law in most societies is simply punitive;

it focuses on the punishments for specific crimes. As mentioned, criminal wrongs are punishable by incarceration, corporal punishment, or even capital punishment. Within the Sharīʿah, criminal law takes a more holistic approach focusing on prevention, punishment, rehabilitation, and forgiveness. There is a lot of emphasis placed on god-consciousness, morality, chastity, repentance, and reformation. That is why punishments in Islam are characterized as both being preventive and reformative; they serve to prevent people from committing crimes and as a means of expiation for those who have committed those crimes.

6. PURPOSE OF JIHĀD

As clarified earlier, the purpose of jihād is not to force people to convert to Islam. The purpose of jihād is to literally raise the word of God (ʿilā' kalimah Allah), establish peace and justice, and to defend Islam. Raising the word of God refers to establishing law according to the Divine system revealed by God Himself through the Quran and teachings of the Prophet ﷺ.

It can be argued that the Sharīʿah is the most successful and most widely practiced legal system in the world. For the last 1400 years it has been practiced by a number of different nations that have strikingly different cultures and customs. One of the reasons for its success is first and foremost that it is divine. It is based on revelation from the Creator of the heavens and the Earth. Every other system of law is man-made and prone to faults, prejudices, deficiencies, injustices, and inequalities. The only system of law that can truly ensure equality, justice, and morality is Islam. Who knows best how to govern human beings than the Creator Himself? It is the most comprehensive and complete way of life that deals with every type of relationship human beings can have. It deals with relationships between individuals, between individuals and the community, between different communities, between the individual and the Creator, and even between the community and the Creator. It is the law that governs the most beautiful way of life that is suitable for all times and places.

7. HOW TO APPROACH ḤADĪTH

If one were to look at this ḥadīth by itself while ignoring all the other aḥādīth and verses of the Quran regarding this topic, while ignoring its context, then they would conclude that a person will be forced to do three things in order to protect their lives and property:

1. Declare the testimony of faith,
2. Pray, and
3. Pay zakāh

However, this conclusion is based on a lack of information and understanding. Whenever a verse of the Quran or ḥadīth of the Prophet ﷺ is taken out of context and divorced from the rich interpretive scholarly tradition of interpretation, it will lead to misunderstandings and incorrect conclusions.

HADITH 9

Do What You Can

عَنْ أَبِي هُرَيْرَةَ عَبْدِ الرَّحْمَنِ بْنِ صَخْرٍ رَضِيَ الله عَنْهُ قَالَ: سَمِعْت رَسُولَ اللَّهِ صلى الله عليه و سلم يَقُولُ: "مَا نَهَيْتُكُمْ عَنْهُ فَاجْتَنِبُوهُ، وَمَا أَمَرْتُكُمْ بِهِ فَأْتُوا مِنْهُ مَا اسْتَطَعْتُمْ، فَإِنَّمَا أَهْلَكَ الَّذِينَ مِنْ قَبْلِكُمْ كَثْرَةُ مَسَائِلِهِمْ وَاخْتِلَافُهُمْ عَلَى أَنْبِيَائِهِمْ".

رَوَاهُ الْبُخَارِيُّ، وَمُسْلِمٌ.

From Abū Hurairah ﷺ who said that I heard the Messenger of Allah ﷺ say, "What I have forbidden you to do, avoid it. What I have ordered you to do, then do as much of it as you can. Verily it was only the excessive questioning and their disagreeing with their Prophets that destroyed those who came before you."

Narrated by al-Bukhārī and Muslim.

THE NARRATOR

His full name is ʿAbd al-Raḥmān ibn Ṣakhr ⬥, who is more well-known as Abū Hurairah, which literally means the father of the kitten. This was a nickname given to him by the Prophet ⬥. He narrated, "I had a cat in my sleeve one day and the Prophet ⬥ noticed me. He asked, 'What is this?' I said, 'It's a cat.' He replied, 'O Abū Hurairah.'"

He accepted Islam in the 7th year after Hijrah, the year that Khaybar was conquered. He participated in that expedition with the Prophet ⬥. He remained in the company of the Prophet ⬥ as much as possible. He dedicated his life to learning, memorizing, and studying the aḥādīth of the Prophet ⬥. The Prophet ⬥ made a dua for him to never forget what he had memorized. 5,374 aḥādīth have been narrated from him, may Allah ⬥ be pleased with him.

IMPORTANCE AND BACKGROUND

The scholars of ḥadīth write that this is an extremely important narration that should be memorized, studied, and understood. Imām al-Nawawī ⬥ in his commentary on *Ṣaḥīḥ Muslim* writes that this ḥadīth is from among the important principles of Islam, from the concise comprehensive speech of the Prophet ⬥, and countless rulings are included in it. Ibn Ḥajar al-Haytamī ⬥ writes that "this is a great ḥadīth from the principles of religion and pillars of Islam. Therefore it is important to memorize it and value it."[82] One of the reasons why it is so important is because it discusses the importance and significance of holding on tight to the teachings of the Quran and Sunnah without any neglect or excessiveness.

The background or context of this ḥadīth is mentioned in a narration recorded in *Ṣaḥīḥ Muslim*. Abū Hurairah ⬥ narrates that the Messenger of Allah ⬥ addressed us and said, "O People! Ḥajj has been made obligatory upon you, so perform ḥajj." A man asked: "Is that every year, O Messenger of Allah?" The Prophet ⬥ remained silent until the man repeated his question three times. Then he said: "If I had said 'yes' then it would have become obligatory upon you (i.e. every year), and you would not have been able to do so. Do not ask me about that which I have left [unspecified], for verily the

---

82   al-Bughā and Mistū, *al-Wāfī fī Sharḥ al-Arbaʿīn al-Nawawiyyah*, p.53

nations before you were destroyed by their excessive questioning and their disagreeing with their Prophets. So if I order you with something then do as much of it as you are able, and if I forbid you from something then keep away from it."[83] Other narrations identify the questioner as al-Aqraʿ ibn Ḥābis ﷺ.

EXPLANATION

The Prophet ﷺ starts by reminding the Companions to stay away from what he has prohibited, "What I have forbidden for you, avoid." Within the framework of the Sharīʿah, there are certain acts that are prohibited or forbidden. The prohibition comes either from a verse of the Quran or the Sunnah of the Prophet ﷺ. The prohibition can be expressed in clear and explicit terms resulting in impermissibility (ḥurmah) or it can be expressed in non-binding terms resulting in dislike (karāhah). Basically, there are different shades of prohibition resulting in something being classified as ḥarām (impermissible) or makrūh (disliked).

Something that is ḥarām is defined as an act that has been prohibited by the Lawgiver in certain and binding terms. The certain and binding terms are understood from the syntax, context, grammar, or external evidence. For example, murder, theft, consuming intoxicants, and false accusations are all ḥarām. An individual who does something that is prohibited is liable and deserving of blame and sin. On the other hand, a person will be rewarded for consciously staying away from those actions.

Something that is makrūh is defined as an act that has been prohibited by the Lawgiver in non-binding terms. The non-binding terms of the prohibition are understood through the syntax, grammar, or context of the prohibition itself as well as through external evidence. For example the Prophet ﷺ said, "Truly Allah has prohibited the disobedience of mothers, burying daughters alive, and withholding while asking. And He has disliked three things for you: vain talk about others ("he said she said"), excessive pointless questioning, and wasting wealth."[84] The distinction in wording of prohibition from "ḥarrama" and dislike from "kariha" is clear. A person who intentionally leaves something that is disliked will be rewarded. There is no sin for choosing to do something that is disliked.

83 Muslim, *k. al-ḥajj, b. farḍ al-ḥajj marrah fī al-ʿumr*, 1337

84 Muslim, *k. Al-aqḍiyah, b. al-nahy ʿan kathrah al-masā'il min ghayr ḥājah*, 593

The Prophet ﷺ is telling the Companions to avoid and stay away from the prohibitions as much as possible.

The Prophet ﷺ then tells the Companions to obey his commandments as much as possible. He says, "What I have ordered you [to do], do as much of it as you can." There are several commands throughout the Quran and Sunnah. The command can be expressed in definitive and binding terms, meaning the act has to be done, creating an obligation (farḍ/wājib). The command can also be expressed in terms that are not absolute or binding. In such a scenario the ḥukm serves as a recommendation (istiḥbāb). The jurists use various rules to determine when a command is expressed in binding or non-binding terms. Basically, there are varying shades of obligation as well. An act can either be obligatory (wājib) or recommended (mustaḥab).

Something that is wājib is technically defined as an act the Lawgiver commands a mukallaf to do in certain and binding terms. The certain and binding nature of the command is either understood from the syntax, context, or language of the statement as well as from external evidence. Examples of acts that are wajib are praying, fasting, paying zakāh, ḥajj, and fulfilling contracts. When something is wājib it has to be done. The one who does it will be rewarded and the one who chooses not to is liable and deserving of punishment.

Something that is mustaḥab is defined as an act the Lawgiver commands a mukallaf to do in non-binding terms. The non-binding nature of the command is understood from the syntax, grammar, or context as well as from external evidence. For example, the Prophet ﷺ said, "Whoever makes wuḍūʾ on Friday then it suffices and it's good, and whoever bathes, then bathing is better." From this ḥadīth, jurists conclude that it is recommended (sunnah) for one to take a ritual bath for Friday prayer. Recommended Acts are then classified into two broad categories:

1. AL-SUNNAH AL-MUʾAKKADAH (السُّنَّةُ الْمُؤَكَّدَةُ): THE RELIGIOUSLY EMPHASIZED SUNNAH

al-Sunnah al-Muʾakkadah is a recommended act that was done by the Prophet ﷺ on a regular and consistent basis while leaving it occasionally, as well as constantly encouraging his Companions ﷺ to do so. Some jurists also refer to this as Sunnah al-Hudā (سُنَّةُ الْهُدَى). These are the practices of the Prophet ﷺ related to religious practices or actions that carry direct religious significance. For example, praying in congregation, the adhān, and select prayers before or after the obligatory prayers. If a person does an act that is classified as sunnah mu'akkadah they will be rewarded. There is no sin or blame for choosing not to. However, it can become blameworthy if left out both consistently and intentionally. If a person consistently and intentionally leaves something that is considered to be sunnah mu'akkadah it is considered "turning away" from the Sunnah, which is blameworthy.

2. AL-SUNNAH GHAYR AL-MU'AKKADAH (السُّنَّةُ غَيرَ المُؤَكَّدَة): THE NON-EMPHASIZED SUNNAH

A non-emphasized sunnah is something the Prophet ﷺ did sometimes and at other times chose not to or did regularly, but didn't make it a point to constantly encourage his Companions ﷺ to do consistently. This type of act is also known as nafl or mustaḥab. For example, the four units of prayer before ʿIshāʾ, fasting on Mondays and Thursdays, facing the qiblah when performing wuḍūʾ, remaining quiet while listening to the adhān, replying to the adhān, and using and beginning with the right side for things that are considered good. A person who does something that is classified as a non-emphasized sunnah will be rewarded and there is no sin for choosing not to. However, by leaving it a person will be depriving themselves of a lot of good and reward.

An act that is considered to be a non-emphasized sunnah can also be part of sunnah al-hudā; meaning, it can be related to a religious practice or an act of worship. It can also be something that the scholars classify as Sunnah al-Zawāʾid (سُنَّةُ الزَّوَايِدِ), or extra Sunnahs. These are ordinary daily tasks the Prophet ﷺ did as a human being such as the way he dressed, ate and drank, the types of food he liked and disliked, the way he walked, and the way he slept. A person who chooses to act upon them seeking to follow the example of the Prophet ﷺ out of love, reverence, and respect will definitely be rewarded. At the same time there is absolutely no blame on a person who chooses not to.

The Prophet ﷺ advised the Companions ﷺ to do as much as they could; to give their best effort and try as hard as possible. There is extremely deep wisdom in this statement. The Prophet ﷺ recognizes that human beings are weak by nature and will not be able to fulfill every single command, nor are they required to. What they are required to do is put forth their best effort. The Prophet ﷺ said, "Indeed you will not be able to do nor will you ever do everything you have been commanded to do. But get as close as possible and seek glad tidings."[85]

The ḥadīth ends by highlighting two causes that led to the downfall and destruction of previous nations:

1. Excessive questioning, and
2. Disagreeing with their Prophets

Excessive questioning refers to asking unnecessary questions that have no purpose or benefit behind them; questions that may lead to making things more difficult, or that may lead towards unnecessary argumentation and debate. It could also be referring to excessive questioning that is a sign of trying to avoid something.

LESSONS AND BENEFITS

1. AVOIDING PROHIBITIONS

Trying one's absolute best to stay away from those things that are impermissible and disliked are an essential part of one's practice of Islam. Just as there is immense reward for obeying the commandments of Allah ﷻ, there are also immense rewards for staying away from His prohibitions. A primary component of worship is staying away from and avoiding those things that Allah ﷻ has prohibited. The Messenger of Allah ﷺ said, "Stay away from the prohibitions and you will be the most obedient of people."[86] al-Ḥasan al-Baṣrī said, "The devout worshippers have not worshipped with anything better than leaving what God has prohibited for them."[87]

According to some scholars, staying away from prohibitions is equally important, if not more important, than obeying commandments. Many people live contradictory lives where they may be praying, fasting, and giving charity but at the same time they have horrible character, lie, cheat, and steal. There may be individuals who are extremely particular about praying regularly in the masjid, but at the same time are involved in interest based transactions. This is similar to driving a car with the A/C on and the win-

85 Abū Dāwūd, *k. al-ṣalāh, b. al-rajul yakhṭub 'alā qaws*, 1096
86 Tirmidhī, *k. al-zuhd ʿan Rasūlillah ﷺ, b. Man ittaqā al-maḥārim fa huwa ʿabad al-nās*, 2305
87 al-Bughā and Mistū, *al-Wāfī fī Sharḥ al-Arbaʿīn al-Nawawiyyah*, p.64

dows rolled down, or placing money in a pocket with holes in it.

2. *OBEYING COMMANDMENTS*

There is no better way to get closer to Allah ﷻ than obeying His commandments; specifically those things that He has made obligatory. The Prophet ﷺ narrated that Allah ﷻ said, "My servant does not draw near to Me with anything more beloved to Me than the religious duties I have obligated upon him."[88] Meaning that the best way to get closer to Allah ﷻ, to increase love for Allah ﷻ, and to increase His love is by fulfilling those things He has made obligatory, whether it is praying, fasting, giving charity or being kind to our parents. If a person wants to be loved by Allah ﷻ, if they want to earn His love and mercy, then they have to do what He has commanded them to do. In terms of prioritizing what actions are most important for a person to do, obligations are on the top of the list.

3. *BEST EFFORT*

Human beings are not expected to be perfect. Perfection is an attribute that belongs to Allah ﷻ alone. Allah ﷻ has created human beings with certain weaknesses and inabilities. That is one of the reasons why Allah ﷻ does not burden an individual with more than they can bear. As Allah ﷻ says, "God does not burden any soul with more than it can bear."[89] Allah ﷻ also says, "God wants ease for you, not hardship."[90] Similarly, the Prophet ﷺ said, "Truly the religion is ease."[91] Ease is a very subjective term; what is easy for a person may be difficult for another, and what is difficult for a person may be easy for another. What is meant by ease is that every human being has the ability to follow the teachings of Islam by trying their best to obey the commandments of Allah ﷻ and staying away from His prohibitions.

4. *GOOD QUESTIONS*

An essential part of learning, seeking knowledge, and education in general is asking questions. However, not all questions are the same. There is a common saying that there is no such thing as a dumb question and that is true to a certain extent. However, there are questions that are useless, non-beneficial, or have ulterior motives behind them. In this ḥadīth the

---

88 Bukhārī, *k. al-Riqāq, b. Al-tawāḍuʿ*, 6502
89 2:286 - لَا يُكَلِّفُ اللَّهُ نَفْسًا إِلَّا وُسْعَهَا
90 2:185 - يُرِيدُ اللَّهُ بِكُمُ الْيُسْرَ وَلَا يُرِيدُ بِكُمُ الْعُسْرَ
91 Bukhārī, *k. al-īmān*, b. Al-dīn yusr, 39

Prophet ﷺ is warning against such questions. On the other hand, asking good, beneficial, and sincere questions is highly encouraged. The Prophet ﷺ said, "Good questions are half of knowledge."[92]

5. OBEYING THE PROPHET ﷺ

In several places throughout the Quran, Allah ﷻ makes it an obligation upon Muslims to obey His Messenger and follow him.

1. "O you who have believed, obey Allah and obey the Messenger and those in authority among you. And if you disagree over anything, refer it to Allah and the Messenger, if you should believe in Allah and the Last Day. That is the best [way] and best in result."[93]
2. "He who obeys the Messenger has obeyed Allah; but those who turn away - We have not sent you over them as a guardian."[94]
3. "It is not for a believing man or a believing woman, when Allah and His Messenger have decided a matter, that they should [thereafter] have any choice about their affair. And whoever disobeys Allah and His Messenger has certainly strayed into clear error."[95]
4. "And whatever the Messenger has given you - take; and what he has forbidden you - refrain from. And fear Allah; indeed, Allah is severe in penalty."[96]
5. "Say, [O Muḥammad], "If you should love Allah, then follow me, [so] Allah will love you and forgive you your sins. And Allah is Forgiving and Merciful."[97]

---

92 al-Bayhaqī, *Shuʿab al-Īmān*, 6568

93 4:59 - يَا أَيُّهَا الَّذِينَ آمَنُوا أَطِيعُوا اللَّهَ وَأَطِيعُوا الرَّسُولَ وَأُولِي الْأَمْرِ مِنكُمْ ۖ فَإِن تَنَازَعْتُمْ فِي شَيْءٍ فَرُدُّوهُ إِلَى اللَّهِ وَالرَّسُولِ إِن كُنتُمْ تُؤْمِنُونَ بِاللَّهِ وَالْيَوْمِ الْآخِرِ ۚ ذَٰلِكَ خَيْرٌ وَأَحْسَنُ تَأْوِيلًا

94 4:80 - مَّن يُطِعِ الرَّسُولَ فَقَدْ أَطَاعَ اللَّهَ

95 33:36 - وَمَا كَانَ لِمُؤْمِنٍ وَلَا مُؤْمِنَةٍ إِذَا قَضَى اللَّهُ وَرَسُولُهُ أَمْرًا أَن يَكُونَ لَهُمُ الْخِيَرَةُ مِنْ أَمْرِهِمْ ۗ وَمَن يَعْصِ اللَّهَ وَرَسُولَهُ فَقَدْ ضَلَّ ضَلَالًا مُّبِينًا

96 59:7 - وَمَا آتَاكُمُ الرَّسُولُ فَخُذُوهُ وَمَا نَهَاكُمْ عَنْهُ فَانتَهُوا

97 3:31 - قُلْ إِن كُنتُمْ تُحِبُّونَ اللَّهَ فَاتَّبِعُونِي يُحْبِبْكُمُ اللَّهُ وَيَغْفِرْ لَكُمْ ذُنُوبَكُمْ ۗ وَاللَّهُ غَفُورٌ رَّحِيمٌ

HADITH 10
Pure Acts

عَنْ أَبِي هُرَيْرَةَ رَضِيَ اللَّه عَنْهُ قَالَ: قَالَ رَسُولُ اللَّهِ صلى الله عليه و سلم "إنَّ اللَّهَ طَيِّبٌ لَا يَقْبَلُ إلَّا طَيِّبًا، وَإِنَّ اللَّهَ أَمَرَ الْمُؤْمِنِينَ بِمَا أَمَرَ بِهِ الْمُرْسَلِينَ فَقَالَ تَعَالَى: "يَا أَيُّهَا الرُّسُلُ كُلُوا مِنْ الطَّيِّبَاتِ وَاعْمَلُوا صَالِحًا"، وَقَالَ تَعَالَى: "يَا أَيُّهَا الَّذِينَ آمَنُوا كُلُوا مِنْ طَيِّبَاتِ مَا رَزَقْنَاكُمْ" ثُمَّ ذَكَرَ الرَّجُلَ يُطِيلُ السَّفَرَ أَشْعَثَ أَغْبَرَ يَمُدُّ يَدَيْهِ إلَى السَّمَاءِ: يَا رَبِّ! يَا رَبِّ! وَمَطْعَمُهُ حَرَامٌ، وَمَشْرَبُهُ حَرَامٌ، وَمَلْبَسُهُ حَرَامٌ، وَغُذِّيَ بِالْحَرَامِ، فَأَنَّى يُسْتَجَابُ لَهُ؟".

رَوَاهُ مُسْلِمٌ.

From Abū Hurairah ﵁ who said that the Messenger of Allah ﷺ said, "Allah the Almighty is Pure and only accepts that which is pure. And verily Allah has commanded the believers to do that which He has commanded the Messengers. The Almighty said, 'Messengers, eat good things and do good deeds: I am well aware of what you do.' [23:51] The Almighty said, 'You who believe, eat the good things We have provided for you and be grateful to God, if it is Him that you worship.' [2:172]" Then he ﷺ mentioned a man who has traveled for a long time, is dishevelled and dusty, raising his hands to the sky saying "O my Lord! O my Lord!" while his food is unlawful, his drink is unlawful, his clothing is unlawful, and he has been nourished with unlawful, so how will his supplication be answered?

Narrated by Muslim.

IMPORTANCE

Ibn Daqīq al-ʿĪd writes that this is one of the aḥādīth upon which the foundation of Islam is built, because it describes deeds and actions that are pleasing to Allah ﷻ. If an act is not pure, sincere, genuine, wholesome, and good, Allah ﷻ will not accept it. It also deals with the issue of having a pure and lawful source of income and consuming things that are pure and lawful; ḥalāl and ḥarām consumption and earning. The ḥadīth also highlights that Allah ﷻ does not respond to the supplication of a person whose sustenance is from impermissible means.

EXPLANATION

The Prophet ﷺ describes Allah ﷻ using the word "ṭayyib", which is also one of His Divine Names and Attributes. Ṭayyib is a word that is used to describe something that is good, pure, wholesome, and healthy. When used to describe Allah ﷻ it means that Allah ﷻ is pure and perfect, above any imperfection or need. Meaning that Allah ﷻ has all of the attributes of perfection and completeness, and is free from any shortcoming, weakness, blemish, defect, or need. Allah ﷻ is perfection.

The Prophet ﷺ then explains that Allah ﷻ does not accept actions or deeds unless they are good and pure. They have to be free from anything that can pollute them, such as showing off, ostentation, and arrogance. In order for a deed or action to be pure it must fulfill two conditions:

1. Sincerity, and
2. It has to be done according to the Sharīʿah.

It is also important to understand the concept of acceptance. Oftentimes actions are described as either being accepted or rejected. What exactly does that mean? Acceptance is of two types:

1. Acceptance based on performance of the legal obligation
2. Acceptance related to earning the pleasure of Allah ﷻ and reward

The first type of acceptance is related to performing the obligation correctly and properly according to the teachings of the Quran and the Sunnah. For example, praying while fulfilling all of its pre-conditions, integrals, wājibāt, sunan, and ādāb. The second type of acceptance is related to the amount of reward one receives for doing the action, which is dependent upon internal factors such as sincerity. For example, praying with humility and concentration. Two people can be praying next to each other, reciting the same phrases and verses, going through the same motions, but their reward can be different. One of them may be distracted thinking about work or family, while the other is fully engaged in an intimate conversation with Allah ﷻ.

Every single aspect of a believer's life is supposed to be pure; their belief, actions, statements, and wealth. Ibn Rajab ﵀ writes, "The believer, his entire being, is good; his heart, his tongue, and his body. Because of the faith that resides in his heart and becomes apparent on his tongue through remembrance, and upon his limbs through righteous deeds that are the fruits of faith."[98]

The Prophet ﷺ then says, "Allah has commanded the believers to do that which he has commanded the Messengers," meaning, whatever the Messengers have been commanded to do, the believers have been commanded to do the same. The Prophet ﷺ then recites two verses specifying which commandment he is referring to. Allah ﷻ says, "Messengers, eat good things and do good deeds: I am well aware of what you do."[99] He also says, "You who believe, eat the good things We have provided for you and be grateful to God, if it is Him that you worship."[100]

Something that is wājib is technically defined as an act the Lawgiver commands a mukallaf to do in certain and binding terms. The certain and binding nature of the command is either understood from the syntax, context, or language of the statement as well as from external evidence. Examples of acts that are wajib are praying, fasting, paying zakāh, ḥajj, and fulfilling contracts. When something is wājib it has to be done. The one who does it will be rewarded and the one who chooses not to is liable and deserving of punishment.

What is meant by ṭayyibāt in the verses is that which is good and permissible. Meaning those things that the Sharīʿah has made permissible to eat;

---

98 Ibn Rajab, *Jāmiʿ al-ʿUlūm wa al-Ḥikam*, p.114

99 23:51 - يَا أَيُّهَا الرُّسُلُ كُلُوا مِنْ الطَّيِّبَاتِ وَاعْمَلُوا صَالِحاً

100 2:172 - يَا أَيُّهَا الَّذِينَ آمَنُوا كُلُوا مِنْ طَيِّبَاتِ مَا رَزَقْنَاكُمْ

things that are pure and lawful to eat. What a person consumes and puts into their bodies has to be pure, good, wholesome, and lawful. Similarly, it must come through lawful means. The Messengers were commanded to eat what is pure and ḥalal and to do righteous deeds. The believers are commanded to do the same. One of the greatest factors that make a person's deeds pure and accepted is consuming pure and lawful food.

From this portion of the hadith till the end, the Prophet ﷺ gives a vivid example of a man who has done things in order for his supplication to be accepted; however, Allah ﷻ will not accept it because he is living his life off unlawful means; things that are impure. This is a very significant point to reflect upon. Allah ﷻ the Most Merciful, the One who loves to respond to His servants who call upon Him, will not respond.

Allah ﷻ says in Sūrah al-Baqarah, "And when my servant asks you concerning Me, surely I am very near. I answer the prayer of the caller when he calls on Me, so they should answer My call and believe in Me in order that they may be led aright."[101] In Sūrah al-Ghāfir, Allah says, "Your Lord says, 'Call on Me and I will answer you; those who are too proud to serve Me will enter Hell humiliated.'"[102] Similarly, there are numerous aḥādīth stating the importance, significance, virtues, and blessings of supplication. These narrations also mention certain things a person can do and certain timings that cause supplications to be accepted. Conversely there are things that a person does that will prevent their supplications from being answered. One of them is eating or drinking things that are impermissible, wearing clothes that are impermissible, or acquiring both through impermissible means.

In this particular ḥadīth the Prophet ﷺ mentions a man, who after a long journey is disheveled and dusty, his hands stretched out to the sky, calling upon Allah ﷻ. Traveling, simplicity, raising one's hands, and calling upon Allah ﷻ are factors that aid in one's supplication being accepted. Regarding traveling, the Prophet ﷺ said, "Three supplications are answered without a doubt: the prayer of the oppressed, the prayer of the traveler, and the prayer of a father against his child."[103] One of the reasons for this is that when one is traveling they are in a foreign place, away from their family, and facing hardships. Because of that, their heart becomes soft and realizes its

101 2:186 - وَإِذَا سَأَلَكَ عِبَادِى عَنِّى فَإِنِّى قَرِيبٌ ۖ أُجِيبُ دَعْوَةَ الدَّاعِ إِذَا دَعَانِ ۖ فَلْيَسْتَجِيبُوا لِى وَلْيُؤْمِنُوا بِى لَعَلَّهُمْ يَرْشُدُونَ

102 40:60 - وَقَالَ رَبُّكُمُ ادْعُونِى أَسْتَجِبْ لَكُمْ ۚ إِنَّ الَّذِينَ يَسْتَكْبِرُونَ عَنْ عِبَادَتِى سَيَدْخُلُونَ جَهَنَّمَ دَاخِرِينَ

103 Tirmidhī, *k. Al-daʿwāt ʿan Rasūlillah* ﷺ, *b. Mā dhukira fī daʿwah al-musāfir*, 3448

dependence upon Allah ﷻ.

Despite having these factors that aid in his supplication being accepted, "his food is unlawful, his drink is unlawful, his clothing unlawful, and his nourishment is unlawful." If one's life is full of forbidden and unlawful things, then how can they expect Allah ﷻ to answer their prayers? If the person does not respond to Allah's teachings, then how will Allah ﷻ respond to their calls? The Prophet ﷺ said, "How is he to be answered?"

One of the factors that can lead to a person's supplications not being answered is earning sustenance and livelihood through unlawful means as well as consuming unlawful items. Ibn ʿAbbās ؓ narrated that when he recited the verse, "O people, eat from whatever is on the Earth lawful and pure," Saʿd ibn Abī Waqqāṣ ؓ stood up and said, "O Messenger of Allah! Ask Allah to make me from those whose prayers are answered." The Prophet ﷺ said, "O Saʿd , purify your food and your prayers will be answered. By the One in whose hand is Muhammad's soul, indeed a servant places an unlawful morsel in his body and Allah will not accept his deeds for 40 days."[104] Another narration mentions that Allah ﷻ will not accept the prayers of a person in whose body there is something unlawful.

LESSONS AND BENEFITS

1. ALLAH ﷻ IS PURE

One of the Divine Names and Attributes of Allah ﷻ is al-Ṭayyib. When used to describe Allah ﷻ it means that Allah ﷻ is pure and perfect, above any imperfection or need. Meaning that Allah ﷻ has all of the attributes of perfection and completeness, and is free from any shortcoming, weakness, blemish, or need. Allah ﷻ is perfection.

2. ACCEPTANCE OF DEEDS

In order for a person's deeds to be accepted, they have to be pure, ṭayyib. A pure deed is one that is done sincerely for the sake of Allah ﷻ along with being done properly according to the Sunnah of the Prophet ﷺ.

---

104 al-Ṭabarānī, *al-Jāmiʿ al-Ṣaghīr*

3. PERMISSIBLE SOURCE OF INCOME

A believer has to ensure that their income and livelihood is from lawful means. The Prophet ﷺ said, "Seeking a lawful source of income is an obligation after other obligations."[105] Meaning, just like praying five times a day, fasting in Ramaḍān, paying zakāh, and performing ḥajj are obligations, it is also an obligation to seek a lawful source of income.

4. CONSUMING LAWFUL FOOD AND DRINK

What a person consumes and puts into their body not only has physical effects, it also has very profound spiritual effects as well. A human being is not simply composed of a physical body. Rather, a human being is a combination of the physical body and the soul. Just like the physical body needs nourishment, the soul also requires nourishment. There are certain types of foods and drinks that are harmful to the body and lead towards all sorts of health issues such as heart problems, weight issues, and various illnesses. There are certain actions that are harmful to the soul, and one of them is consuming food and drinks that are unlawful or have been acquired through unlawful means.

5. ACCEPTED SUPPLICATIONS

Allah ﷻ promises that He will respond to His servants if they call upon Him seeking His help, assistance, and guidance. However, from experience, people know that they don't always get what they ask for. A common question people ask is "why are my prayers not being answered?". The Prophet ﷺ provides a response to this question in the following ḥadīth. Abū Hurairah رضي الله عنه narrates that the Prophet ﷺ said, "There is not a man who calls upon Allah with a supplication, except that he is answered. Either it shall be granted to him in the world, or reserved for him in the Hereafter, or his sins shall be expiated for it according to the extent that he supplicated - as long as he does not supplicate for some sin, or for the severing of the ties of kinship, and he does not become hasty." The companions said: "O Messenger of Allah, and how would he be hasty?" He ﷺ said: "He says: 'I called upon my Lord, but He did not answer me.'"[106]

105 al-Bayhaqī, *Shuʿab al-Īmān*, 2920

106 Tirmidhī, *k. Al-daʿwāt ʿan rasūlillah* ﷺ

HADITH 11

Leaving Doubt

عَنْ أَبِي مُحَمَّدٍ الْحَسَنِ بْنِ عَلِيٍّ بْنِ أَبِي طَالِبٍ سِبْطِ رَسُولِ اللَّهِ صلى الله عليه و سلم وَرَيْحَانَتِهِ رَضِيَ اللَّهُ عَنْهُمَا، قَالَ: حَفِظْت مِنْ رَسُولِ اللَّهِ صلى الله عليه و سلم "دَعْ مَا يُرِيبُك إلَى مَا لَا يُرِيبُك".

رَوَاهُ التِّرْمِذِيُّ [رقم:2520]، وَالنَّسَائِيُّ وَقَالَ التِّرْمِذِيُّ: حَدِيثٌ حَسَنٌ صَحِيحٌ.

From Abū Muḥammad al-Ḥasan ibn ʿAlī ibn Abī Ṭālib ﷺ, the grandson of the Messenger of Allah ﷺ, and the one much loved by him, who said that I memorized from the Messenger of Allah ﷺ, "Leave that which makes you doubt for that which does not make you doubt."

Narrated by al-Tirmidhī and al-Nasā'ī and al-Tirmidhī said that it is a good and authentic (ḥasan ṣaḥīḥ) ḥadīth.

THE NARRATOR

Abū Muḥammad al-Ḥasan ibn ʿAlī ibn Abī Ṭālib ﷺ, the son of ʿAlī and Fāṭimah ﷺ, the grandson of the Prophet ﷺ, was born in the third year after migration in the city of Madinah and grew up in the Prophet's ﷺ household. He was extremely intelligent, patient, righteous, and eloquent. He passed away in the year 50 in the city of Madinah where he is buried in al-Baqīʿ. He narrated 13 aḥādīth from his grandfather, the Prophet ﷺ.

IMPORTANCE

This ḥadīth is also among the concise comprehensive sayings of the Prophet ﷺ that are extremely deep in meaning. It is from the deep, profound, farsighted, and eloquent wisdom of the Prophet ﷺ. In this ḥadīth the Prophet ﷺ mentions a general principle that can be applied to all aspects of one's life. If a person applies this principle in their life, they will feel a sense of peace, tranquility, and contentment. This principle has far reaching psychological and spiritual effects. If a person follows the teachings of this ḥadīth they will be free of general stress and anxiety and be on the path to true piety. Regarding this ḥadīth, ibn Ḥajar al-Haytamī writes, "This ḥadīth is an extremely important religious principle, the foundation for personal piety that is the essence of God-consciousness, and a savior from the darkness of worries and doubts that prevent a person from the light of certainty."[107]

EXPLANATION

In simple words, the Prophet ﷺ is saying to avoid and stay away from doubtful matters, affairs, situations, circumstances, and issues and to choose what one is certain about. "Leave that which makes you doubt for that which does not make you doubt." This is closely related to the meaning of ḥadīth six in this collection, "That which is lawful is clear and that which is unlawful is clear, and between the two of them are doubtful matters."

Doubt can exist in several different areas including acts of worship, financial transactions, social dealings, food and drink, sayings, and thoughts. Wherever the doubt may be and whatever is causing it, whether it is related

107 al-Bughā and Mistū, *al-Wāfī fī Sharḥ al-Arbaʿīn al-Nawawiyyah*, p.85

to worldly affairs or religious affairs, it is best to leave it aside. Building a habit of avoiding doubts allows one to avoid unnecessary stress and worries. Adopting this particular outlook towards one's affairs leads towards a form of personal piety known as warʿ.

LESSONS AND BENEFITS

1. AVOIDING DOUBTS

A person who has a sound heart that is connected to Allah ﷻ may find themselves in a certain situation or engaging in something that makes them feel uncomfortable, which is described as "rayb". al-Rayb is defined as doubt, suspicion, uncertainty, uneasiness, and discomfort. The opposite of "rayb" in this context would be "yaqīn", which is translated as certainty. According to this ḥadīth, a person should avoid situations that create doubt and adopt what leads towards certainty.

2. CERTAINTY IS NOT REMOVED BY DOUBT

Within the framework of the Sharīʿah there are certain maxims known as al-Qawāʿid al-Fiqhiyyah, or Legal Maxims of Islamic Law. "Legal Maxims are theoretical abstractions, usually in the form of short epithetical statements, that are expressive, often in a few words, of the goals and objectives of the Sharīʿah."[108] The legal maxims of fiqh are general principles that are derived and extracted from the detailed and specific legal rulings of Islamic Jurisprudence. A maxim is defined as a general rule which applies to all of its related particulars. One of the Legal Maxims of Islamic Law is, "Certainty is not removed by doubt." A practical application of this principle can be seen in the case of one who is unsure if they have nullified their wuḍū'. If a person performs wuḍū' in the morning for fajr prayer, and then before dhuhr prayer they don't remember if they nullified their wuḍū' or not, the ruling is that they still have wuḍū'. In this scenario having wuḍū' is certain and nullifying wuḍū' is uncertain, and the legal maxim is, "Certainty is not removed by doubt".

---

108 Kamali. *Qawa'id al-Fiqh: The Legal Maxims of Islamic Law*. The Association of Muslim Lawyers

3. PERSONAL PIETY

As mentioned under ḥadīth six, personal piety is a higher level of consciousness or awareness of Allah ﷻ that leads one to staying away from doubtful matters as well, which is described as warʿ. This is a personal level of piety where a person chooses to avoid things that are doubtful, or even things that may be permissible, in order to stay far away from those things that are impermissible. By doing so they are striving to protect their religion and their honor, as described by the Prophet ﷺ. Sufyān ibn ʿUyaynah ؒ said, "A servant does not achieve the reality of īmān until they place between themselves and the impermissible a barrier of the permissible, and until they leave sins and what comes close to them."[109]

4. MENTAL HEALTH

When a person engages in doubtful matters it creates a sense of uneasiness, discomfort, and uncertainty. This sense and feeling of uneasiness and discomfort can lead to a lot of internal stress and anxiety. By avoiding doubts, a person relieves themselves of this unnecessary stress and anxiety.

109 Ibn Rajab, *Jāmiʿ al-ʿUlūm wa al-Ḥikam*, v. 2 p. 161-2

HADITH 12

Leave What Doesn't Concern You

عَنْ أَبِي هُرَيْرَةَ رَضِيَ اللَّه عَنْهُ قَالَ: قَالَ رَسُولُ اللَّهِ صلى الله عليه وسلم "مِنْ حُسْنِ إسْلَامِ الْمَرْءِ تَرْكُهُ مَا لَا يَعْنِيهِ".

حَدِيثٌ حَسَنٌ، رَوَاهُ التِّرْمِذِيُّ [رقم:2318]، ابن ماجه [رقم:3976].

From Abū Hurairah ﵁ who said that the Messenger of Allah ﷺ said, "Part of the perfection of one's Islam is his leaving that which does not concern him."

A good (ḥasan) ḥadīth narrated by al-Tirmidī and ibn Mājah.

IMPORTANCE

This ḥadīth is also from those concise and comprehensive sayings of the Prophet ﷺ that are extremely deep in meaning. It is considered to be one of the foundations for manners, etiquette, and behavior in Islam. According to a number of scholars all good manners and behavior are alluded to in four aḥādīth:

1. "Whoever believes in Allah and the Last Day should speak well or remain silent."[110]
2. "Part of the perfection of one's Islam is to leave that which does not concern them."[111]
3. "Do not get angry."[112]
4. "None of you [truly] believes until he loves for his brother that which he loves for himself."[113]

EXPLANATION

The Prophet ﷺ is describing an essential aspect of one's practice of Islam. He ﷺ says, "Part of the perfection of one's Islam is to leave that which does not concern them." In order to be a complete Muslim, in order for a person's faith to be complete, they have to leave those things that don't concern them. In simpler words, a person should mind their own business. They should not be concerned with matters, affairs, and issues they are not directly or indirectly involved with; those things that are none of their business, whether they are things related to this world or to the affairs of religion, should be left alone.

LESSONS AND BENEFITS

1. HOLISTIC PRACTICE OF ISLAM

Islam is not limited to ritual acts of worship. Islam is a complete and

110 Ḥadīth #15 in this collection

111 Ḥadīth #12 in this collection, the current ḥadīth under discussion

112 Ḥadīth #16 in this collection

113 Ḥadīth #13 in this collection

holistic way of life that provides human beings guidance for all of their affairs; personal, social, economic, political, physical, emotional, and spiritual. Part of one's practice of Islam is to prioritize and focus on what is important and relevant to them.

2. *HEALTHY SOCIETY*

Islam works towards building a healthy, wholesome, and peaceful society; a society where individuals, families, and communities feel welcome, safe, secure, and at peace. It helps develop a society that is free from arguments, conflicts, ill-will, and any other negativity. Islam wants individuals to be happy, friendly, affable, approachable, to honor and respect others, and not to inconvenience others. One of the greatest things that leads to conflicts among individuals, families, and communities is getting involved in other people's private affairs.

3. *PRIORITIES*

If a person truly understands their purpose and role in this world, if they truly recognize their responsibilities, then they will busy themselves with things that concern them; those affairs that will benefit them in this world and the next. Life is extremely complex and complicated with the world being full of several things competing for a person's attention. There are numerous distractions and relationships that a person has to deal with. Muslims need to realize that they are ultimately responsible for what they do and how they spend their time. They are responsible for their own actions, statements, and time, as well as those under their care. If a person occupies themselves with things that don't concern them, then they will not have time or energy to fulfill their own responsibilities. Similarly, if they occupy their thoughts and time with those things that concern them, they will not have time to waste. Imām Mālik ﷺ mentions a report regarding Luqmān al-Ḥakīm in his *al-Muwaṭṭa'*. Someone asked him, "What caused you to reach the level you have attained?" He said, "Truthful speech, fulfilling trusts, and leaving that which doesn't concern me."[114]

---

114 Mālik, *al-Muwaṭṭa'*, 2:990

HADITH 13

Love for Your Brother What You Love for Yourself

عَنْ أَبِي حَمْزَةَ أَنَسِ بْنِ مَالِكٍ رَضِيَ اللَّهُ عَنْهُ خَادِمِ رَسُولِ اللَّهِ صلى اللَّه عليه و سلم عَنْ النَّبِيِّ صلى اللَّهُ عليه وسلم قَالَ: "لَا يُؤْمِنُ أَحَدُكُمْ حَتَّى يُحِبَّ لِأَخِيهِ مَا يُحِبُّ لِنَفْسِهِ".

رَوَاهُ الْبُخَارِيُّ [رقم:13]، وَمُسْلِمٌ [رقم:45].

From Abū Ḥamzah Anas ibn Mālik ﵁ — the servant of the Messenger of Allah ﷺ — that the Prophet ﷺ said, "None of you [truly] believes until he loves for his brother that which he loves for himself."

Narrated by al-Bukhārī and Muslim.

THE NARRATOR

Abū Ḥamzah Anas ibn Mālik is among the well-known Companions of the Prophet ﷺ. He served the Prophet ﷺ as an assistant earning the title of "Servant of the Messenger of Allah ﷺ". His mother, Umm Sulaym, is also a famous female Companion of the Prophet ﷺ. The Prophet ﷺ made a special supplication for him saying, "O Allah increase his wealth and children, grant him a long life, bless him, and enter him into Paradise." As a result of this supplication he was extremely wealthy, had a lot of children, and lived a long and blessed life. He passed away in the city of Basra in the year 93. He has narrated 2,286 aḥādīth, may Allah ﷻ be pleased with him.

IMPORTANCE

This ḥadīth teaches one of the most important rules of behavior in Islam. It highlights the type of relationship that is supposed to exist between Muslims and how they should behave and interact with one another. It is considered to be a general principle of relationships in Islam. As mentioned before, all good manners and behavior are alluded to in four aḥādīth:

1. "Whoever believes in Allah and the Last Day should speak well or remain silent."[115]
2. "Part of the perfection of one's Islam is to leave that which does not concern them."[116]
3. "Do not get angry."[117]
4. "None of you [truly] believes until he loves for his brother that which he loves for himself."[118]

EXPLANATION

The Prophet ﷺ starts by saying, "None of you truly believes." This is a very significant and heavy statement from the Prophet ﷺ. In this sentence the Prophet ﷺ is not negating one's entire belief, rather he is negating the

115 Ḥadīth #15 in this collection
116 Ḥadīth #12 in this collection
117 Ḥadīth #16 in this collection
118 Ḥadīth #13 in this collection, the current ḥadīth under discussion

completeness of one's belief. Meaning that a person does not truly believe, or their belief is not complete until they act upon the advice and teachings of the Prophet ﷺ. In order for a person to have true and complete faith, they must love for their brothers and sisters what they love for themselves. Īmān, faith, manifests through a person's thoughts, feelings, speech, and behavior. Under the discussion of the second ḥadīth in this collection, it is mentioned that īmān is manifested through three avenues:

1. Heart,
2. Tongue, and
3. Limbs

The Prophet ﷺ then mentions part of what completes one's faith, "until he loves for his brother what he loves for himself." This is the condition that the Prophet ﷺ stated for true and complete faith. Part of having true and complete faith is adopting this particular attitude and outlook towards others. Individuals should not only want good for themselves and their families but for others as well. What is meant by good are those things that are beneficial to one's life in this world and the next. That includes acts of obedience and things that are permissible. Individuals should treat others how they themselves want to be treated. Similarly, they should dislike for others what they dislike for themselves. Imām al-Nawawī رحمه الله also mentions that this includes non-Muslims, meaning, a person should love for them to be guided to Islam. That is one of the reasons why it is recommended to pray for the guidance of people.

LESSONS AND BENEFITS

1. AVOIDING ENVY AND UNHEALTHY COMPETITION

Envy and jealousy are extremely destructive diseases of the heart. Scholars consider them to be the root of all other spiritual ailments. It is considered to be the first manifestation of wrongdoing and the first cause of disobedience against Allah ﷻ. It is one of the first sins ever committed. It is the reason why Satan refused to prostrate before Adam عليه السلام. It is a satanic trait and leads towards enmity and hatred between people. One way of dealing with ḥasad is trying to implement the message of this ḥadīth.

2. UNITY AND MUTUAL LOVE

Unity in Islam is not simply a slogan or an ideal. It is a goal that can be achieved through implementing the guidance of the Quran and the Prophet ﷺ. Allah ﷻ says in the Quran, "The believers are brothers."[119] Similarly the Prophet ﷺ said, "The believers are like a single person. If the head hurts the entire body feels the pain and if the eye hurts the entire body feels the pain."[120] One of the ways of achieving unity and mutual love is by implementing the principle highlighted in this ḥadīth.

3. HEALTHY FAMILIES AND COMMUNITIES

Practically working towards building healthy families and communities is a priority of every Muslim. The attitude family members and community members have towards one another plays a significant role in doing so.

4. AL-ĪTHĀR

al-Īthār, or being selfless is an expression of one's Īmān. It is a quality that is born from mercy, empathy, generosity, care, concern, and pure brotherhood. It is described as giving preference to the needs and benefits of others over one's own personal needs and benefits. The reason for doing so is to earn reward from Allah ﷻ and to act upon natural human emotions that Allah ﷻ has placed within us to be kind, caring, and generous.

This may sound like some sort of cliché or one-liner; but, believers are supposed to be selfless not selfish. They are supposed to be more concerned with the needs of others than their own. This type of attitude has a very powerful impact upon personal lives and society at large. Imagine a community where everyone was concerned about the welfare and well-being of others? Where everyone was concerned about the physical, financial, emotional, psychological, and spiritual well-being of others? This may sound like some sort of idealistic notion, but that is what Islam nurtures within hearts.

---

119 إِنَّمَا الْمُؤْمِنُونَ إِخْوَةٌ - 49:10

120 Muslim, k. *Al-birr wa al-ṣilah wa al-ādāb*, b. *Tarāḥum al-mu'minīn wa taʿāṭufihim wa taʿāḍudihim*, 2586

HADITH 14

Crime and Punishment

عَنْ ابْنِ مَسْعُودٍ رَضِيَ اللَّه عَنْهُ قَالَ: قَالَ رَسُولُ اللَّهِ صلى الله عليه وسلم "لَا يَحِلُّ دَمُ امْرِئٍ مُسْلِمٍ يشهد أن لا إله إلا اللَّه، وأني رسول اللَّه إلَّا بِإِحْدَى ثَلَاثٍ: الثَّيِّبُ الزَّانِي، وَالنَّفْسُ بِالنَّفْسِ، وَالتَّارِكُ لِدِينِهِ الْمُفَارِقُ لِلْجَمَاعَةِ".

رَوَاهُ الْبُخَارِيُّ، وَمُسْلِمٌ.

From ibn Masʿūd ﵁ who said that the Messenger of Allah ﷺ said, "The blood of a Muslim is not permissible except in three instances: the married person who commits adultery, a life for a life, and the one who abandons his religion and separates from the community."

Narrated by al-Bukhārī and Muslim.

IMPORTANCE

This ḥadīth discusses the sanctity of a Muslim's life. A Muslim's life may not be taken unjustly under any circumstance unless they commit a crime so heinous, harmful, and detrimental to society that they no longer deserve to live. The criteria for determining the seriousness of a crime is not subjective. It is not subject to an individual's thoughts, ideas, philosophies, ideologies, or worldview. The seriousness of the crime and its punishment is determined by Allah ﷻ. This particular ḥadīth describes a few of these instances and crimes.

EXPLANATION

The ḥadīth starts by declaring the sanctity of a Muslim's life, "It is not permissible to spill the blood of a Muslim except in three circumstances." In Islam, human life is something that is sacred. One of the primary objectives of the Sharīʿah is to protect life, honor, and wealth. There are several verses of the Quran and aḥadīth of the Prophet ﷺ that emphasize the sanctity of human life.

Although life is sacred, there are cases and instances where a person may do something that is so heinous, harmful, and destructive that they forfeit their right to live. The cases and instances that cause one to forfeit their right to live are determined by Allah ﷻ. In Islam the concerns of society as a whole, generally speaking, take precedence over the wants and desires of an individual, especially one who has no respect for the welfare of society itself and is willing to commit the crimes mentioned in the ḥadīth.

The first crime highlighted by the Prophet ﷺ is "the married person who commits adultery." The word used is al-thayyib al-zānī, which refers to an adulterer who had legal relations (in marriage) at one time. A "thayyib" is a person who is married or was married at one time and has had legal intercourse within that marriage. Within Islamic Jurisprudence, such a person is also termed as a muḥṣan. Zinā refers to unlawful sexual intercourse, which includes both adultery and fornication. Adultery is when a married individual has relations with someone other than their spouse and fornication is when an unmarried individual has illicit relations. Within the framework of the Sharīʿah both are classified as zinā, but the punishment for both is different. The punishment for fornication is 100 lashes, as mentioned in verse two of Sūrah al-Nūr.[121] The punishment for adultery is stoning to death, as is mentioned in several aḥādīth of the Prophet ﷺ.

A muḥṣan who commits the crime of zinā is deserving of death because they have committed a crime that slowly eats away at and destroys the family, community, and society. Islam views zinā as a very serious crime and act of disobedience. It is something that destroys individuals and families. The person who commits zinā destroys their own life, the life of their spouse, the life of the one who consented with him or her, and the life of their children. It leads to the breakdown of the family, which is the foundation of society.

As mentioned above, the prescribed punishment (ḥad) for such a person is stoning. This punishment is established from a verse whose recitation has been abrogated; however its ruling is still valid.[122] In Ṣaḥīḥ Muslim 'Abdullah ibn 'Abbās reports that 'Umar ؓ sat on the pulpit of the Messenger of Allah ﷺ and said, "Verily, Allah sent Muḥammad ﷺ with the truth, and He sent the book down upon him. The verse of stoning was revealed with it, we recited it, memorized it, and understood it. The Prophet ﷺ awarded the punishment of stoning to death, and after him we did the same. I am afraid that with the passage of time, people will forget it and say, 'We do not find the punishment of stoning in the Book of Allah,' and go astray by abandoning this duty prescribed by Allah. Stoning is a duty laid down in Allah's book for married men and women who commit adultery when proof is established."[123] This punishment was also carried out during the time of the Prophet ﷺ.

This punishment can only be enacted once the crime has been proven without the slightest doubt or ambiguity. Under Islamic Law, there are only two ways to prove the crime:

1. Testimony of four credible male eye-witnesses
2. Confession

Ḥudūd penalties are to be exacted by the state and only after trial. One must never forget this. The Quran and hadith address the collective, the

---

121   24:2 - الزَّانِيَةُ وَالزَّانِي فَاجْلِدُوا كُلَّ وَاحِدٍ مِنْهُمَا مِائَةَ جَلْدَةٍ

122   According to another view, this verse was never part of the Quran. It was part of a previous revealed law and its ruling was affirmed and upheld within Islamic Law.

123   Muslim, k. al-ḥudūd, b. rajm al-thayyib fī al-zinā,

state, those in power, and not the individual on this matter.

The second crime mentioned by the Prophet ﷺ is murder, "a life for a life". If a person intentionally kills someone unjustly, commits murder, then they are deserving of the death penalty. Allah ﷻ says, "And We ordained for them therein a life for a life."[124] Similarly Allah ﷻ says, "O you who have believed, prescribed for you is legal retribution for those murdered."[125] If a person is found guilty in a court of law of premeditated murder then there are two possible outcomes:

1. They receive the death penalty, or
2. If the family forgives them, they will pay blood money.

The third crime mentioned in the ḥadīth is "one who abandons his religion and separates from the community." This is referring to the traditional Islamic punishment for Muslims who consciously and voluntary leave their own religion, which is known as riddah or irtidād in Arabic. Riddah is usually translated as apostasy in English, which is the generic act of renouncing or leaving one's religion. Within the framework of Islam it refers to a public renunciation of Islam within an Islamic State. It has both a religious and political aspect to it. In the pre-modern era, before the advent of the "Nation State", most people and governments identified with the religion they followed and practiced. When a person renounced their religion publicly it was seen as an act of betrayal and opposing one's community with political implications. The details and nuances of this discussion are beyond the scope of this short commentary. For a more detailed perspective on the issue please read "The Issue of Apostasy in Islam" by Dr. Jonathan Brown.[126]

LESSONS AND BENEFITS

1. SANCTITY OF HUMAN LIFE

Human life is considered to be sacred. By default, every human being is entitled to a safe, secure, peaceful, and free life.

---

124 5:45 - وَكَتَبْنَا عَلَيْهِمْ فِيهَا أَنَّ النَّفْسَ بِالنَّفْسِ

125 2:178 - يَا أَيُّهَا الَّذِينَ آمَنُوا كُتِبَ عَلَيْكُمُ الْقِصَاصُ فِي الْقَتْلَى

126 Brown, Jonathan. "The Issue of Apostasy in Islam." *Yaqeen*, Yaqeen Institute, 5 July 2017, https://yaqeeninstitute.org/en/jonathan-brown/the-issue-of-apostasy-in-islam/

2. *UNDERSTANDING SHARĪʿAH*

In today's current social and political climate, the word Sharīʿah has become an ugly term associated with politics, the chopping off of hands, terrorism, stoning of women, oppression of women in general, and religious intolerance. When people hear the word "Sharīʿah" they automatically think of the Taliban or ISIS and their actions. This is partially the result of how the mainstream media and popular culture portray the image of Islam. The reality is that most Americans, and it can be argued that a good number of Muslims, don't really know exactly what the Sharīʿah is.

The word Sharīʿah is an Arabic word derived from the root letters ش ر ع, which literally convey the meaning of coming to water to drink. That is why, linguistically speaking, Sharīʿah is defined as a watering hole or a place where a person or animal drinks water. Technically, it is defined as what Allah ﷻ has legislated for His servants from religion. In simpler words, the Sharīʿah is God's revealed law that governs and regulates human life and activity. It is a code of life that believers have to follow in order to obtain guidance in this world and salvation in the next.

Oftentimes Sharīʿah is understood to be Islamic Law; however, that is only partially correct. The Sharīʿah includes creed, ritual acts of worship, morals, ethics, and law. That is why a better understanding would be that the Sharīʿah is a complete code of life based on revealed scripture from God, which is meant to regulate and guide human behavior. While the common translation, "Islamic law," is not entirely wrong, it is under-inclusive. Islamic Law is a portion of the Sharīʿah, not all of it.

Islamic Law really has no parallel in history. It can be argued that it is the most successful and widely practiced legal system in the world. For the last 1400 years it has been practiced by a number of different nations that have strikingly different cultures and customs. One of the reasons for its success is first and foremost that it is divine. It is based on Revelation from the Creator of the heavens and the Earth. Every other system of law is man-made and prone to faults, prejudices, deficiencies, injustices, and inequalities. The only system of law that can ensure equality, justice, and morality is Islam. Who knows best how to govern human beings than the Creator Himself? It is the most comprehensive and complete way of life that deals with every type of relationship we as human beings can have. It deals with relationships between individuals, between individuals and the community, between different communities, between the individual and the Creator, and even between the community and the Creator. It is the law that governs the most beautiful way of life that is suitable for all times and places.

3. CRIMINAL LAW WITHIN THE SHARĪʿAH

The current mainstream narrative surrounding the Sharīʿah has created a false equivalency within the minds of most people. To most people the Sharīʿah is equivalent to a set of harsh criminal punishments known as the Ḥudūd. Perhaps to the surprise of many, this false equivalency even exists in the Muslim world. As mentioned above, this can't be further from the truth. The Sharīʿah is not simply a set of laws or a legal code; it is a very comprehensive and inclusive way of life covering all the guidance from Allah ﷻ prescribed for human beings. Law is one aspect of the Sharīʿah, and the ḥudūd make up a very small portion of it. If one were to do a survey of all the topics covered within a typical Islamic Law manual, a book of fiqh, they would find that less than 2% would be dedicated to crimes and their punishments.

Every single society, whether big or small, rural or urban, tribal or otherwise, is in need of a system of governance. In order for a society to be healthy, productive, and flourish, in order for a society to function properly, there needs to be a working system of governance; a particular system of laws and regulations that regulate behavior. Without these laws and regulations a society will quickly devolve into absolute chaos. That is why throughout history societies have developed and refined various forms of governance and law.

Just like any other system of law that exists or has existed, one aspect of the Sharīʿah is criminal law. Criminal law in most societies is simply punitive; it focuses on the punishments for specific crimes. Within the Sharīʿah criminal law takes a more holistic approach focusing on prevention, punishment, rehabilitation, and forgiveness. There is a lot of emphasis placed on God-consciousness, morality, chastity, repentance, and reformation. That is why punishments in Islam are characterized as both being preventive and reformative; they serve to prevent people from committing crimes and as a means of expiation for those who have committed those crimes.

One of the most controversial aspects of the Sharīʿah, at least to the modern mind, is a set of punishments known as the Ḥudūd. These are a specific set of laws found in the Quran and Sunnah that determine the punishment for very specific crimes. al-Ḥudūd is often translated as the fixed punishments or the divinely ordained punishments. The word ḥad literally means a boundary or limit that separates and prevents one thing from intruding on another. Technically, within the Sharīʿah, it refers to a quantitatively fixed punishment that is imposed for a violation of the right of Allah. In simpler terms they are fixed punishments that are prescribed by the Quran and Sunnah.

There are five divinely ordained punishments:

1. Ḥadd al-Zinā (adultery/fornication),
2. Ḥadd al-Qadhf (accusing someone of adultery/fornication without eyewitness testimony),
3. Ḥadd al-Sariqah (specific theft)
4. Ḥadd Shurb al-Khamr (consuming wine), and
5. Ḥadd al-Ḥirābah (highway robbery)

Each of these terms is referring to a very specific crime within the scope of the Shari'ah. They have been ascribed fixed punishments because they are considered to be extremely heinous crimes that are harmful to both the individual and society. Each of these crimes, their punishments, and how they are to be applied have detailed legal rulings and very specific procedures that are elaborated in works of Islamic Jurisprudence.

HADITH 15

Expressions of Iman

عَنْ أَبِي هُرَيْرَةَ رَضِيَ اللَّهُ عَنْهُ أَنَّ رَسُولَ اللَّهِ صلى اللَّهُ عليه و سلم قَالَ: "مَنْ كَانَ يُؤْمِنُ بِاَللَّهِ وَالْيَوْمِ الْآخِرِ فَلْيَقُلْ خَيْرًا أَوْ لِيَصْمُتْ، وَمَنْ كَانَ يُؤْمِنُ بِاَللَّهِ وَالْيَوْمِ الْآخِرِ فَلْيُكْرِمْ جَارَهُ، وَمَنْ كَانَ يُؤْمِنُ بِاَللَّهِ وَالْيَوْمِ الْآخِرِ فَلْيُكْرِمْ ضَيْفَهُ".

رَوَاهُ الْبُخَارِيُّ، وَمُسْلِمٌ.

From Abū Hurairah ﵁ that the Messenger of Allah ﷺ said, "Whoever believes in Allah and the Last Day should say something good or keep silent; and whoever believes in Allah and the Last Day should be generous to their neighbor; and whoever believes in Allah and the Last Day should be generous to his guest."

Narrated by al-Bukāhrī and Muslim.

IMPORTANCE

This ḥadīth is also among the concise and comprehensive sayings of the Prophet ﷺ. The words may be few in number but the meanings and wisdom behind them are extremely vast and deep. This is one of the aḥādīth that form the foundation of manners, etiquette, and behavior in Islam. The Prophet ﷺ mentions three things that are considered to be the foundation of good character. These foundations of good character are a result and consequence of īmān that lies in one's heart; they are expressions of true sincere faith.

EXPLANATION

In this ḥadīth the Prophet ﷺ is describing three specific characteristics or qualities that are an expression of faith or īmān. They are a part of the branches of īmān referred to by the Prophet ﷺ when he said, "Faith has seventy some odd branches."[127] Without these branches one's faith is lacking.

The first characteristic is the ability to control one's tongue. The Prophet ﷺ said, "Whoever believes in Allah ﷻ and the last day should say something good or remain silent." This is a very significant statement. If a person truly believes in Allah ﷻ, if they have full certainty in the reality of life after death, judgment, and accountability then they will be conscious of how they use their tongue. They will be conscious of how their words affect them and those around them.

Words can be very painful. A person may say something to someone that they think is harmless, but it breaks the other person's heart. Similarly, they may say something that they feel is insignificant and small but it fills the other person's heart with joy and happiness. The tongue, this small piece of flesh, is very powerful. It has the power to drag a person into a pit of Hell and at the same time to lead a person to Paradise. The Prophet ﷺ said, "Truly a servant may utter a word which pleases Allah without giving it much importance, and because of that Allah will raise him by degrees. And truly a servant may utter a word that displeases Allah without thinking of its gravity and because of that he will be thrown into the Fire."[128]

---

127 Muslim, *k. al-īmān, b. Bayān ʿadad shuʿab al-īmān*, 35

128 Bukhārī, *k. al-Riqāq, b.ḥifẓ al-lisān*, 6478

That is why it is important to recognize the significance of the words a person speaks and nowadays even the words they type. Communication has evolved and changed so much that one of the primary ways people communicate with others is through emails, texts, and social media. The same principle applies. Just as a person should think before they speak they should also think before they type. It leads to the breakdown of the family, which is the foundation of society.

Something that helps with that is to always remember that whatever a person says or types is being recorded, not just by the FBI or the NSA, but by Angels appointed by Allah ﷻ. "Man does not utter any word except that with him is an observer prepared [to record]."[129] This consciousness is part of faith.

The second characteristic is being good to one's neighbors. The Prophet ﷺ starts by repeating the same statement, "whoever believes in Allah and the last day should be good to their neighbor." Meaning if a person is sincere in their faith, if their īmān is actually rooted in their heart, then it will translate to treating their neighbors well. This includes helping them, visiting them when they are sick, congratulating them, giving them condolences, and not harming them in any way. Throughout the Quran and Sunnah a lot of emphasis has been placed on treating neighbors well. The Prophet ﷺ said, "Jibrīl kept advising me regarding the neighbor to the point that I thought the neighbor would inherit."[130] In another narration the Prophet ﷺ told Abū Dhar رضي الله عنه, "When you cook stew increase its water and share it with your neighbors."[131]

The last characteristic mentioned is being kind and generous to one's guest. The Prophet ﷺ said, "Whoever believes in Allah and the Last Day, then let them honor their guest." How to honor one's guest can be different based on time, place, culture, and context. However, there are general guidelines that include welcoming them, making them feel comfortable, offering them food and drink, and serving them. All of this should be done within one's own limits and convenience in mind without any extravagance or waste.

---

129 مَّا يَلْفِظُ مِن قَوْلٍ إِلَّا لَدَيْهِ رَقِيبٌ عَتِيدٌ - 50:18

130 Bukhārī, *k. al-adab, b. al-waṣāh bi al-jār*, 6015

131 Muslim, *k. al-birr wa al-ṣilah wa al-ādāb, b. Al-waṣiyyah bi al-jār wa al-iḥsān ilayhi*, 2625

LESSONS AND BENEFITS

1. COMPLETE FAITH

Īmān plays a role in every single aspect of a believer's life. It is the main catalyst behind everything they do in the life of this world. It expresses itself through a person's speech, behavior, conduct, the way they carry themselves, morals, principles, and values. An extremely important aspect of one's īmān is how they deal with others and interact with them.

Human beings are by nature social beings; they require relationships, communication, love, attention, and care. These relationships are healthy if they are built upon mutual love, compassion, respect, care, etiquettes, and manners. That is exactly what the Prophet ﷺ is teaching through these beautiful words.

2. CONTROLLING THE TONGUE

The tongue is considered to be a double edged sword. It can be the cause of great good and at the same time it can be the cause of great harm. It can be a means for a person to earn unimaginable amounts of reward and it can also be the means of earning sin and committing disobedience. Every single word a person says is recorded by the Angelic Scribes. On the Day of Judgment a person will be held accountable for whatever they said or did in the life of this world. That is why it is so important to learn how to control one's tongue. The Prophet ﷺ said, "Whoever can guarantee for me what is between their jaws and what is between their legs, I will guarantee Paradise for them."[132] The Prophet ﷺ speaking to Muʿādh ﷺ said, "Shall I not tell you of the foundation of all of that?" I said, "Yes, O Messenger of Allah." So he took hold of his tongue and said, "Restrain this." I said, "O Prophet of Allah, will we be taken to account for what we say with it?" He ﷺ said, "May your mother be bereaved of you, O Muʿādh! Is there anything that throws people into the Hellfire upon their faces — or on their noses — except the harvests of their tongues?"[133]

Anas ﷺ narrates that the Prophet ﷺ said, "A person's faith is not sound until their heart is sound, and their heart is not sound until their tongue is

132 Bukhārī, *k. al-raqā'iq*, *b. ḥifẓ al-lisān*, 6474

133 Ḥadīth #29 in this collection.

sound."[134] Similarly, the Prophet ﷺ said, "A person will not reach the reality of faith until they control their tongue."[135]

3. BE A GOOD NEIGHBOR

One of the ways in which īmān expresses itself is through how one interacts with their neighbors. Īmān requires a person to be kind, respectful, courteous, and helpful to their neighbors. They should not cause any harm or be a source of inconvenience to their neighbors. This is also perhaps the best way to change the negative attitudes of people towards Islam and Muslims, especially where they are a minority.

4. BE A GENEROUS HOST

Islam encourages generosity in all of its different shapes and forms. One of them is to be a kind and generous host, which is an expression of one's faith. Faith requires one to be accommodating, welcoming, and generous as opposed to being cold and stingy. A person should be pleasant with their guest, make them feel welcome, engage them in conversation, and serve them with food and drink.

---

134 Mundhirī, *al-Targhīb wa al-Tarhīb*, 4:21

135 Ṭabarānī, *al-Muʿjam al-Awsaṭ*, 5:378

HADITH 16

Control Your Anger

عَنْ أَبِي هُرَيْرَةَ رَضِيَ اللَّهُ عَنْهُ أَنَّ رَجُلًا قَالَ لِلنَّبِيِّ صلى اللَّهُ عليه و سلم أَوْصِنِي. قَالَ: لَا تَغْضَبْ، فَرَدَّدَ مِرَارًا، قَالَ: لَا تَغْضَبْ".
رَوَاهُ الْبُخَارِيُّ.

From Abū Hurairah ﷺ that a man said to the Prophet ﷺ, "Advise me." The Prophet ﷺ said, "Do not become angry." The man repeated [his request for advice] several times, and [each time] he ﷺ said, "Do not become angry."

Narrated by al-Bukhārī.

IMPORTANCE

This is one of the narrations that is considered to be the foundation of manners, etiquette, and behavior in Islam. It is also one of the concise comprehensive statements of the Prophet ﷺ that may be few in words, but is extremely deep and profound in terms of meaning. The amount of evil and headaches this advice prevents and the amount of good it brings is unimaginable. Oftentimes anger is the root cause of poor choices, regret, remorse, sorrow, and strained and broken relationships. Think about all the problems anger brings about in a one's personal and social life; between brothers, siblings, parents and children, husbands and wives. If a person were to truly act upon this advice of the Prophet ﷺ it would lead to a wholesome, healthy, sound, and peaceful life.

EXPLANATION

In this narration a man comes to the Prophet ﷺ and asks for some advice saying, "Advise me." This shows that the Companions of the Prophet ﷺ were constantly willing to learn from the Prophet ﷺ and seek advice and counsel from him in all of their affairs. Another version mentions that the man asked the Prophet ﷺ to advise him with something that was light and easy so that he could safeguard it and act upon it.

The Prophet ﷺ responded to his request by advising him to not get angry. He advised him with a few simple words, "Don't get angry." Don't lose your temper and let your emotions get the best of you. Don't get upset with people and say or do something that will be a source of regret later on. This is extremely succinct advice. However, the questioner did not realize how comprehensive and important this advice was. That is one of the reasons why he kept asking the Prophet ﷺ to advise him. Another narration mentions that later on he said, "I thought about what the Prophet ﷺ said and I came to the conclusion that anger gathers all the evils."

LESSONS AND BENEFITS

1. ANGER

Anger is a natural human emotion. It is something that every single human being feels and experiences. The Arabic word for anger is "ghaḍab". Linguistically, anger is the opposite of contentment. It is derived from the root letters غ ض ب that indicate towards severity and strength.

Some scholars describe anger as "a flame of fire, lit from Allah's fire, that overtakes hearts. Whoever it overcomes has inclined toward the hereditary disposition of the devil, for indeed he was created from fire."[136] The Prophet ﷺ said, "Truly anger is from Satan and Satan was truly created from fire."[137] It is an emotion that enters into one's heart and can be both positive and negative. Other scholars have described it as a "movement of the soul as a result of revenge, or an internal quality that results in a movement of the soul to seek revenge." Imām al-Ghazālī ؒ writes that it is when the heart's blood boils out of a desire to seek revenge. Imām Mawlūd describes it as a "swelling ocean". It is a swelling mass of emotion that is difficult to hold back once it is unleashed.

It is not necessarily a negative emotion in and of itself. Without anger there are many things that would not have been achieved. It can be a positive motivator. At the same time it can possess, consume, and ultimately destroy a person. In a state of anger a person is unable to see clearly; they don't think of consequences. When a person becomes angry, they lose control of their ability to think, speak, and act rationally. Oftentimes they will say or do things that they regret later on. How many people have ruined their lives because of something they said or did while in a fit of anger? How many people don't have healthy relationships because they are known to be short-tempered? How many relationships has anger ruined and destroyed?

Anger is an emotion that needs to be trained, tamed, and kept in-check; it has to be controlled. It is an emotion that requires balance and moderation; a middle way. It is acceptable only at the right time, in the right place, for the right reasons, and with the right intensity. That is why scholars mention that there are two types of anger. One is for the sake of Allah, and this is good anger, which can be channeled into positive actions. The other is bad anger, which is for the sake of ego and attributed to the devil. That is why the Sharīʿah encourages controlling one's anger.

The Prophet ﷺ said, "The strong person is not one who overcomes you.

---

136 al-Ghazālī, *al-Arbaʿīn fī Uṣūl al-Dīn*, p.133

137 Abū Dāwūd, *k. al-adab*, *b. Mā yuqāl ʿinda al-ghaḍab*, 4784

A true strong person is one who is able to control himself when angry."[138] Similarly, the Prophet ﷺ said, "Whoever swallows their anger while having the ability to act upon it, Allah will fill him with security and faith."[139]

2. *WAYS TO CONTROL ANGER*

The following is a list of some practical ways to control and break one's anger:

a. Remember the extensive praise, virtues, rewards, and blessings associated with patience, forbearance, and humility. There are unimaginable blessings associated with swallowing one's anger and it is considered to be an expression of one's consciousness of Allah ﷻ. A person's desire to earn these rewards and blessings can protect them from losing their temper.
b. Controlling one's anger by remaining silent. The Prophet ﷺ said, "When one of you becomes angry, remain silent."[140]
c. Seek refuge and protection with Allah ﷻ from Satan. It is narrated that two men began to argue and curse each other in the presence of the Prophet ﷺ and the face of one of them turned red and the veins of his neck were swollen (from rage). The Prophet ﷺ said, "I know of a word, if he were to utter that, his rage would vanish and that is: I seek refuge with Allah from Satan the accursed."[141]
d. Change physical position or leave; a person should sit if they are standing, and lay down if they are sitting. The Prophet ﷺ said, "If one of you becomes angry while they're standing, they should sit. If his anger doesn't subside then he should lie down."
e. Perform wuḍū'. The Prophet ﷺ said, "Indeed anger is from Satan and Satan has been created from fire. So if one of you becomes angry, make wuḍū'."[142]
f. Be forgiving and overlook people's rude behavior. There is a correla-

138 Muslim, *k. al-birr wa al-ṣilah wa al-ādāb, b. faḍl man yamliku nafsahu ʿinda al-ghaḍab wa bi ayyai shay yadhabu al-ghaḍab*, 2609

139 Bukhārī, *al-Tārīkh al-Kabīr*, 6:123

140 Bukhārī, *al-Adab al-Mufrad*, 12:245

141 Muslim, *k. al-birr wa al-ṣilah wa al-ādāb, b. faḍl man yamliku nafsahu ʿinda al-ghaḍab wa bi ayyai shay yadhabu al-ghaḍab*, 2610

142 Abū Dāwūd, *k. al-adab, b. Mā yuqālu ʿinda al-ghaḍab*, 4784

tion between what a person does and what they receive from Allah ﷻ in kind – a correspondence that the Almighty has placed in the workings of creation. If a person doesn't want to incur the anger of Allah ﷻ, then they should not be angry with people unjustly. A man asked the Prophet ﷺ, "What is the worst thing that one incurs concerning Allah?" The Prophet ﷺ replied, "His wrath." The man then asked, "How do we avoid it?" The Prophet ﷺ said, "Do not become angry."[143] Similarly, if a person wants to receive mercy from Allah ﷻ they should be merciful to others.

143 Ḥanbal, *Musnad*, 175:2

HADITH 17

Excellence

عَنْ أَبِي يَعْلَى شَدَّادِ بْنِ أَوْسٍ رَضِيَ اللَّه عَنْهُ عَنْ رَسُولِ اللَّهِ صلى الله عليه و سلم قَالَ: "إِنَّ اللَّهَ كَتَبَ الْإِحْسَانَ عَلَى كُلِّ شَيْءٍ، فَإِذَا قَتَلْتُمْ فَأَحْسِنُوا الْقِتْلَةَ، وَإِذَا ذَبَحْتُمْ فَأَحْسِنُوا الذِّبْحَةَ، وَلْيُحِدَّ أَحَدُكُمْ شَفْرَتَهُ، وَلْيُرِحْ ذَبِيحَتَهُ".

رَوَاهُ مُسْلِمٌ.

From Abū Yaʻlā Shaddād ibn Aws ☙ that the Messenger of Allah ☙ said, "Verily Allah ☙ has prescribed iḥsān (proficiency, perfection) in all things. So if you kill then kill well; and if you slaughter, then slaughter well. Let each one of you sharpen his blade and let him spare suffering to the animal he slaughters."

Narrated by Muslim.

THE NARRATOR

The narrator of this ḥadīth is Abū Yaʿlā Shaddād ibn Aws al-Khazrajī al-Anṣāri ﷺ. He was a noble companion of the Prophet ﷺ as well as one of the governors appointed by ʿUmar ibn Khaṭṭāb ﷺ. He was the governor of Hims and later when ʿUthmān ﷺ was martyred, he stepped out of the public view and devoted himself to worship. He was known for his eloquence, forbearance, and wisdom. He passed away in al-Quds in the year 58. He has narrated 50 aḥādīth, may Allah ﷻ be pleased with him.

IMPORTANCE

In this ḥadīth the Prophet ﷺ explains an extremely important principle within the framework of Islam; everything should be done with perfection and excellence; iḥsān. This is a general principle that should be applied to every single aspect of one's life. Everything big and small, significant and insignificant, major and minor, should be done with iḥsān.

EXPLANATION

The Prophet ﷺ starts by mentioning a general principle, "Verily Allah has prescribed iḥsān in all things." Meaning, Muslims are supposed to strive for excellence and perfection in everything they do, whether the action is big or small, important or insignificant. It is a standard that one should strive to achieve in all aspects of their life; personal, family, social, professional, and economic. It should be applied in all of one's relationships as well. The Prophet ﷺ then mentions two examples of how this principle can be applied. "So if you kill then kill well; and if you slaughter, then slaughter well. Let each one of you sharpen his blade and let him spare suffering to the animal he slaughters." The unique thing about these two examples is that they are actions that people may not consider being related to iḥsān. People may think that iḥsān has no role on the battlefield or when slaughtering animals. The Prophet ﷺ explains that iḥsān is prescribed even in these scenarios.

LESSONS AND BENEFITS

1. IḤSĀN

The word iḥsān literally means perfection or goodness. Iḥsān is the concept of doing things in the best way possible; it is the hallmark of an upright, moral, and God-conscious believer. A believer should strive for excellence and perfection in everything they do. Iḥsān is considered to be the highest level or station a person can reach when performing an act of worship. It is worship or any other deed accompanied with God-consciousness, which leads to humility, concentration, and sincerity in actions. This state of iḥsān is achieved by recognizing that Allah ﷻ is watching and is aware of a person's innermost thoughts and feelings.

The concept of iḥsān is so important that it is actually obligatory. Allah ﷻ says, "God commands justice, doing good, and generosity towards relatives and He forbids what is shameful, blameworthy, and oppressive. He teaches you, so that you may take heed."[144] Similarly, Allah ﷻ says in Sūrah al-Baqarah, "And do things with perfection. Indeed Allah loves those who do things with perfection."[145]

Iḥsān is a comprehensive approach and attitude towards everything in life. It includes doing things with sincerity, purpose, completely, quality, nicely, while observing proper etiquettes and manners in a timely manner.

2. ANIMAL RIGHTS

Islam approaches animal rights in a very balanced and holistic fashion. Part of that approach is that the animal should not be harmed in any way, shape, or form.

---

144 16:90 - إِنَّ اللَّـهَ يَأْمُرُ بِالْعَدْلِ وَالْإِحْسَانِ وَإِيتَاءِ ذِي الْقُرْبَىٰ وَيَنْهَىٰ عَنِ الْفَحْشَاءِ وَالْمُنكَرِ وَالْبَغْيِ ۚ يَعِظُكُمْ لَعَلَّكُمْ تَذَكَّرُونَ

145 2:195 - وَأَحْسِنُوا ۛ إِنَّ اللَّـهَ يُحِبُّ الْمُحْسِنِينَ

HADITH 18

Fear Allah Wherever You Are

عَنْ أَبِي ذَرٍّ جُنْدَبِ بْنِ جُنَادَةَ، وَأَبِي عَبْدِ الرَّحْمَنِ مُعَاذِ بْنِ جَبَلٍ رَضِيَ اللَّهُ عَنْهُمَا، عَنْ رَسُولِ اللَّهِ صلى الله عليه و سلم قَالَ: "اتَّقِ اللَّهَ حَيْثُمَا كُنْت، وَأَتْبِعْ السَّيِّئَةَ الْحَسَنَةَ تَمْحُهَا، وَخَالِقْ النَّاسَ بِخُلُقٍ حَسَنٍ".

رَوَاهُ التِّرْمِذِيُّ وَقَالَ: حَدِيثٌ حَسَنٌ، وَفِي بَعْضِ النُّسَخِ: حَسَنٌ صَحِيحٌ.

From Abū Dharr Jundub ibn Junādah and Abū ʿAbd al-Raḥmān Muʿādh ibn Jabal that the Messenger of Allah ﷺ said, "Fear Allah wherever you are, and follow up a bad deed with a good deed, which will wipe it out, and interact with people with good manners."

Narrated by al-Tirmidhī, who said it is a ḥasan (good) ḥadīth, and in some copies it is stated to be a ḥasan ṣaḥīḥ ḥadīth.

THE NARRATOR

This ḥadīth has been narrated by two companions:

1. Abū Dharr Jundub ibn Junādah 🙵 and
2. Muʿādh bin Jabal 🙵

Jundub ibn Junādah, better known as Abū Dharr 🙵, was one of the Companions who accepted Islam very early on. He himself says that he was the fifth person to accept Islam. He was known for his honesty, so much so that he was given as an example of honesty. He is the first person to greet the Prophet 🙵 with the greeting of Islam. He passed away in the year 32 and narrated 281 aḥādīth, may Allah 🙵 be pleased with him.

The second narrator is Abū ʿAbd al-Raḥmān Muʿādh ibn Jabal 🙵 al-Anṣārī al-Khazrajī. He was the most knowledgeable of the Companions when it came to the issues of lawful and unlawful. The Prophet 🙵 said, "The most knowledgeable of my nation with respect to ḥalāl and ḥarām is Muʿādh ibn Jabal 🙵."[146] Meaning, he was a jurist. He was a handsome young man, known for his forbearance, generosity, and modesty. He accepted Islam as a teenager at the age of 18. He participated in all of the expeditions with the Prophet 🙵. Because of his knowledge the Prophet 🙵 sent him to Yemen as a governor and teacher. He passed away in the year 18 at the age of 34. He narrated 157 aḥādīth, may Allah 🙵 be pleased with him.

IMPORTANCE

This ḥadīth, like those before it, is from the concise yet comprehensive sayings of the Prophet 🙵 whose words are few in number but great in meaning. In this short ḥadīth the Prophet 🙵 has presented an entire roadmap for life, combining between fulfilling the rights of Allah 🙵 and the rights of others. Regarding this ḥadīth ibn Rajab al-Ḥanbalī 🙵 wrote, "This is powerful advice, bringing together the rights of Allah and the rights of His servants."[147] The first two statements deal with the rights of Allah 🙵 and the last statement deals with the rights humans have upon one another.

---

146   Tirmidhī, k. al-manāqib ʿan Rasūlillah 🙵, 3791
147   Ibn Rajab, Jāmiʿ al-ʿUlūm wa al-Ḥikam, p.184

EXPLANATION

The Prophet ﷺ starts by advising, "Fear Allah wherever you are." Meaning be conscious, mindful, and aware of Allah ﷻ in both public and private. Oftentimes taqwā is translated as fear; however, this translation does not capture the true essence and meaning of the word. Fear is only one aspect or part of taqwā. Linguistically, taqwā is defined as forbearance, fear, or abstinence. It is derived from the verb waqā/yaqī, which means to protect or prevent. To make a shield or barrier between one's self and what they fear for protection.

In the context of the Quran and Sunnah it refers to being mindful, conscious, and aware of Allah ﷻ. Being conscious and aware that Allah ﷻ is the All-Knowing, All-Seeing, and All-Hearing and that everything a person says or does is being recorded. It means being aware of the fact that there is a Day of Judgment and on that Day a person will be held accountable for whatever they have said or done. This consciousness then drives a person's behavior and motivates them to try their best to obey the commandments of Allah ﷻ and stay away from His prohibitions. Practically speaking, the scholars define taqwā as obeying the commands of Allah ﷻ and staying away from His prohibitions. The Prophet ﷺ is advising his followers to be conscious and aware of Allah ﷻ at all times and under all circumstances.

The second piece of advice in this ḥadīth is, "follow up a bad deed with a good one and it will erase it." The Prophet ﷺ is mentioning a very important principle within Islam: good deeds erase bad deeds. This can refer to performing a good deed immediately after falling into sin or an act of disobedience. It can also refer to seeking forgiveness and repentance. Allah ﷻ says in Sūrah Hūd, "Establish ritual prayer at both ends of the day and in the early hours of the night. Surely good deeds erase bad deeds. That is a reminder for the mindful."[148]

The Prophet ﷺ concludes this statement by reminding people to deal with others in the best way possible, "and behave well towards people". This is referring to having good character, morals, values, and ethics. Character includes how a person speaks and behaves, their conduct and behavior, especially with others. The Prophet ﷺ is reminding his companions to adorn their speech and behavior with noble qualities and characteristics such as

---

148 11:114 - وَأَقِمِ الصَّلَاةَ طَرَفَيِ النَّهَارِ وَزُلَفًا مِّنَ اللَّيْلِ ۚ إِنَّ الْحَسَنَاتِ يُذْهِبْنَ السَّيِّئَاتِ

gentleness, humility, compassion, sympathy, care, concern, patience, forbearance, and mercy.

LESSONS AND BENEFITS

1. THE IMPORTANCE OF TAQWĀ

God-Consciousness, being aware of Allah ﷻ, is one of the greatest and most important qualities that a person is supposed to develop and nurture within themselves. It is described as a comprehensive trait that gathers all forms of good and protects one from all types of harm. It is one of the most essential aspects of a person's relationship with Allah ﷻ and is considered to be the catalyst behind everything a person does. There are numerous verses of the Quran and aḥādīth of the Prophet ﷺ that speak about the virtue and value of taqwā.

The rewards, blessings, benefits, and virtues of taqwā are extremely profound and powerful. The following are a few highlighted by Allah ﷻ in the Quran:

a. "Surely, Allah is with those who are mindful of Him and those who are good in their deeds."[149]
b. "God will find a way out for those who are mindful of Him, and will provide for them from an unexpected source; God will be enough for those who put their trust in Him. God achieves His purpose; God has set a due measure for everything."[150]
c. "But if you are steadfast and conscious of God, their scheming will not harm you in the least: God encircles everything they do."[151]
d. "My mercy encompasses all things. I shall ordain My mercy for those who are conscious of God and pay the prescribed alms; who believe in Our Revelations."[152]

---

149 16:128 - إِنَّ اللَّـهَ مَعَ الَّذِينَ اتَّقَوا وَّالَّذِينَ هُم مُّحْسِنُونَ

150 65 :2-3 - وَمَن يَتَّقِ اللَّـهَ يَجْعَل لَّهُ مَخْرَجًا وَيَرْزُقْهُ مِنْ حَيْثُ لَا يَحْتَسِبُ ۚ وَمَن يَتَوَكَّلْ عَلَى اللَّـهِ فَهُوَ حَسْبُهُ ۚ إِنَّ اللَّـهَ بَالِغُ أَمْرِهِ قَدْ جَعَلَ اللَّـهُ لِكُلِّ شَيْءٍ قَدْرًا

151 3:120 - وَإِن تَصْبِرُوا وَتَتَّقُوا لَا يَضُرُّكُمْ كَيْدُهُمْ شَيْئًا ۗ إِنَّ اللَّـهَ بِمَا يَعْمَلُونَ مُحِيطٌ

152 7:156 - وَرَحْمَتِي وَسِعَتْ كُلَّ شَيْءٍ ۚ فَسَأَكْتُبُهَا لِلَّذِينَ يَتَّقُونَ وَيُؤْتُونَ الزَّكَاةَ وَالَّذِينَ هُم بِآيَاتِنَا يُؤْمِنُونَ

2. *THE POWER OF ISTIGHFĀR AND TAWBAH*

Every single human being has faults, deficiencies, and shortcomings. There are times when people will make mistakes, poor choices, and have lapses in judgment. As the Prophet ﷺ said, "Every son of Adam is a profuse wrongdoer and the best of profuse wrongdoers are those who repent."[153] Istighfār means to seek forgiveness from Allah ﷻ for one's mistakes, sins, and acts of disobedience that were done knowingly or unknowingly. There are numerous narrations that encourage istighfār and highlight its virtues, blessings, and rewards. In addition to that, there are several actions a person does throughout the day that serve as a means for having one's minor sins forgiven. For example, performing wuḍū', walking to the masjid, and praying wipe away a person's minor sins.

Tawbah is usually translated as repentance, and is required for one's major sins to be forgiven. It is a very powerful tool that allows one to turn back to Allah ﷻ. Linguistically the word التوبة is derived from the root letters ت و ب, which convey the meaning of returning. When a person repents they are returning to the obedience of Allah ﷻ after having disobeyed Him. Some scholars have defined it as "returning to Allah from the path of being distant to the path of nearness." It has also been defined as leaving sin because of its ugliness, regret upon one's shortcoming, making a firm resolution not to return, and making up the shortcoming if possible.[154] It is also said that repentance is acknowledgement, remorse, and to abandon (leave off/desist).[155] As the Prophet ﷺ said, "Remorse is repentance."[156]

In summary, repentance is returning to Allah ﷻ after having done something wrong by doing the following:

a. Feeling remorse
b. Seeking forgiveness
c. Making a firm resolution not to do it again
d. Redress – making up

Once a person repents, it is as if they never sinned in the first place. The

153 Ibn Mājah, *k. al-Zuhd*, 4251

154 تَركُ الذَّنبِ لِقُبحِهِ وَالنَّدَمُ عَلَى مَا فَرَطَ مِنهُ وِالعَزِيمَةُ عَلَى تَركِ المُعَاوَدَةِ، وَتَدَارَكُ مَا أَمكَنَهُ أَن يَتَدَارَكَ مِن الَأعمَالِ بِالإِعَادَةِ

155 التَّوبَةُ الِاعتَرِافُ وَالنَّدَمُ وَالإِقلاَعُ.

156 Ibn Mājah, *k. al-Zuhd*, 4252

Prophet ﷺ said, "The one who repents from a sin is like one who has no sin at all."[157]

3. THE IMPORTANCE OF GOOD CHARACTER

The importance of akhlāq, or good character, in Islam, can't be overstated. In today's society, when a person thinks of religion, they think of rules and regulations, restrictions, and devotional acts of worship. Even Muslims are guilty of limiting Islam to devotional acts of worship. Generally, when a person hears the word Islam, automatically they think of praying, fasting, giving charity, and reading Quran. These devotional acts of worship are a fundamental part of Islam as a way of life, but they aren't the only part. As a matter of fact, our success simply isn't in prayers, fasting, charity, or ḥajj. Rather, it is in good manners coupled with these acts of worship.

The Prophet ﷺ himself described perfecting good manners as the reason why he was sent as a Prophet. "I have only been sent to perfect good character."[158] Through this statement the Prophet ﷺ explained that one of the primary objectives of his mission was to perfect good character. Interestingly, the acts of worship that have been prescribed in Islam help a person build good character.

Akhlāq isn't simply a few manners or qualities; rather, it is a group of praiseworthy characteristics and qualities that a person has. For example, generosity, forbearance, forgiveness, leniency, chastity, fairness, gentleness, humility, justice, mercy, kindness, honesty, and bravery. That is why when a person is polite and respectful to others, humble and kind to the poor and needy, they are showing good character.

The Prophet ﷺ throughout his life stressed the importance of having good character both in speech and deed. The Prophet ﷺ said, "The believers most complete in faith are those who have the best character." When asked about what deeds will lead people to Paradise, the Prophet ﷺ responded, "God-consciousness and good character."[159] When he was sending Muʿādh ؓ as a governor to Yemen he ﷺ reminded him, "and show good manners in your dealing with others."[160]

---

157 al-Bayhaqī, *Shuʿab al-Īmān*, 6780

158 Haythamī, *Majmaʿ al-Zawā'id*, 9:18

159 Tirmidhī, *k. Al-birr wa al-ṣilah ʿan rasūlillah* ﷺ, *b. Mā jā'a fī ḥusn al-khuluq*, 2004

160 Tirmidhī, *k. Al-birr wa al-ṣilah ʿan rasūlillah* ﷺ, *b. Mā jā'a fī muʿāsharah al-nās*, 1987

Not only did the Prophet ﷺ encourage others to have good character but he showed them how to as well practically. The Prophet ﷺ had the best character himself. Anything he said about character he practiced himself. Allah ﷻ addressed the Prophet ﷺ saying, "And verily, you (Muḥammad) are on an exalted standard of character."[161] Anything the Quran mentioned regarding character, the Prophet ﷺ embodied it. That is why when ʿĀ'ishah رضي الله عنها was asked about the character of the Prophet ﷺ, she said, "His character was the Quran."[162] Literally, he was a walking and talking Quran.

161 وَإِنَّكَ لَعَلَىٰ خُلُقٍ عَظِيمٍ - 68:4

162 Bukhārī, *al-Adab al-Mufrad*, 308

HADITH 19

Be Mindful of Allah

عَنْ عَبْدِ اللّٰهِ بْنِ عَبَّاسٍ رَضِيَ اللّٰهُ عَنْهُمَا قَالَ: "كُنْت خَلْفَ رَسُولِ اللّٰهِ صلى الله عليه و سلم يَوْمًا، فَقَالَ: يَا غُلَامِ! إنِّي أُعَلِّمُك كَلِمَاتٍ: احْفَظْ اللّٰهَ يَحْفَظْك، احْفَظْ اللّٰهَ تَجِدْهُ تُجَاهَك، إذَا سَأَلْت فَاسْأَلْ اللّٰهَ، وَإِذَا اسْتَعَنْت فَاسْتَعِنْ بِاَللّٰهِ، وَاعْلَمْ أَنَّ الْأُمَّةَ لَوْ اجْتَمَعَتْ عَلَى أَنْ يَنْفَعُوك بِشَيْءٍ لَمْ يَنْفَعُوك إلَّا بِشَيْءٍ قَدْ كَتَبَهُ اللّٰهُ لَك، وَإِنْ اجْتَمَعُوا عَلَى أَنْ يَضُرُّوك بِشَيْءٍ لَمْ يَضُرُّوك إلَّا بِشَيْءٍ قَدْ كَتَبَهُ اللّٰهُ عَلَيْك؛ رُفِعَتْ الْأَقْلَامُ، وَجَفَّتْ الصُّحُفُ".

رَوَاهُ التِّرْمِذِيُّ وَقَالَ: حَدِيثٌ حَسَنٌ صَحِيحٌ.

وَفِي رِوَايَةِ غَيْرِ التِّرْمِذِيِّ: "احْفَظْ اللّٰهَ تَجِدْهُ أَمَامَك، تَعَرَّفْ إلَى اللّٰهِ فِي الرَّخَاءِ يَعْرِفْك فِي الشِّدَّةِ، وَاعْلَمْ أَنَّ مَا أَخْطَأَك لَمْ يَكُنْ لِيُصِيبَك، وَمَا أَصَابَك لَمْ يَكُنْ لِيُخْطِئَك، وَاعْلَمْ أَنَّ النَّصْرَ مَعَ الصَّبْرِ، وَأَنَّ الْفَرَجَ مَعَ الْكَرْبِ، وَأَنَّ مَعَ الْعُسْرِ يُسْرًا".

From ʿAbdullah ibn ʿAbbās ﵄ who said, "One day I was behind the Prophet ﷺ [riding on the same mount] and he said, 'O young man, I shall teach you some words [of advice]: Be mindful of Allah ﷻ and Allah ﷻ will protect you. Be mindful of Allah ﷻ and you will find Him in front of you. If you ask, then ask Allah ﷻ; and if you seek help, then seek help from Allah ﷻ. And know that if the nation were to gather together to benefit you with anything, they would not benefit you except with what Allah ﷻ has already prescribed for you. And if they were to gather together to harm you with anything, they would not harm you except with what Allah ﷻ has already prescribed against you. The pens have been lifted and the pages have dried.'"

Narrated by al-Tirmidhī, who said it is a good and authentic ḥadīth.

Another narration, other than that of al-Tirmidhī, reads: "Be mindful of Allah ﷻ, and you will find Him in front of you. Recognize and acknowledge Allah ﷻ in times of ease and prosperity, and He will remember you in times of adversity. And know that what has passed you by [and you have failed to attain] was not going to befall you, and what has befallen you was not going to pass you by. And know that victory comes with patience, relief with affliction, and hardship with ease."

IMPORTANCE

Regarding this ḥadīth ibn al-Jawzī ﷺ writes, "I pondered over this ḥadīth and it amazed me to the point that I almost became lightheaded...what a pity for the one who is ignorant of this ḥadīth and has little understanding of its meaning."[163] This statement is enough to show how important, profound, and powerful this particular narration is.

EXPLANATION

Ibn ʿAbbās ﷺ starts the narration by describing the situation and context in which he heard these words from the Prophet ﷺ. He says, "One day I was riding behind the Prophet ﷺ." Meaning that ibn ʿAbbās ﷺ was riding behind the Prophet ﷺ on the same animal. The reason why he mentions this specific detail is to stress that he heard these words directly from the Prophet ﷺ, and he remembered them so well that he even remembered the circumstance in which he heard them.

The Prophet ﷺ grabbed his attention by calling out to him, "O young Man!" When the Prophet ﷺ gave this advice to ibn ʿAbbās he was just about to enter the age of puberty. This is significant because it shows the methodology of the Prophet ﷺ in teaching youth. What can be derived from this is that one of the most important things to teach youth is a proper understanding of faith and īmān, planting the seed of faith in their hearts from a very young age so that they always have a strong relationship with Allah ﷻ, literally instilling within their hearts and minds the concept of who Allah ﷻ truly is.

The Prophet ﷺ continues, "I shall teach you some words. Be mindful of Allah and Allah will protect you." Being mindful of Allah ﷻ means being conscious of the limits set by Allah ﷻ, being aware of His commandments and obeying them, and being mindful of His prohibitions and staying away from them. If a person is mindful, conscious, and aware of Allah ﷻ then He will provide protection both in this world and the next. He will provide protection in this world from various trials, difficulties, and problems. He will also protect them by safeguarding their religion. He will protect them in the next world from the punishment of Hell.

Allah ﷻ Himself says in the Quran, "Whoever, male or female, has acted

163 Ibn al-Jawzī, *Ṣayd al-Khāṭir*, 9

righteously, while being a believer, We shall certainly make him live a good life."[164] However, if a person is not careful of the limits set by Allah ﷻ, then they are not guaranteed any such protection. As a matter of fact a lot of the trials and tribulations in this life are a result of ignoring the rules of Allah ﷻ. He tells us in Sūrah al-Shūra, "Whatever hardship befalls you is because of what your own hands have committed, while He overlooks (many of your faults)."[165]

The Prophet ﷺ emphasizes his advice saying, "Be mindful of Allah and you will find Him in front of you." The Prophet ﷺ is repeating the importance of obeying Allah's commands and staying away from His prohibitions. If a person does so, then, not only will Allah ﷻ protect them, but He will also help them in their affairs, support them, and guide them. He will be there to help in times of difficulty, hardship, trials, tribulations, sorrow, and sadness.

The Prophet ﷺ then teaches ibn ʿAbbās رضي الله عنهما about the importance of relying upon Allah ﷻ alone and asking Him for all of one's needs. He ﷺ says, "If you ask, ask Allah." With this statement the Prophet ﷺ is advising believers to turn towards Allah ﷻ and to ask Him alone for all of their needs. People should be completely dependent upon Allah ﷻ, not His creation because it is Allah ﷻ and Allah ﷻ alone who is able to take care of all needs. There is a world of difference between asking others to fulfill their needs and asking Allah ﷻ. Others don't like to be asked for favors or bounties; whereas, Allah ﷻ loves to be asked. A famous scholar once said, "Do not ask one who runs from your requests, instead ask the One who has ordered you to ask Him."

Essentially the Prophet ﷺ is advising ibn ʿAbbās رضي الله عنهما to make asking Allah ﷻ a regular habit. In another narration the Prophet ﷺ said, "Ask Allah from His grace, for indeed Allah loves to be asked."[166] Similarly the Prophet ﷺ said, "Allah becomes angry with one who doesn't ask Him. So you should ask your Lord for all your needs, even the strap of your sandal if it breaks."[167]

The Prophet ﷺ then emphasizes the concepts of supplication and tawakkul (reliance upon Allah) by saying, "If you seek help, seek help from Allah." In this portion of the ḥadīth the Prophet ﷺ is advising ibn ʿAbbās

---

164 16:97 - مَنْ عَمِلَ صَالِحاً مِن ذَكَرٍ أَوْ أُنثَىٰ وَهُوَ مُؤْمِنٌ فَلَنُحْيِيَنَّهُ حَيَاةً طَيِّبَةً

165 42:30 - وَمَا أَصَابَكُم مِن مُصِيبَةٍ فَبِمَا كَسَبَتْ أَيْدِيكُمْ وَيَعْفُو عَن كَثِيرٍ

166 Tirmidhī, *k, al-daʿwāt ʿan Rasūlillah* ﷺ, *b. fī intiḍār al-faraj wa ghayr dhālika*, 3571

167 Tirmidhī, *k, al-daʿwāt ʿan Rasūlillah* ﷺ, b., 3604

to rely solely on Allah ﷻ for help, support, and assistance. These two phrases spoken by the Prophet ﷺ echo the same message of Sūrah al-Fātiḥah that is recited by believers multiple times a day. At least seventeen times a day Muslims recite in prayer "You alone do we worship and from You alone we seek help." The Prophet ﷺ is informing his Companions about the importance of duʿā, the importance of asking Allah ﷻ and the importance of seeking help from Him in all of our affairs.

The Prophet ﷺ then tells ibn ʿAbbās ؓ something extremely profound and powerful. He says, "Know that even if the Nation (or the whole community) were to gather together to benefit you with something, they would not benefit you with anything except that which Allah has already recorded for you. And if they were to gather together to harm you with anything, they would not harm you except with what Allah had already prescribed against you. The pens have been lifted and the pages have dried." In this last portion of the ḥadīth the Prophet ﷺ is explaining the concept of qadr. Having a proper understanding of the concept of qaḍā and qadr, the divine decree and will of Allah ﷻ, is the source of true happiness and contentment in the life of this world. Being pleased with the divine decree of Allah ﷻ is the key to living a stress free, worry free, and anxiety free life. It brings peace of mind and clarity.

The Prophet ﷺ is explaining to a young ibn ʿAbbās that every single thing that happens in this world, both the good and the bad, happens according to the Divine will, decree, plan, and wisdom of Allah ﷻ. Everything that happens in this world has some deep divine wisdom behind it. The Prophet ﷺ wants ibn ʿAbbās to realize from a young age that nothing and no one has the ability to cause benefit or harm without the decree, will, and permission of Allah ﷻ. Everything comes from Allah ﷻ. Recognizing this is an essential part of īmān. The Prophet ﷺ said, "Indeed everything has a reality. No servant will recognize the reality of faith until they know that what has befallen them would not have missed them, and what has missed them would not have befallen them."[168]

Imam al-Nawawī ؒ then brings another version of the same ḥadīth with slightly different wording and some additional advice. The Prophet ﷺ says, "Be mindful of Allah, and you will find Him in front of you. Recognize and acknowledge Allah in times of ease and prosperity, and He will remember

---

168   Aḥmad, *Musnad Aḥmad ibn Ḥanbal*, 27490

you in times of adversity. And know that what has passed you by [and you have failed to attain] was not going to befall you, and what has befallen you was not going to pass you by. And know that victory comes with patience, relief with affliction, and hardship with ease."

In this version of the ḥadīth the Prophet ﷺ advises ibn ʿAbbās ؓ to always remember Allah ﷻ, in times of ease and in times of difficulty. Oftentimes when people are living a life of comfort and ease they tend to forget about Allah ﷻ, but as soon as they are afflicted or tested with hardship and difficulty they turn to Allah ﷻ asking for help and assistance. A believer should be mindful of Allah ﷻ in all circumstances. In times of ease, comfort, and prosperity they should be mindful of Allah ﷻ through gratitude, thankfulness, and appreciation, and in times of difficulty and hardship they should be mindful of Allah ﷻ through patience, strength, and perseverance. A believer should be flowing between the states of shukr and ṣabr.

The Prophet ﷺ then consoles the young ibn ʿAbbās reminding him to always keep a positive outlook and to be optimistic about the future. "And know that victory comes with patience, relief with affliction, and hardship with ease." This same message is mentioned by Allah ﷻ in Sūrah al-Sharḥ, "Truly with difficulty comes ease, and truly with difficulty comes ease."[169]

LESSONS AND BENEFITS

1. TARBIYYAH AND EDUCATION

One of the most important aspects of raising children, educating them, and nurturing them is to instill the greatness of Allah ﷻ within their hearts from a very young age. To teach them about Allah ﷻ so that they can recognize and internalize His existence, oneness, might, power, glory, magnificence, and omnipotence from a very young age. Instilling the love of Allah ﷻ within a child's heart is one of the most important things a parent and teacher can do. Planting the seed of faith in their hearts from a very young age so that they always have a strong relationship with Allah ﷻ. Literally instilling within their hearts and minds the concept of who Allah ﷻ truly is.

2. BE MINDFUL OF ALLAH

In this ḥadīth the Prophet ﷺ mentions two very powerful benefits of

---

169 فَإِنَّ مَعَ الْعُسْرِ يُسْرًا إِنَّ مَعَ الْعُسْرِ يُسْرًا - 94 :6-7

being mindful of Allah:

1. Protection and
2. Assistance

If a person is mindful of Allah ﷻ in their daily lives, in their speech, behavior, attitude, and conduct, then Allah ﷻ will protect them from all types of harm and will grant them His divine support and assistance.

3. DUʿĀ

As discussed above, duʿā is one of the most powerful tools a person has. It is a direct line of communication between a person and their Lord. The Prophet ﷺ described it as the weapon of a believer and the essence of worship.

4. TAWAKKUL

The reality of tawakkul is recognizing with absolute firm conviction and certainty that nothing and no one in this world can cause harm or benefit, give or take, without the decree, will, and permission of Allah ﷻ. It includes relegating the consequences of one's affairs to Allah ﷻ, relying upon His help, and trusting and accepting His decisions.

5. QAḌĀ' AND QADR

This concept has been discussed before in detail. Being content and pleased with the decree of Allah ﷻ is one of the most difficult things to do, but once internalized it leads to a life of true happiness and contentment.

6. OPTIMISM

People of īmān are people of optimism; they always keep a positive outlook and recognize that everything that happens in this universe happens according to the Divine will, decree, and wisdom of Allah ﷻ.

HADITH 20

Al-Haya

عَنْ أَبِي مَسْعُودٍ عُقْبَةَ بْنِ عَمْرٍو الْأَنْصَارِيِّ الْبَدْرِيِّ رَضِيَ اللَّه عَنْهُ قَالَ: قَالَ رَسُولُ اللَّهِ صلى اللَّه عليه و سلم "إنَّ مِمَّا أَدْرَكَ النَّاسُ مِنْ كَلَامِ النُّبُوَّةِ الْأُولَى: إذَا لَمْ تَسْتَحِ فَاصْنَعْ مَا شِئْتَ".

رَوَاهُ الْبُخَارِيُّ.

From Abū Masʿūd ʿUqbah ibn ʿAmr al-Anṣārī al-Badrī ﵁ who said that the Messenger of Allah ﷺ said, "Verily, from what was learnt by the people from the speech of the earlier Prophets is: If you feel no shame, then do as you wish."

Narrated by al-Bukhārī.

THE NARRATOR

Abū Masʿūd Uqbah ibn ʿAmr al-Anṣārī al-Badrī ﷺ is well-known by his nickname of al-Badrī, but he didn't participate in the Battle of Badr. He was given that nickname because he lived in Badr. He participated in the second pledge of al-ʿAqabah as well as Uḥud and all the other expeditions after it. He settled in Kufah and was placed in charge of Kufah when ʿAlī ﷺ went for the battle of Ṣiffīn. He passed away after the year 40, may Allah ﷻ be pleased with him.

IMPORTANCE

In this ḥadīth, the Prophet ﷺ is highlighting the importance and significnace of the concept of ḥayā in Islam. Along with īmān and taqwā, ḥayā is one of the most important and impactful qualities and characteristics that a person can possess. A person's ḥayā is directly related to the level of their faith, and is one of the qualities that drives a person's decisions, statements, and actions. Imām al-Nawawī writes regarding this ḥadīth, that all of Islam revolves around this one statement.

EXPLANATION

This ḥadīth starts with the Prophet ﷺ describing a particular statement regarding ḥayā as part of the legacy of previous Prophets and Messengers. The quality and characteristic of ḥayā was taught, encouraged, and exemplified by all of the previous Prophets and Messengers sent by Allah ﷻ. It is something that they nurtured and developed within themselves as well as in their followers and was then passed on from generation to generation.

The Prophet ﷺ then mentions the statement, "If you feel no shame, then do as you wish." This statement is expressed in the form of a command and the scholars have understood this command in three different ways. One is that the statement means if a person has no modesty or shame, then they will do whatever they want and desire, but they will be responsible for their choices. If they choose to do something wrong, commit an act of disobedience, or sin they will be liable and deserving of punishment. Meaning that this statement is actually a threat or warning against making poor choices.

The second way this statement has been understood is that modesty should be used as a standard to weigh one's actions. Meaning, if a person is thinking about doing something and there is no reason to be ashamed about it in front of Allah ﷻ or anyone else, then they may do it.

The third way that this statement is understood is that it is a statement of fact. Meaning, if a person has no shame or modesty, then there is nothing preventing them from disobeying Allah ﷻ and doing whatever they want. Ḥayā serves as a protective barrier between a person and making bad decisions.

LESSONS AND BENEFITS

1. ḤAYĀ IS A SIGN OF ĪMĀN

Ḥayā is one of the most important factors that keeps a person from committing a sinful act. If a person has no ḥayā, then they will do almost anything without any feeling of guilt, shame, or modesty. It is almost as if they don't care what Allah ﷻ or others think about them. In order to understand this ḥadīth properly and realize its importance, it is necessary to understand exactly what ḥayā is.

The single greatest blessing that Allah ﷻ has given any human being is the blessing of īmān. A major part of īmān is this characteristic or trait known as ḥayā. The Prophet ﷺ said, "Īmān has seventy some-odd branches. The most virtuous is the statement there is no God except Allah, and the lowest of them is removing harm from the path. And ḥayā is a branch of īmān."[170] In another ḥadīth the Prophet ﷺ said, "Ḥayā and īmān are two companions that go together. If one of them is lifted, the other is also lifted."[171] This ḥadīth demonstrates how essential this characteristic of ḥayā is to a person's faith. For a person to have true complete faith, they must have ḥayā. In another narration the Prophet ﷺ said, "Ḥayā is a part of īmān."[172] What is understood from all of these narrations is that the Prophet ﷺ placed a lot of stress and gave a lot of importance to the characteristic of ḥayā.

Ḥayā is derived from the word al-ḥayāh, which means life. It is said that a person who has no ḥayā is a person who has no life. It is defined as shame

170 Muslim, *k. al-Īmān, b. bayān ʿadad shuʿab al-īmān*, 35

171 Bayhaqī, *Shuʿab al-Īmān*, 7331

172 Abū Dāwūd, *k. al-adab, b. fī al-ḥayā*, 4795

or a sense of shame, shyness or bashfulness, a shrinking of the soul from foul behavior through fear of blame. Ḥayā is the feeling in a person's heart that keeps them from committing sins. It is a characteristic that causes one to avoid evil deeds and to fulfill other's rights. It is the feeling in a person's heart that causes them to feel shame when thinking about doing something bad. It can be described as a person's moral conscience. It is that feeling inside of a person that keeps them from acting on their desires or lusts.

This feeling of modesty, shame, or moral conscience is something that every single human being naturally possesses. Like all natural characteristics it is something that can be nurtured and allowed to grow, or it can be stunted to the point that a person no longer has a feeling of shame. This natural feeling of shame or modesty is what stops an individual from doing bad deeds and having bad manners. At the same time it causes them to have the best of manners.

There is also a form of ḥayā that can be acquired. This is the type of ḥayā that is related to a person's faith. It is acquired by recognizing Allah ﷻ, His existence, greatness, nearness, awareness of all actions, and that He knows what the eyes steal and what the hearts conceal. This type of ḥayā comes from realizing that Allah ﷻ is always present; that He sees everything a person does, hears everything a person says, and knows everything that is going on in a person's heart and mind. It arises from the realization that every single thing a person does or says is being recorded and one day they will be held accountable for them.

Once a person realizes this they will be ashamed to do anything that is displeasing to Allah ﷻ. This consciousness or awareness of Allah ﷻ is one of the main factors that will help increase and strengthen ḥayā.

Another way to acquire this type of ḥayā is to think about all of the blessings that Allah ﷻ has bestowed upon a human being. If a person thinks about all of the blessings they have received and continue to receive from Allah ﷻ, then they will be ashamed to use these blessings in ways that are displeasing to Him. This is one of the definitions of ḥayā given by the scholars. For example, if a person thinks about how great the blessing of eyesight is, they will be ashamed to use it to look at things that are displeasing to Allah ﷻ.

The characteristic of ḥayā is one of the hallmarks of Islam. As the Prophet ﷺ said, "Every religion has a particular characteristic, and the characteristic of Islam is ḥayā."[173] This is because ḥayā is part of the completeness of good, moral character, and part of the mission of the Prophet ﷺ was to perfect morals and behavior.

173 Ibn Mājah, *k. al-zuhd*, 4321

HADITH 21

Steadfastness

عَنْ أَبِي عَمْرٍو وَقِيلَ: أَبِي عَمْرَةَ سُفْيَانَ بْنِ عَبْدِ اللَّهِ رَضِيَ اللَّه عَنْهُ
قَالَ: "قُلْت: يَا رَسُولَ اللَّهِ! قُلْ لِي فِي الْإِسْلَامِ قَوْلًا لَا أَسْأَلُ عَنْهُ أَحَدًا
غَيْرَك؛ قَالَ: قُلْ: آمَنْت بِاللَّهِ ثُمَّ اسْتَقِمْ".

رَوَاهُ مُسْلِمٌ.

From Abū 'Amr — and it said Abū 'Amrah — Sufyān ibn 'Abdullah al-Thaqafī 🙵 who said that I said, "O Messenger of Allah, tell me something about Islam which I can ask of no one but you." He 🙵 said, "Say I believe in Allah — and then be Steadfast."

Narrated by Muslim.

THE NARRATOR

Abū ʿAmr Sufyān ibn ʿAbdullah al-Thaqafī ﵁ is a Companion of the Prophet ﷺ from the people of Ṭā'if. He accepted Islam with the delegation of Thaqīf and served as a zakāh collector during the time of ʿUmar ﵁ for the people of Ṭā'if. This is the only ḥadīth that Imām Muslim narrrated from him in his entire collection.

IMPORTANCE

This ḥadīth is also from the concise, yet comprehensive sayings of the Prophet ﷺ that have captured the essence of Islam. Islam is built upon the twin pillars of īmān and obedience, and obedience is istiqāmah. The Prophet ﷺ summarized the entire essence of Islam in two words: faith and steadfastness.

EXPLANATION

In this narration, we are told that Sufyān ﵁ came to the Prophet ﷺ and said, "O Messenger of Allah, tell me something about Islam which I can ask of no one but you." He's asking the Prophet ﷺ to tell him something concise about Islam that is also comprehensive and easy to act upon. He is asking for a general principle that would help him in his life to be a good, practicing, upright, and God-conscious Muslim.

The Prophet ﷺ responded with something that was so comprehensive that it captured his entire mission of 23 years. The religion of Islam, both in terms of belief and practice, is based on the foundations of tawḥīd and obedience. The Prophet ﷺ answered, "Say, 'I believe in Allah,' and then be steadfast." He told him to renew his faith, to renew his commitment to Allah ﷻ, and then to remain steadfast upon it. This is one of the most concise yet comprehensive statements of the Prophet ﷺ. In a few simple words the Prophet ﷺ captured the entire essence of Islam; imān and istiqāmah.

LESSONS AND BENEFITS

1. THE IMPORTANCE OF ISTIQĀMAH

As the Prophet ﷺ grew older and aged, some of his blessed hair started to turn white. Abū Bakr ؓ, his closest friend and father-in-law, started to notice this. One day Abū Bakr ؓ said to the Prophet ﷺ, "O Messenger of Allah! Your hair has turned gray."[174] The Prophet ﷺ responded, "Sūrah Hūd and its sisters have caused my hair to turn gray." The commentators mention that what caused some of the Prophet's ﷺ hair to turn gray was the command to have istiqāmah; the command to remain steadfast, upright, and consistent upon the path of Islam. Allah ﷻ says in Sūrah Hūd, "So, stand firm (remain steadfast) as you have been commanded, as well as those who have repented, and do not cross the limits. Indeed He sees whatever you do."[175] Imagine; this command was so heavy on the Prophet ﷺ, the last and final Messenger, the most perfect man to walk on the face of this Earth, that it caused some of his hair to turn gray.

Ibn ʿAbbās ؓ mentioned that this particular verse was the hardest and most difficult verse of the Quran on the Prophet ﷺ. That is because having istiqāmah, being steadfast upon faith, being upright and consistent in religion is something very difficult. Consistently staying on the straight path is one of the most difficult things to do, but it can be attained through hard work, dedication and determination. That is why Imām al-Ghazālī ؒ wrote, "Istiqāmah on the straight path in this world is as difficult as crossing the bridge over Hell. Both paths are more delicate than hair and sharper than the sword."[176]

Remaining steadfast, being upright and consistent in one's practice of faith religion is a very great characteristic. In several places throughout the Quran, Allah ﷻ reminds the believers to remain steadfast upon the straight path, to be upright and consistent.

Istiqāmah is derived from the Arabic verb istaqāma/yastaqīmu, which means to become balanced, straight, even, or upright. It is one of those words that does not have an exact equivalent in English because it is such an all-encompassing term. It has been defined as to follow the straight path,

---

174 Tirmidhī, k. *tafsīr al-Quran ʿan rasūl Allah*, 3297

175 11:112 - فَاسْتَقِمْ كَمَا أُمِرْتَ وَمَن تَابَ مَعَكَ وَلاَ تَطْغَوْاْ إِنَّهُ بِمَا تَعْمَلُونَ بَصِيرٌ

176 al-Qārī, *Mirqāt al-Mafātīḥ*, v.1 p.85

which is the straight religion without deviating right or left. It includes undertaking all acts of obedience, both external and internal, and leaving all forbidden things. Practically speaking, it is obeying the commands of Allah ﷻ to the best of one's ability and staying away from His prohibitions to the best of one's ability.

Istiqāmah includes internalizing and actualizing the meaning of lā ilāha illa Allah and remaining steadfast upon it. It is described as being sincere in one's statements and actions - both in public and in private- while remaining sincere in faith, prayer, and worship. In simpler words, istiqāmah means being a Muslim in the truest sense of the word; trying to be the best Muslim a person can be. Throughout their daily lives they put forth a sincere effort in being conscious, upright, practicing Muslims, whether they're alone, at home with their families, at work, or anywhere else.

This does not mean that they have to be perfect; human beings are not angels and perfection is not required from them. What is required is a sincere and honest effort. As the Prophet ﷺ said, "O people, you won't be able to do everything you've been commanded to do. But try to be upright and have glad tidings."[177]

The path to developing this characteristic is through the heart. Ibn Rajab رحمه الله mentions, "The foundation of steadfastness is steadfastness of the heart upon the oneness of Allah. When the heart becomes steadfast upon the recognition of Allah, fearing Him, honoring Him, respecting Him, loving Him, wanting Him, having hope in Him, asking Him, relying upon Him and turning away from everyone else besides Him, then the limbs will be steadfast upon His obedience. The heart is the king (ruler) of the limbs, and they are his army. If the ruler is steadfast and upright, then his army will also be steadfast and upright."[178] This is a very deep and profound statement and it is based upon the famous ḥadīth of the Prophet ﷺ mentioned above, "Indeed, there's a piece of flesh in the body. If it becomes good then the entire body becomes good. If it becomes corrupt then the entire body becomes corrupt. Indeed it is the heart."[179] The key to developing this characteristic is through nurturing the heart, working on faith, and the recognition of Allah ﷻ.

Imam al-Muḥāsibī رحمه الله mentions that the source of consistency lies in

---

177 Abū Dāwūd, *k. al-ṣalāh, b. al-rajul yakhṭub ʿalā qaws*, 1096

178 Ibn Rajab, *Jāmiʿ al-ʿUlūm wa al-Ḥikam*, p. 240

179 Ḥadīth #6 in this collection.

three things: following the Quran, following the Sunnah, and adhering to the community of faith.[180] Following the Quran means to actually engage with it, to make it a part of one's daily life. To read it attentively and to benefit from its teachings. Reading the Quran strengthens faith, reminds one of Allah ﷻ and life after death. It reminds one of their real purpose in life and the temporary nature of this world. It will remind them that there's nothing in this world that's worth taking them off the straight path. The same thing goes for the Sunnah of the Prophet ﷺ. The last thing is keeping good company. A person should be aware of their environment and how it affects them. In particular, one should focus on their:

1. House and family
2. School
3. Mosque
4. Society
5. Media and
6. Work

The reward for istiqāmah is Paradise. Allah ﷻ says, "Indeed, those who have said, 'Our Lord is Allah' and then remained on a right course - the angels will descend upon them, [saying], 'Do not fear and do not grieve but receive good tidings of Paradise, which you were promised. We were your allies in the worldly life and in the Hereafter. And you will have therein whatever your souls desire and you will have therein whatever you request as hospitality from the Forgiving, the Merciful.'"[181]

180 al-Muḥāsibī, *Risālah al-Mustarshidīn*, p. 189

181 41 :30-32 إِنَّ الَّذِينَ قَالُوا رَبُّنَا اللَّهُ ثُمَّ اسْتَقَامُوا تَتَنَزَّلُ عَلَيْهِمُ الْمَلَائِكَةُ أَلَّا تَخَافُوا وَلَا تَحْزَنُوا وَأَبْشِرُوا بِالْجَنَّةِ الَّتِي كُنتُمْ تُوعَدُونَ نَحْنُ أَوْلِيَاؤُكُمْ فِي الْحَيَاةِ الدُّنْيَا وَفِي الْآخِرَةِ وَلَكُمْ فِيهَا مَا تَشْتَهِي أَنفُسُكُمْ وَلَكُمْ فِيهَا مَا تَدَّعُونَ نُزُلًا مِّنْ غَفُورٍ رَّحِيمٍ

HADITH 22

The Path to Paradise

عَنْ أَبِي عَبْدِ اللَّهِ جَابِرِ بْنِ عَبْدِ اللَّهِ الْأَنْصَارِيّ رَضِيَ اللَّهُ عَنْهُمَا: "أَنَّ رَجُلًا سَأَلَ رَسُولَ اللَّهِ صلى الله عليه و سلم فَقَالَ: أَرَأَيْت إذَا صَلَّيْتُ الْمَكْتُوبَاتِ، وَصُمْتُ رَمَضَانَ، وَأَحْلَلْتُ الْحَلَالَ، وَحَرَّمْتُ الْحَرَامَ، وَلَمْ أَزِدْ عَلَى ذَلِكَ شَيْئًا؛ أَأَدْخُلُ الْجَنَّةَ؟ قَالَ: نَعَمْ". رَوَاهُ مُسْلِمٌ.

From Abū ʿAbdullah Jābir ibn ʿAbdullah al-Anṣārī ❧ that a man questioned the Messenger of Allah ❧ and said, "Do you think that if I perform the obligatory prayers, fast in Ramaḍān, treat as lawful that which is lawful, and treat as forbidden that which is forbidden, and do not increase upon that [in voluntary good deeds], then I shall enter Paradise?" He ❧ replied, "Yes."

Narrated by Muslim.

THE NARRATOR

The narrator of this ḥadīth is Abū ʿAbdullah Jābir ibn ʿAbdullah al-Anṣārī al-Khazrajī 🙂. He accepted Islam before hijrah, and was present as a child with his father during the Pledge of ʿAqabah. He is known as a very brave and courageous warrior who participated in 19 expeditions with the Prophet 🙂. He himself mentioned that his father didn't allow him to participate in the Battle of Badr and the Battle of Uḥud, but after his father was martyred he joined every expedition. He is among the Companions who narrated a large number of ḥadīth, 1,540 to be exact. He passed away in the city of Madinah in the year 74, may Allah 🙂 have mercy upon him.

IMPORTANCE

In this ḥadīth, a Companion asks the Prophet 🙂 if certain deeds will be enough to take him to Paradise. This in and of itself is a very significant point. The companions were human beings who wanted to go to Paradise. They wanted to know the best and easiest way to earn eternal salvation. There are many companions who asked the same exact question or at least a very similar question; what can we do to get to Paradise? Ibn Daqīq al-ʿEid mentions that the Questioner is Nuʿmān ibn Qawqal 🙂, which is supported by another narration. al-Nuʿmān ibn Qawqal 🙂 participated in the battle of Badr and was martyred in the battle of Uḥud.

EXPLANATION

In this narration, Nuʿmān 🙂 comes to the Prophet 🙂 and asks, "Do you think that if I perform the obligatory prayers, fast in Ramaḍān, treat as lawful that which is lawful, and treat as forbidden that which is forbidden, and do not increase upon that [in voluntary good deeds], then I shall enter Paradise?" Nuʿmān asks specifically about prayer and fasting, but he does not ask about zakāh or ḥajj. The scholars of ḥadīth have given several reasons why he didn't ask about the other two pillars. One is that they may not have been obligatory at the time that he asked the question. Another is that zakāh and ḥajj may not have been applicable to him specifically, or it could be a combination of both. Nuʿmān is saying that he will perform the pillars of Islam.

He also said that he would treat the lawful as permissible and the forbidden as prohibited. Imām al-Nawawī ﷺ writes that this means he believed the lawful to be permissible and acted upon it, and he believed the unlawful to be prohibited and stayed away from it. This attitude is essential to one's faith; it is a basic principle of īmān. A person has to believe in the permissibility of what Allah ﷻ has allowed. They must also believe in the prohibition of whatever Allah ﷻ has forbidden.

He then says, "I will not add anything to that." Meaning that this particular companion said that he would not perform anything more than the obligatory acts. He would not perform any voluntary prayers or keep any voluntary fasts. The reason why he said this was because he was new to Islam and the love for performing these extra deeds had not entered into his heart yet. That is why the Prophet ﷺ responded to him in such a way that would ensure that he performs the obligatory acts. The Prophet ﷺ also knew that once this Companion entered into Islam completely, he would automatically start performing these extra deeds. This is exactly what happened, as Nuʿmān participated in the Battle of Badr and was later martyred during the Battle of Uḥud.

Nuʿmān ﷺ asks the Prophet ﷺ that if he performs what is obligatory and believes and acts upon what is lawful and what is unlawful, will that be enough to enter him into Paradise. The Prophet ﷺ answered, "Yes." This ḥadīth shows that if a person performs all of the obligatory deeds and stays away from sin, then they will enter Paradise. There are numerous narrations that prove this point. The Prophet ﷺ said, "There is no slave of Allah who prays the five daily prayers, fasts the month of Ramaḍān, gives zakāh, and stays away from the seven major sins (zinā, drinking, magic, false accusation of zinā, murder, interest, running away from battle) except that the gates of Paradise are opened for him and he can enter through whichever one he chooses."[181]

All of the aḥādīth of this nature in which the Prophet ﷺ says, "whoever does such and such will enter paradise" or something similar are to be understood at face value. A person who performs these acts with sincerity will enter Paradise, as long as they don't do anything that would prevent them from entering Paradise.

Islam is meant to be easy. It is very easy to be a good, upright, practic-

181 Mundhirī, *al-Targhīb wa al-Tarhīb*, 2

ing, God-conscious, and moral Muslim. The path to Paradise is clear and is extremely easy. However, it does require effort, work, steadfastness, consistency, and sincerity.

LESSONS AND BENEFITS

1. PARADISE IS THE GOAL

One of the ultimate goals and objectives of every believer is to earn eternal salvation in the life of the hereafter; to be among the people of Paradise. They recognize the temporary nature of this world and understand that the life of the hereafter is a life of eternity.

2. PILLARS OF ISLAM

Please refer to ḥadīth #3 above for a discussion on the importance of the five pillars.

3. ḤALĀL AND ḤARĀM

Allah ﷻ has made certain things permissible and has made certain things impermissible. This knowledge is conveyed directly through Revelation in the form of the Quran and the Sunnah of the Prophet ﷺ. Once a person submits to Allah ﷻ, they have made a commitment to themselves and their Lord to live by these rules, regulations, limitations, and boundaries. An essential part of one's īmān is to believe and acknowledge what is permissible and what is impermissible and then try their best to live by that.

4. EASE

As this ḥadīth shows, the path to Paradise is easy, clear, and straightforward. All it requires is effort, commitment, patience, discipline, and consistency.

5. VOLUNTARY DEEDS

Performing voluntary deeds is an expression of one's love, obedience, submission, and devotion to Allah ﷻ. They are a means of making up for any deficiencies in fulfilling one's obligations and drawing near to Allah ﷻ.

HADITH 23

Purification is Half of Iman

عَنْ أَبِي مَالِكٍ الْحَارِثِ بْنِ عَاصِمٍ الْأَشْعَرِيِّ رَضِيَ اللَّه عَنْهُ قَالَ: قَالَ رَسُولُ اللَّهِ صلى الله عليه و سلم "الطَّهُورُ شَطْرُ الْإِيمَانِ، وَالْحَمْدُ لِلَّهِ تَمْلَأُ الْمِيزَانَ، وَسُبْحَانَ اللَّهِ وَالْحَمْدُ لِلَّهِ تَمْلَآنِ -أَوْ: تَمْلَأُ- مَا بَيْنَ السَّمَاءِ وَالْأَرْضِ، وَالصَّلَاةُ نُورٌ، وَالصَّدَقَةُ بُرْهَانٌ، وَالصَّبْرُ ضِيَاءٌ، وَالْقُرْآنُ حُجَّةٌ لَك أَوْ عَلَيْك، كُلُّ النَّاسِ يَغْدُو، فَبَائِعٌ نَفْسَهُ فَمُعْتِقُهَا أَوْ مُوبِقُهَا".

رَوَاهُ مُسْلِمٌ.

From Abū Mālik al-Ḥārith ibn ʿĀsim al-Ashʿarī ﵁ who said that the Messenger of Allah ﷺ said, "Purity is half of īmān (faith). Alḥamdulillah (praise be to Allah) fills the scales, and SubḥānAllah (how far is Allah from every imperfection) and Alḥamdulillah fill that which is between heaven and earth. And ṣalāh (prayer) is a light, charity is an evidence, patience is illumination, and the Quran is a proof either for you or against you. Every person starts his day as a vendor of his soul, either freeing it or causing its ruin."

Narrated by Muslim.

THE NARRATOR

His full name is Abū Mālik al-Ḥārith ibn ʿĀṣim al-Ashʿarī ﷺ. al-Ashʿarī is an attribution to a well-known tribe from Yemen and he came along with the people of his tribe to meet the Prophet ﷺ. He passed away during the khilāfah of ʿUmar ﷺ in the plague. He has narrated 27 aḥādīth from the Prophet ﷺ, may Allah ﷻ be pleased with him.

IMPORTANCE

This is a very beautiful and profound ḥadīth that mentions the virtues, rewards, and blessings of specific deeds such as purification, dhikr (remembering Allah), prayer, charity, patience, and living by the Quran. It also mentions the true way of purchasing one's freedom and attaining liberty.

EXPLANATION

The Prophet ﷺ starts by highlighting the importance of purification and cleanliness and its relationship to faith. He ﷺ says, "Purification is half of faith." Īmān, true faith, is an amazing thing. True faith expresses itself in several different ways. Īmān is not some abstract concept or some intangible that can't be touched. It is not simply an emotion. Rather īmān is something that is living and organic; it can be felt and seen. A person's entire life is an expression of this faith; the way they worship their Creator, the way they deal with their parents and siblings, friends and relatives, co-workers, and classmates. It is how they treat their husbands and wives, siblings, children, and other family members. Faith is how they interact with others in society and how they react when someone cuts them off on the freeway. It is how they park in the masjid on Fridays, how they earn money and how they spend money. It is how they behave at work and on campus. As the Prophet ﷺ told us, "Faith is made up of some seventy odd branches."[182] One of those branches is cleanliness and purification. And that is why the Prophet ﷺ emphasized the importance of both physical and ritual purity along with personal hygiene.

After highlighting the importance of cleanliness and purification, the

182 Muslim, *k. al-īmān, b. Bayān ʿadad shuʿab al-īmān*, 35

Prophet ﷺ is now mentioning the rewards and virtues for simply saying alḥamdulillah. "Alḥamdulillah (praise be to Allah) fills the scales." It is important to note that this reward is granted to a person who says it consciously, while thinking, pondering, and reflecting over its meaning.

Alḥamdulillah is translated as "all praise is for Allah". However, its meaning is much more comprehensive than simply praise. It means both praise and thankfulness. It is praise coupled with gratitude done out of genuine love, reverence, and appreciation. It includes praising Allah ﷻ and giving thanks to Him for all of the favors and blessings He has given to human beings in this world and the reward He will give them in the next. Ibn ʿAbbās ؓ said, "Alḥamdulillah is the statement of every thankful servant." This is the phrase that Allah ﷻ has taught human beings to use in order to praise Him. Every single blessing a person enjoys in this world is directly from Allah ﷻ. "And every blessing you have is from Allah."[183] It is impossible to quantify or even imagine all of the blessings that Allah ﷻ has given to human beings. As Allah ﷻ says, "If you try to count the blessings of Allah, you will not be able to do so."[184] One of the ways for a person to express their gratitude to Allah ﷻ is by simply saying alḥamdulillah. This simple statement will fill their scale of good deeds on the Day of Judgement.

The Prophet ﷺ continues, "SubḥānAllah and alḥamdulillah fill what is between the heavens and the Earth." SubḥānAllah is generally translated as 'Glory be to Allah'; however, this translation doesn't capture the essence of the phrase. It means to declare the absolute and unquestionable perfection of Allah ﷻ. That Allah ﷻ is free from any blemish, shortcoming, imperfection, or defect.

With these two statements, the Prophet ﷺ is indicating towards the importance, virtues, and merits of dhikr. Dhikr is considered to be the nourishment of hearts, the connection between a person and their Lord. It is something that brings them closer to Allah ﷻ. Dhikr is one of the most powerful and effective ways of expressing gratitude, thanks, and appreciation for all of the blessings that Allah ﷻ bestows upon a person. Throughout the Quran Allah ﷻ commands believers to engage in dhikr, praises the people of dhikr, and describes their rewards. Allah ﷻ says in the Quran, "O you who believe,

---

183   16:53 - وَمَا بِكُم مِّن نِّعْمَةٍ فَمِنَ اللَّهِ

184   16:18 - وَإِن تَعُدُّوا نِعْمَةَ اللَّهِ لاَ تُحْصُوهَا

remember Allah often, and proclaim His perfection morning and evening."[185] Similarly Allah ﷻ says, "The ones who believe and their hearts are peaceful with the remembrance of Allah. Listen, the hearts find peace only in the remembrance of Allah."[186] All of the acts of worship we have revolve around the concept of remembering Allah ﷻ. For example, Allah ﷻ says regarding prayer, "And establish prayer for my Remembrance."[187] The Prophet ﷺ referred to dhikr as the best of our deeds.

The Prophet ﷺ then mentions one of the benefits of prayer saying, "Prayer is light." As discussed before, ṣalāh is the most important and significant act of worship that a person is required to do. It is the absolute most important thing after īmān in terms of a person's relationship with Allah ﷻ. The Prophet ﷺ is saying that prayer is a light that guides to the path of success. It illuminates hearts and minds lighting the path to guidance and righteousness. It has a profound spiritual effect on an individual and sometimes that spiritual effect can be seen on a person's face.

Next, the Prophet ﷺ mentions one of the virtues of charity saying, "Charity is evidence." Ṣadaqah, or charity, is giving one's wealth for the sake of Allah ﷻ. It is evidence or proof of one's faith, generosity, kindness and mercy. It shows that a person's heart isn't attached to money and materialism.

The Prophet ﷺ then highlights one of the benefits of patience describing it as "brightness." Patience is a brightness that provides clarity and light during times of difficulties and hardships. It allows people to process the trials they are experiencing allowing them to remain firm, steadfast, and forbearing.

The Prophet ﷺ then highlights one aspect of the Quran saying, "The Quran is a proof either for you or against you." If a person believes in the Quran, recites it on a regular and consistent basis, thinks, reflects, and ponders over its meanings, and most importantly tries to live a life based on the Quran, then it will be a proof for them on the Day of Judgment. If a person doesn't recite the Quran, or they don't reflect upon its meanings, and they don't live by it, then it will be a proof against them on the Day of Judgment.

The Prophet ﷺ ends the ḥadīth by describing how a person can "pur-

---

185 33:41-42 - يَا أَيُّهَا الَّذِينَ آمَنُوا اذْكُرُوا اللَّـهَ ذِكْرًا كَثِيراً وَسَبِّحُوهُ بُكْرَةً وَأَصِيلاً

186 13:28 - الَّذِينَ آمَنُوا وَتَطْمَئِنُّ قُلُوبُهُم بِذِكْرِ اللَّـهِ ۗ أَلَا بِذِكْرِ اللَّـهِ تَطْمَئِنُّ الْقُلُوبُ

187 20:14 - وَأَقِمِ الصَّلَاةَ لِذِكْرِي

chase" their success. The Prophet ﷺ says, "Every person starts his day as a vendor of his soul, either freeing it or causing its ruin." Every morning a person wakes up they have a choice of two paths in front of them. One path leads to success and paradise and the other path leads to loss and punishment. They can free their soul by following the commandments of Allah ﷻ and the Sunnah of the Prophet ﷺ; by engaging in the virtuous deeds mentioned in this ḥadīth. They can also choose to destroy their soul by living a life of heedlessness or following one's whims and desires. Freedom and liberation of the soul comes through submission to Allah ﷻ.

LESSONS AND BENEFITS

1. IMPORTANCE OF PURITY AND CLEANLINESS

Allah ﷻ says, "Truly Allah loves those who repent often and those who purify themselves."[188] Islam places a lot of importance on physical and spiritual purity. Physical purity is ensuring one's body, clothes, and environment are clean. It also includes personal hygiene. Purification of one's body, clothes, and place of prayer is a precondition for the validity of prayer. Spiritual purity is cleansing one's soul through seeking forgiveness and repentance and cleansing one's heart. The spiritual heart can become polluted and diseased through spiritual illnesses such as jealousy, envy, hatred, arrogance, and pride.

2. DHIKR

Just like the physical body requires nutrition to remain healthy and alive so too does the soul. The nourishment of the soul is the remembrance of Allah ﷻ. It is one of the greatest ways of expressing gratitude to Allah ﷻ for all of His immense blessings and favors. There are several aḥādīth that highlight the virtues, rewards, blessings, and benefits of dhikr. Abū Saʿīd and Abū Hurayrah ﷺ both narrate that the Prophet ﷺ said, "Allah has chosen four statements: subḥānallah, alḥamdulillah, lā ilāha illa Allah, and Allahu Akbar. Whoever says subḥānallah, twenty rewards will be recorded for them and twenty sins will be removed from them. Whoever says Allahu Akbar will receive something similar. Whoever says lā ilāha illa Allah will receive some-

188 2:222 - إِنَّ اللَّـهَ يُحِبُّ التَّوَّابِينَ وَيُحِبُّ الْمُتَطَهِّرِينَ

thing similar. Whoever says alḥamdulillah will receive something similar. Whoever says alḥamdu lillāhi rab al-ʿālamīn with sincerity will receive thirty rewards and thirty sins will be removed from them."[189] Whoever says these phrases of remembrance, recognizing and internalizing their meanings with mindfulness will receive unimaginable rewards. Abū Hurayrah ﵁ narrates that the Prophet ﷺ said, "Whenever a servant says lā ilāha illa Allah with sincerity, the gates of Paradise are opened for them until they reach the Throne."[190]

As mentioned above, dhikr creates a feeling of peace, tranquility, and contentment within a heart. If a person truly reflects upon what they're saying, focusing on its deep meanings, with mindfulness, and connecting their hearts with Allah ﷻ, it will remove feelings of stress, anxiety, and worry.

3. PRAYER IS LIGHT

Establishing prayer is a very powerful means of producing a spiritual light that illuminates the path towards Allah ﷻ. Allah ﷻ says regarding prayer, "[Prophet], recite what has been revealed to you of the Scripture; keep up the prayer: prayer restrains outrageous and unacceptable behaviour. Remembering God is greater: God knows everything you are doing."[191]

It will be a source of light and radiance for people on the Day of Judgment illuminating their path to Paradise. Regarding this light, Allah ﷻ says, "Their light will go before them and to their right."[192] This light can even be seen on their faces in the life of this world. Allah ﷻ says, "... from the traces of their sujūd."[193] ʿUbādah ibn Ṣāmit ﵁ narrates that the Prophet ﷺ said, "If a servant safeguards their prayer, perfecting its wuḍū', bowing, prostration, and recitation, the prayer will say to him: 'May Allah protect you as you protected me. It will elevate to the sky with a light reaching Allah ﷻ and intercede on his behalf.'"[194]

Praying in congregation increases this light and illumination. The Prophet ﷺ said, "Whoever prays the five obligatory prayers in congregation

---

189 Aḥmed, *Musnad*, 15:227

190 Tirmidhī, *k. al-Daʿwāt ʿan Rasūlillāh, b. Duʿā Umm Salamah*, 3590

191 29:45 - اتْلُ مَا أُوحِيَ إِلَيْكَ مِنَ الْكِتَابِ وَأَقِمِ الصَّلَاةَ ۖ إِنَّ الصَّلَاةَ تَنْهَىٰ عَنِ الْفَحْشَاءِ وَالْمُنكَرِ ۗ وَلَذِكْرُ اللَّهِ أَكْبَرُ ۗ وَاللَّهُ يَعْلَمُ مَا تَصْنَعُونَ

192 66:8 - نُورُهُمْ يَسْعَىٰ بَيْنَ أَيْدِيهِمْ وَبِأَيْمَانِهِمْ

193 48:29 - سِيمَاهُمْ فِي وُجُوهِهِم مِّنْ أَثَرِ السُّجُودِ

194 Ṭabarānī, *al-Muʿjam al-Awsaṭ*, 3095

will cross the bridge like a bolt of lightning among those who cross first. They will come on the Day of Judgment like the full moon."[195] The Prophet ﷺ also said, "Give glad tidings to those who walk to the mosques in darkness with complete illumination on the Day of Judgment."[196]

4. VOLUNTARY DEEDS

Performing voluntary deeds is an expression of one's love, obedience, submission, and devotion to Allah ﷻ. They are a means of making up for any deficiencies in fulfilling one's obligations and drawing near to Allah ﷻ.

5. CHARITY IS EVIDENCE

As mentioned above, charity is generally understood as giving one's wealth for the sake of Allah ﷻ. Within the framework of Islam, the concept of charity is not limited to financial assistance. It includes every good act that is done with sincerity and excellence, especially those good acts that are done to help others. The Prophet ﷺ said, "Every good deed is charity." All good deeds are evidence of a person's īmān.

6. THE IMPORTANCE OF ṢABR

Ṣabr is usually translated as patience. However, this translation is underinclusive. Part of ṣabr is definitely patience; however, it also includes forbearance, strength, discipline, self-restraint, and being content with the decree of Allah ﷻ. That is why the scholars mention that there are three types of ṣabr:

1. al-ṣabr ʿalā al-ṭāʿāt (ṣabr upon acts of obedience),
2. al-ṣabr ʿan al-maʿāṣī (ṣabr against acts of disobedience), and
3. al-ṣabr ʿalā aqdārillah (ṣabr with the decree of Allah)

It requires ṣabr in the form of discipline to obey the commandments of Allah ﷻ such as praying and fasting. It requires ṣabr in the form of self-restraint and self-control to stay away from His prohibitions. It also requires ṣabr in the form of patience, perseverance, and strength when dealing with difficulties and hardships.

---

195 Ibn Rajab, *Jāmiʿ al-ʿUlūm wa al-Ḥikam*, 2:23

196 Abū Dāwūd, k. *Al-ṣalāh, b. mā jā'a fī al-mashy ilā al-ṣalāh fī al-dhulam*, 561

7. IMPORTANCE OF THE QURAN

The importance of the Quran in the life of a Muslim cannot be overemphasized. Without a doubt, the Quran is the most important book in the life of a Muslim. That is because the Quran is not simply a book; it is the divine uncreated speech of Allah ﷻ — His words revealed to the Prophet ﷺ. It is the last and final Revelation sent for the guidance of humanity for all times and all places. It is our primary source of beliefs, rituals, ethics, morals, and laws in Islam. Our entire lives as Muslims revolve around the teachings of the Quran. Its words are so powerful, emotive, and effective that if they were to be revealed on a mountain, it would be humbled and would burst apart out of the awe of Allah ﷻ. Its recitation, memorization, interpretation, understanding, teaching, and learning are all acts of worship that bring blessings and reward. These words are a source of light, guidance, cure, and mercy.

True love and respect for the Quran is expressed through reading it, understanding its message, and applying it to one's daily life. It is a source of guidance to navigate through the world and live a life that is pleasing to Allah ﷻ. It is literally a manual for life that is used to build a path towards the Divine. It is supposed to be a source of inspiration, encouragement, and a tool used to deal with the challenges of life. It contains guidance for every single aspect of life: theological, spiritual, individual, communal, economic, and political.

8. TAKING ADVANTAGE OF TIME AND MAKING SMART DECISIONS

Time is a very limited commodity. It is considered to be one of the most valuable possessions of a human being. Time is a priceless commodity; there's no way possible to assign a value to it. There is a famous saying that a person can spend money to make more money but they can never spend time to make more time. Once it's gone, it's gone, and there's no way to get it back.

Time is the capital of life. Hours, days, months and years move quickly. At the beginning of one's life a person possesses a lot of this capital but every single day a portion of it disappears; and it disappears on its own. A poet once said, "Your life is a few breaths that can be counted. Every time one passes, a part of your life decreases." Time is capital just like money is capital. When it comes to business, everyone is very smart and cautious. They do their research and make sure that there's a high rate of return. They know that if they make smart investments they will profit and if they make bad investments they will be at a loss. Allah ﷻ has given humans this capital so that they can invest in something profitable, something that will give them high returns. If a person invests their time in faith and righteous deeds then the return on that investment literally can't be quantified; it's unlimited. However, if they invest it in disobedience and sin, then there's nothing but complete loss and bankruptcy.

HADITH 24

Prohibition of Injustice

عَنْ أَبِي ذَرٍّ الْغِفَارِيِّ رَضِيَ اللَّهُ عَنْهُ عَنْ النَّبِيِّ صلى الله عليه و سلم فِيمَا يَرْوِيهِ عَنْ رَبِّهِ تَبَارَكَ وَتَعَالَى، أَنَّهُ قَالَ: "يَا عِبَادِي: إنِّي حَرَّمْتُ الظُّلْمَ عَلَى نَفْسِي، وَجَعَلْتُهُ بَيْنَكُمْ مُحَرَّمًا؛ فَلَا تَظَالَمُوا. يَا عِبَادِي! كُلُّكُمْ ضَالٌّ إلَّا مَنْ هَدَيْتُهُ، فَاسْتَهْدُونِي أَهْدِكُمْ. يَا عِبَادِي! كُلُّكُمْ جَائِعٌ إلَّا مَنْ أَطْعَمْتُهُ، فَاسْتَطْعِمُونِي أُطْعِمْكُمْ. يَا عِبَادِي! كُلُّكُمْ عَارٍ إلَّا مَنْ كَسَوْتُهُ، فَاسْتَكْسُونِي أَكْسُكُمْ. يَا عِبَادِي! إنَّكُمْ تُخْطِئُونَ بِاللَّيْلِ وَالنَّهَارِ، وَأَنَا أَغْفِرُ الذُّنُوبَ جَمِيعًا؛ فَاسْتَغْفِرُونِي أَغْفِرْ لَكُمْ. يَا عِبَادِي! إنَّكُمْ لَنْ تَبْلُغُوا ضُرِّي فَتَضُرُّونِي، وَلَنْ تَبْلُغُوا نَفْعِي فَتَنْفَعُونِي. يَا عِبَادِي! لَوْ أَنَّ أَوَّلَكُمْ وَآخِرَكُمْ وَإِنْسَكُمْ وَجِنَّكُمْ كَانُوا عَلَى أَتْقَى قَلْبِ رَجُلٍ وَاحِدٍ مِنْكُمْ، مَا زَادَ ذَلِكَ فِي مُلْكِي شَيْئًا. يَا عِبَادِي! لَوْ أَنَّ أَوَّلَكُمْ وَآخِرَكُمْ وَإِنْسَكُمْ وَجِنَّكُمْ كَانُوا عَلَى أَفْجَرِ قَلْبِ رَجُلٍ وَاحِدٍ مِنْكُمْ، مَا نَقَصَ ذَلِكَ مِنْ مُلْكِي شَيْئًا. يَا عِبَادِي! لَوْ أَنَّ أَوَّلَكُمْ وَآخِرَكُمْ وَإِنْسَكُمْ وَجِنَّكُمْ قَامُوا فِي صَعِيدٍ وَاحِدٍ، فَسَأَلُونِي، فَأَعْطَيْتُ كُلَّ وَاحِدٍ مَسْأَلَتَهُ، مَا نَقَصَ ذَلِكَ مِمَّا عِنْدِي إلَّا كَمَا يَنْقُصُ الْمِخْيَطُ إذَا أُدْخِلَ الْبَحْرَ. يَا عِبَادِي! إنَّمَا هِيَ أَعْمَالُكُمْ أُحْصِيهَا لَكُمْ، ثُمَّ أُوَفِّيكُمْ إيَّاهَا؛ فَمَنْ وَجَدَ خَيْرًا فَلْيَحْمَدْ اللَّهَ، وَمَنْ وَجَدَ غَيْرَ ذَلِكَ فَلَا يَلُومَنَّ إلَّا نَفْسَهُ".

رَوَاهُ مُسْلِمٌ.

From Abū Dharr al-Ghifārī ﵁ from the Prophet ﷺ from his Lord, that He said: "O My servants! I have forbidden ẓulm(oppression) for Myself, and I have made it forbidden amongst you, so do not oppress one another. O My servants, all of you are astray except those whom I have guided, so seek guidance from Me and I shall guide you. O My servants, all of you are hungry except those whom I have fed, so seek food from Me and I shall feed you. O My servants, all of you are naked except those whom I have clothed, so seek clothing from Me and I shall clothe you. O My servants, you commit sins by day and by night, and I forgive all sins, so seek forgiveness from Me and I shall forgive you. O My servants, you will not attain harming Me so as to harm me, and you will not attain benefitting Me so as to benefit Me. O My servants, if the first of you and the last of you, and the humans of you and the jinn of you, were all as pious as the most pious heart of any individual amongst you, then this would not increase My Kingdom an iota. O My servants, if the first of you and the last of you, and the humans of you and the jinn of you, were all as wicked as the most wicked heart of any individual amongst you, then this would not decrease My Kingdom an iota. O My servants, if the first of you and the last of you, and the humans of you and the jinn of you, were all to stand together in one place and ask of Me, and I were to give everyone what he requested, then that would not decrease what I possess, except what is decreased of the ocean when a needle is dipped into it. O My servants, it is but your deeds that I account for you, and then recompense you for. So he who finds good, let him praise Allah, and he who finds other than that, let him blame no one but himself."

Narrated by Muslim.

IMPORTANCE

This ḥadīth is also classified as a ḥadīth qudsī; meaning it is a ḥadīth that the Prophet ﷺ narrated from Allah ﷻ. The meaning is from Allah ﷻ and the words are those of the Prophet ﷺ. This narration stresses the prohibition of all types of oppression, injustice, and wrongdoing and commands Muslims to practice justice, which is one of the primary objectives of the Sharīʿah. It also encourages supplicating to Allah ﷻ for guidance and worldly needs. The ḥadīth also encourages the concept of tawakkul (reliance upon Allah ﷻ), while at the same time destroying the concept of materialism and establishing the greatness of Allah ﷻ.

This ḥadīth is extremely profound and powerful in terms of shaping human understanding of the greatness, might, power, glory, magnificence, and justice of Allah ﷻ. Imām al-Nawawī mentions that Abū Idrīs al-Khawlānī, who narrates the ḥadīth from Abū Dharr, would fall onto his knees out of awe and reverence whenever he would narrate this ḥadīth.[196]

EXPLANATION

Allah ﷻ begins this statement by directly addressing each and every single one of His servants. He is speaking to all of mankind, "O my servants!" This is done to grab the attention of the listener. It also highlights the reality of mankind's relationship with Allah ﷻ; He is their Lord and they are His servants.

Allah ﷻ then says, "Indeed I have prohibited ẓūlm (injustice/oppression/wrongdoing) for Myself." Meaning that Allah ﷻ is exalted and pure from committing any type of ẓulm by His essence. It is impossible and unimaginable that Allah ﷻ would do something that is unjust.

Generally ẓulm is defined as "putting something in the wrong place", violating another's right unjustly, or going beyond the limit. This is impossible for Allah ﷻ because He is the Owner and Lord of all creation and nothing has a right upon Him. That is why it is mentioned in numerous places throughout the Quran that Allah ﷻ does not wrong any soul. Allah ﷻ says, "And your Lord treats no one with injustice."[197] "Allah is not unjust even to the

196 Ibn Rajab, *Jāmiʿ al-ʿUlūm wa al-Ḥikam*, 263

197 وَلَا يَظْلِمُ رَبُّكَ أَحَدًا - 18:49

extent of the weight of an atom."[198] "Allah wills no injustice to the world."[199] It is clear that Allah ﷻ never has and never will commit any form of injustice.

This first statement gives deep insight into how one is supposed to understand Allah ﷻ and their relationship with Him. Allah ﷻ, the Divine, the Almighty, the All-Powerful, is the absolute most fair and just. Everything He wills and decrees is just. It is human beings who are unjust towards one another.

Allah ﷻ then says, "And I have made it prohibited for you." Just as Allah ﷻ has forbidden injustice for Himself, he has prohibited human beings from being unjust as well. This prohibition includes all types of wrongdoing, oppression, and injustice. The worst form of injustice a human can do is disbelieve in Allah ﷻ or associate partners with Him. Allah ﷻ is the only being worthy of worship. To associate any partners with Him is an offensive crime as Allah ﷻ says, "Truly shirk is a great wrongdoing."[200]

The Scholars mention that there are three major types or categories of ẓulm:

1. Ẓulm al-nafs: being unjust to ourselves by committing sins. Acts of disobedience are considered to be unjust; the worst being shirk.
2. Ẓulm that we do towards others: any type of harm that we cause to another person is considered to be oppression.
3. Ẓulm done to other creatures: any type of harm that is caused to animals or the planet.

Ibn Taymiyyah ﵀ mentions that this prohibition encompasses the entire religion. Everything that Allah ﷻ has forbidden is a type of ẓulm, and everything He has ordered is a form of ʿadl.[201] Allah ﷻ then emphasizes the prohibition by saying, "Therefore do not wrong one another."

It is also understood from this statement that the establishment of justice is a desired goal and objective of Islam. This is something that the Companions understood extremely well. When the Emperor of Persia asked the Muslims what brought them to his lands they replied, "Allah has sent us to

---

198 4:40 - إِنَّ اللَّـهَ لاَ يَظْلِمُ مِثْقَالَ ذَرَّةٍ

199 3:108 - وَمَا اللَّـهُ يُرِيدُ ظُلْمًا لِّلْعَالَمِينَ

200 31:13 - إِنَّ الشِّرْكَ لَظُلْمٌ عَظِيمٌ

201 Ibn Taymiyyah, *Majmūʿ*, 18:166

take people from the servitude of mankind to the the servitude of Allah, from the narrowness of this world to its expanse, and from injustice to the justice of Islam."[202] True justice is established by building a society on Quranic principles.

The next portion of the ḥadīth deals with the concept of guidance. Allah ﷻ says, "O My servants, all of you are lost except for those whom I have guided. Therefore, seek guidance from Me and I will guide you." This ḥadīth states that all of humanity is lost or astray except those whom Allah ﷻ has guided. Being lost or astray means to be away from the Straight Path, which is the path towards Allah ﷻ, mercy, forgiveness, and salvation, which is Islam. The greatest blessing Allah ﷻ has bestowed upon any human being is the blessing of guidance; being guided towards belief in Allah ﷻ, His Angels, His books, His Messengers, life after death, and the divine decree. This guidance then translates into action that leads a person down the path of earning eternal salvation. There is no greater blessing than being guided towards faith and righteousness; it is priceless. This blessing is a unique gift from Allah ﷻ; He gives to whom He wills and withholds it from whom He wills.

Since guidance comes only from Allah ﷻ, He commands His servants to seek guidance from Him. "Therefore, seek guidance from Me and I will guide you." Whoever turns to Allah ﷻ with an open heart and an open mind sincerely searching for the truth, Allah ﷻ will guide them towards it. Once a person has received the gift of guidance they should be extremely grateful and ask for steadfastness upon it.

After highlighting the importance of spiritual nourishment, Allah ﷻ now mentions that He alone is the One who provides physical nourishment. "O My servants! All of you are hungry except for those whom I have fed. Therefore, seek food from me and I will feed you." Food is another great blessing of Allah ﷻ. In today's modern world, especially affluent societies, food is something that is taken for granted. People don't recognize the value of food because it is readily available. As a matter of fact there is an excess of food that leads to a problem of waste. Those who are made to live through droughts and have experienced hunger recognize the true value of food.

Oftentimes people are under the assumption that they are the ones who put food on the table; that they earned the food through their own efforts, abilities, and capabilities. Allah ﷻ is clarifying and reminding humanity

---

202 Ibn Kathīr, *al-Bidāyah wa al-Nihāyah*, v.7

that He alone is the One Who provides food and drink. As Allah ﷻ mentions in Sūrah al-Wāqiʿah, "Consider the seeds you sow in the ground - is it you who make them grow or We? If We wished, We could turn your harvest into chaff and leave you to wail, 'We are burdened with debt; we are bereft.' Consider the water you drink- was it you who brought it down from the raincloud or We? If We wanted, We could make it bitter: will you not be thankful?"[203] Allah ﷻ reminds mankind to seek provisions from Him and Him alone, "Therefore, seek food from me and I will feed you."

The ḥadīth then gives a reminder about the blessings of clothes. "O My servants! All of you are naked except for those whom I have clothed. Therefore, seek clothing from me and I will clothe you." To reiterate, the last two sentences of the ḥadīth are powerful reminders that Allah ﷻ is the One who truly provides; that He is al-Rāziq. Allah ﷻ is the One who gives food, drink, and clothes. Even though human beings are required to put forth their effort in carrying out their daily activities, they should not become materialistic and rely on their efforts alone. They should not be deceived by the apparent nature of this world. This portion of the ḥadīth is in essence a refutation of materialism.

Allah ﷻ then reminds mankind of His infinite and limitless mercy. "O My servants! You sin by night and by day, and I forgive all sins. Therefore, seek forgiveness from Me and I will forgive you." Every single human being has shortcomings, makes mistakes, poor choices, sins, slips up and falls into acts of disobedience. This is part of human nature. However, no matter how much a person has sinned before, no matter how ugly or bad it was, they can still earn the forgiveness of Allah ﷻ, the Most Merciful of those who are merciful. All they have to do is turn to Allah ﷻ with remorse and humility and ask for forgiveness. Allah ﷻ is the Most Forgiving, the Always Forgiving, the One Who accepts repentance, the Most Merciful. This portion of the ḥadīth helps one understand the magnitude of the mercy, forgiveness, and grace of Allah ﷻ.

The ḥadīth then goes on to describe the infinite might and power of Allah ﷻ reminding humanity that He is the Almighty, the All-Powerful, the Self-Sufficient, Who is not in need of anyone or anything, but everyone and everything is in need of Him. "O My servants! You will not be able to harm

---

203 أَفَرَأَيْتُم مَّا تَحْرُثُونَ أَأَنتُمْ تَزْرَعُونَهُ أَمْ نَحْنُ الزَّارِعُونَ لَوْ نَشَاءُ لَجَعَلْنَاهُ حُطَامًا فَظَلْتُمْ تَفَكَّهُونَ إِنَّا لَمُغْرَمُونَ بَلْ نَحْنُ مَحْرُومُونَ أَفَرَأَيْتُمُ الْمَاءَ الَّذِي تَشْرَبُونَ أَأَنتُمْ أَنزَلْتُمُوهُ مِنَ الْمُزْنِ أَمْ نَحْنُ الْمُنزِلُونَ لَوْ نَشَاءُ جَعَلْنَاهُ أُجَاجًا فَلَوْلَا تَشْكُرُونَ 56:63-70

Me so as to bring Me any harm, and you will not be able to benefit Me so as to bring Me any benefit." Allah ﷻ is not in need of any of His creation. He is self-sufficient and perfect. No one can benefit or harm Allah ﷻ in any way, shape or form. Allah ﷻ loves for His servants to be pious and repent to Him, yet He does not benefit from it in any way. Similarly, He dislikes it when someone disbelieves and commits sins, yet it does not harm Him in any way. It is only out of His love, mercy, kindness and goodness to His creation that He likes what is beneficial for them and dislikes what is harmful for them.

Allah ﷻ then highlights the vastness of His kingdom and sovereignty. "O my servants, if the first and last of you and the human and jinn of you were as pious as the most pious heart of anyone among you; it would not add anything to my dominion. O my servants, if the first and last of you and the human and jinn of you were as wicked as the most wicked heart of anyone among you, it would not decrease anything from My dominion." Meaning that Allah's kingdom is not enriched or made greater by obedience to Him by humans and jinn. Similarly, if all of mankind and jinn were as evil as Shaytān, it would not diminish Allah's kingdom and dominion in any way.

Allah ﷻ then highlights the vastness of His generosity and magnitude of His infinite grace. "O my servants, if the first and last of you and the human and jinn of you were to gather on the same piece of land and ask Me and if I were to give every one of them what they asked, that would not decrease what I have any more than a needle decreases what is in the ocean when it is put into it." Allah ﷻ is absolutely Generous, Free of all wants and needs, Rich and able to give anything to whomever He wills. He is able to provide for all of mankind and jinn without decreasing anything from His dominion and treasures.

Allah ﷻ then reminds humanity about the concepts of accountability and recompense, highlighting His infinite mercy and justice. "O my servants, it is but your deeds that I reckon. Then I recompense you for them." Every single thing a person says or does is being recorded. On the Day of Judgment, they will stand before Allah ﷻ and be questioned about their statements and actions. Allah ﷻ will then recompense them accordingly. Allah ﷻ through His infinite mercy will reward good deeds, and through His justice can choose to hold people accountable for their bad deeds. This portion of the ḥadīth is related to the first portion of the ḥadīth that relates to injustice.

Allah ﷻ then mentions the consequence of that, "The one who finds good is to give praise to Allah." If an individual was guided towards faith, which translated into righteous deeds, and because of that he is rewarded in the Hereafter, they should thank Allah ﷻ and praise Him. It is only through the guidance, will, and decree of Allah ﷻ that the individual was guided towards the truth and righteous actions. On the other hand, if a person is not guided to the truth and they choose to disbelieve and engage in acts of disobedience, then they have no one to blame but themselves. "The one who finds other than this should not blame anyone but himself."

LESSONS AND BENEFITS

1. THE GRAVITY OF ẒULM

Ẓulm, in all of its various shapes and forms, is absolutely forbidden. Not only does it have negative consequences in the life of this world, but it will lead to sorrow and difficulty in the life to come. The Prophet ﷺ said, "Ẓulm will be layers of darkness on the Day of Judgment."[204]

2. GUIDANCE

Hidāyah is the single greatest blessing that Allah ﷻ bestows upon a human being. It is through divine guidance that an individual is able to lead a life that is pleasing to Allah ﷻ allowing them to earn His mercy, grace, forgiveness, and ultimately salvation in the Hereafter.

3. BLESSINGS

Allah ﷻ is constantly showering humanity with His blessings and mercy. Every single blessing a person enjoys comes directly from Allah ﷻ. He says, "And whatever blessing you have it is from Allah."[205] The blessings of Allah are innumerous; they can't be quantified or even imagined. Allah ﷻ says, "If you tried to count God's favours you could never calculate them: man is truly unjust and ungrateful."[206]

4. ALLAH'S KINGDOM

Allah ﷻ is Mālik al-Mulk; the sole Owner, Master, King, and Sovereign

---

204 Muslim, *k. al-birr wa al-ṣilah wa al-ādāb, b. taḥrīm al-dhulm*, 2579

205 16:53 - وَمَا بِكُم مِّن نِّعْمَةٍ فَمِنَ اللَّـهِ

206 14:34 - وَإِن تَعُدُّوا نِعْمَتَ اللَّـهِ لَا تُحْصُوهَا ۗ إِنَّ الْإِنسَانَ لَظَلُومٌ كَفَّارٌ

of the entire universe and everything it contains. He is the King of all kings.

5. ALLAH'S TREASURES

Allah's bounties and treasures are infinite and everlasting. He gives to whom He wills and withholds from whom He wills.

6. DEEDS AND RECOMPENSE

Every single sane adult human being is accountable before Allah ﷻ.

7. RESPONSIBILITY

Human beings are responsible for their own actions.

HADITH 25

Acts of Charity

عَنْ أَبِي ذَرٍّ رَضِيَ اللَّه عَنْهُ أَيْضًا، "أَنَّ نَاسًا مِنْ أَصْحَابِ رَسُولِ اللَّهِ صلى اللَّه عليه وسلم قَالُوا لِلنَّبِيِّ صلى اللَّه عليه وسلم يَا رَسُولَ اللَّهِ ذَهَبَ أَهْلُ الدُّثُورِ بِالْأُجُورِ؛ يُصَلُّونَ كَمَا نُصَلِّي، وَيَصُومُونَ كَمَا نَصُومُ، وَيَتَصَدَّقُونَ بِفُضُولِ أَمْوَالِهِمْ. قَالَ: أَوَلَيْسَ قَدْ جَعَلَ اللَّهُ لَكُمْ مَا تَصَّدَّقُونَ؟ إنَّ بِكُلِّ تَسْبِيحَةٍ صَدَقَةً، وَكُلِّ تَكْبِيرَةٍ صَدَقَةً، وَكُلِّ تَحْمِيدَةٍ صَدَقَةً، وَكُلِّ تَهْلِيلَةٍ صَدَقَةً، وَأَمْرٌ بِمَعْرُوفٍ صَدَقَةٌ، وَنَهْيٌ عَنْ مُنْكَرٍ صَدَقَةٌ، وَفِي بُضْعِ أَحَدِكُمْ صَدَقَةٌ. قَالُوا: يَا رَسُولَ اللَّهِ أَيَأْتِي أَحَدُنَا شَهْوَتَهُ وَيَكُونُ لَهُ فِيهَا أَجْرٌ؟ قَالَ: أَرَأَيْتُمْ لَوْ وَضَعَهَا فِي حَرَامٍ أَكَانَ عَلَيْهِ وِزْرٌ؟ فَكَذَلِكَ إذَا وَضَعَهَا فِي الْحَلَالِ، كَانَ لَهُ أَجْرٌ".

رَوَاهُ مُسْلِمٌ.

Also from Abū Dharr ﷺ: Some people from among the Companions of the Messenger of Allah ﷺ said to the Prophet ﷺ, "O Messenger of Allah, the affluent have made off with the rewards; they pray as we pray, they fast as we fast, and they give [much] in charity by virtue of their wealth." He ﷺ said, "Has Allah not made things for you to give in charity? Truly every tasbīḥah is a charity, and every takbīrah is a charity, and every taḥmīdah is a charity, and every tahlīlah is a charity. And commanding the good is a charity, and forbidding an evil is a charity, and in marital relations there is a charity." They said, "O Messenger of Allah, when one of us fulfills his carnal desire will he have some reward for that?" He ﷺ said, "Do you not see that if he were to act upon it [his desire] in an unlawful manner then he would be deserving of punishment? Likewise, if he were to act upon it in a lawful manner then he will be deserving of reward."

Narrated by Muslim.

IMPORTANCE

In this beautiful ḥadīth the Prophet ﷺ is explaining the concept of ṣadaqah to his Companions ﷺ. He is clarifying to them that charity is a very broad and comprehensive act that is not limited to being financial. Charity can be in the form of remembering Allah ﷻ, giving advice, and doing things in a lawful manner. Ṣadaqah is not limited to wealth but it includes several other acts of worship and kindness. There are multiple avenues or multiple paths of righteousness, getting close to Allah ﷻ, and earning reward.

EXPLANATION

This narration starts with a genuine concern from the Companions ﷺ of the Prophet ﷺ. This concern is not coming from a place of displeasure, discomfort, or difficulty. Rather it is a concern rooted in their desire and eagerness to earn reward and get closer to Allah ﷻ. They said, "O Messenger of Allah, the affluent have made off with the rewards; they pray as we pray, they fast as we fast, and they give [much] in charity by virtue of their wealth." One of the important lessons to draw from this question or concern of the Companions ﷺ is to realize how eager they were to perform deeds that are pleasing to Allah ﷻ. Instead of competing with one another for the things of this world, for material things, they raced with each other for the sake of pleasing Allah ﷻ. Their mindset and attitude was completely different. They understood the reality of this world and the importance of earning as much reward as possible.

The Prophet ﷺ understood their concern and consoled, comforted, and reassured them in the most beautiful way possible. He asked, "Has Allah not made things for you to give in charity?" Although you may not have wealth or material things to give away in charity, Allah ﷻ has still blessed you with opportunities to earn the same reward as charity by performing other deeds. The Prophet ﷺ then lists some of those deeds. "Truly every tasbīḥah is a charity, and every takbīrah is a charity, and every taḥmīdah is a charity, and every tahlīlah is a charity. And commanding the good is a charity, and forbidding an evil is a charity, and in marital relations there is a charity." Remembering Allah ﷻ, praising Him, and glorifying Him by saying subḥānallah, Allahu Akbar, al-ḥamdulillah, and lā ilāha illa Allah brings the same rewards as charity. Commanding good by reminding people and encouraging towards good deeds brings the same reward as charity. Forbidding evil also brings the same reward as charity.

The Prophet ﷺ then told them that even having relations with one's spouse is a source of reward and a type of charity. When the Companions heard this they were a little surprised so they asked, "O Messenger of Allah, when one of us fulfills his carnal desire will he have some reward for that?" The Prophet ﷺ responded, "Do you not see that if he were to act upon it [his desire] in an unlawful manner then he would be deserving of punishment? Likewise, if he were to act upon it in a lawful manner then he will be deserving of reward."

LESSONS AND BENEFITS

1. *COMPETING IN GOOD DEEDS*

It is healthy and beneficial to compete with others in performing good deeds and earning reward as long as it's done with sincerity. Allah ﷻ says, "Race with one another towards forgiveness from your Lord and towards a paradise the width of which spans the heavens and the earth. It has been prepared for the God-fearing."[207] He also says, "Compete with each other in proceeding towards forgiveness from your Lord and to Paradise the width of which is like the width of the sky and the earth. It has been prepared for those who believe in Allah and His Messengers. That is the bounty of Allah; He gives it to whomsoever He wills and Allah is the Lord of the great bounty."[208] After describing some of the pleasures and delights of Paradise, Allah ﷻ says, "It is this (bliss) in aspiring for which the competitors should race each other."[209]

2. *THE REWARD OF DHIKR*

As mentioned earlier, dhikr is considered to be the nourishment of hearts, the connection between a person and their Lord. It is something that brings them closer to Allah ﷻ. Dhikr is one of the most powerful and effec-

207 3:133 - وَسَارِعُوا إِلَىٰ مَغْفِرَةٍ مِّن رَّبِّكُمْ وَجَنَّةٍ عَرْضُهَا السَّمَاوَاتُ وَالْأَرْضُ أُعِدَّتْ لِلْمُتَّقِينَ

208 57:21 - سَابِقُوا إِلَىٰ مَغْفِرَةٍ مِّن رَّبِّكُمْ وَجَنَّةٍ عَرْضُهَا كَعَرْضِ السَّمَاءِ وَالْأَرْضِ أُعِدَّتْ لِلَّذِينَ آمَنُوا بِاللَّهِ وَرُسُلِهِ ۚ ذَٰلِكَ فَضْلُ اللَّهِ يُؤْتِيهِ مَن يَشَاءُ ۚ وَاللَّهُ ذُو الْفَضْلِ الْعَظِيمِ

209 83:26 - وَفِي ذَٰلِكَ فَلْيَتَنَافَسِ الْمُتَنَافِسُونَ

tive ways of expressing gratitude, thanks, and appreciation for all of the blessings that Allah ﷻ bestows upon a person. Throughout the Quran, Allah ﷻ commands believers to engage in dhikr, praises the people of dhikr, and describes the rewards for the people of dhikr. Allah ﷻ says in the Quran, "O you who believe, remember Allah often, and proclaim His perfection morning and evening."[210] Similarly Allah ﷻ says, "The ones who believe and their hearts are peaceful with the remembrance of Allah. Listen, the hearts find peace only in the remembrance of Allah."[211] All of the acts of worship we have revolve around the concept of remembering Allah ﷻ. For example, Allah ﷻ says regarding prayer, "And establish prayer for My remembrance."[212] The Prophet ﷺ referred to dhikr as the best of our deeds.

3. IMPORTANCE OF COMMANDING GOOD AND FORBIDDING EVIL

Islam is not an individualistic religion; it doesn't simply focus on the individual and their relationship with God. Islam is a religion of community that works towards building a healthy, moral, upright, principled, and God-conscious society; a society that reminds each other of their responsibilities towards God and towards each other by enjoining good and forbidding evil. This is one of the defining qualities of a Muslim community and is why Allah ﷻ praises them in the Quran. Allah ﷻ says regarding the believers, "[Believers], you are the best community singled out for people: you order what is right, forbid what is wrong, and believe in God."[213] Allah ﷻ also says in Sūrah al-ʿAṣr, "By the declining day, man is [deep] in loss, except for those who believe, do good deeds, urge one another to the truth, and urge one another to steadfastness."[214]

4. POWER OF INTENTIONS

Intentions have the power to turn ordinary actions into acts of worship that bring reward and blessings. They can transform a person's entire life into one of worship, servitude, submission, devotion, and purpose. Please

---

210 33: 41-42 - يَا أَيُّهَا الَّذِينَ آمَنُوا اذْكُرُوا اللَّـهَ ذِكْرًا كَثِيراً وَسَبِّحُوهُ بُكْرَةً وَأَصِيلاً

211 13:28 - الَّذِينَ آمَنُوا وَتَطْمَئِنُّ قُلُوبُهُم بِذِكْرِ اللَّـهِ ۗ أَلاَ بِذِكْرِ اللَّـهِ تَطْمَئِنُّ الْقُلُوبُ

212 20:14 - وَأَقِمِ الصَّلاَةَ لِذِكْرِى

213 3:110 - كُنتُمْ خَيْرَ أُمَّةٍ أُخْرِجَتْ لِلنَّاسِ تَأْمُرُونَ بِالْمَعْرُوفِ وَتَنْهَوْنَ عَنِ الْمُنكَرِ وَتُؤْمِنُونَ بِاللَّـهِ

214 103 :1-3 - وَالْعَصْرِ إِنَّ الإِنْسَانَ لَفِي خُسْرٍ إِلاَّ الَّذِينَ آمَنُوا وَعَمِلُوا الصَّالِحَاتِ وَتَوَاصَوْا بِالْحَقِّ وَتَوَاصَوْا بِالصَّبْرِ

see ḥadīth #1 above for more details.

5. FOLLOWING THE SHARĪʿAH

The Sharīʿah is Allah's revealed law that governs and regulates human life and activity. It is a code of life that believers are supposed to follow in order to obtain guidance in this world and salvation in the next. It includes creed, ritual acts of worship, morals, ethics, and law. It is a complete code of life based on revealed scripture from Allah ﷻ. Allah ﷻ knows human beings better than they know themselves. He has made certain things attractive to human beings; things that they are naturally drawn towards. There are certain enjoyments, delights, pleasures, and entertainment that they are allowed to partake and participate in. They are allowed to enjoy certain types of food, drinks, clothes, homes, and marriages. Humans are allowed to enjoy wealth, desires, and the pleasures and delights of this world within certain boundaries and limits set by Allah ﷻ. If enjoyed within the limits and boundaries set by Allah ﷻ, they will be a source of reward.

HADITH 26

Charity Upon Every Joint

عَنْ أَبِي هُرَيْرَةَ رَضِيَ اللَّه عَنْهُ قَالَ: قَالَ رَسُولُ اللَّهِ صلى الله عليه و سلم "كُلُّ سُلَامَى مِنْ النَّاسِ عَلَيْهِ صَدَقَةٌ، كُلَّ يَوْمٍ تَطْلُعُ فِيهِ الشَّمْسُ تَعْدِلُ بَيْنَ اثْنَيْنِ صَدَقَةٌ، وَتُعِينُ الرَّجُلَ فِي دَابَّتِهِ فَتَحْمِلُهُ عَلَيْهَا أَوْ تَرْفَعُ لَهُ عَلَيْهَا مَتَاعَهُ صَدَقَةٌ، وَالْكَلِمَةُ الطَّيِّبَةُ صَدَقَةٌ، وَبِكُلِّ خُطْوَةٍ تَمْشِيهَا إلَى الصَّلَاةِ صَدَقَةٌ، وَتُمِيطُ الْأَذَى عَنْ الطَّرِيقِ صَدَقَةٌ".
رَوَاهُ الْبُخَارِيُّ، وَمُسْلِمٌ.

From Abū Hurairah ﵁ who said that the Messenger of Allah ﷺ said, "Every joint of a person must perform a charity each day that the sun rises: to judge justly between two people is charity. To help a man with his mount, lifting him onto it or hoisting up his belongings onto it, is charity. And a good word is charity. And every step that you take towards the prayer is charity, and removing a harmful object from the road is charity."

Narrated by al-Bukhārī and Muslim.

IMPORTANCE

In this ḥadīth, the Prophet ﷺ is reminding the Companions about the great blessings and favors of Allah ﷻ that are impossible to count or even imagine. He ﷺ provides guidance on how to show gratitude for the blessings and bounties of Allah ﷻ by performing certain acts of righteousness. It also emphasizes the lesson from the last ḥadīth, that charity is not restricted to wealth, but every act of goodness is considered charity. The acts of goodness highlighted in this ḥadīth revolve around the concept of helping and serving others in order to create an environment of mutual love, cooperation, and unity.

EXPLANATION

The ḥadīth starts with the Prophet ﷺ explaining that every morning a person wakes up they owe a charity for every joint in their body. "Every joint of a person must perform a charity each day that the sun rises." Imām al-Nawawī رحمه الله mentions that there are approximately 360 joints in the human body, which means that a person owes 360 acts of charity every single day. ʿĀfiyah, or health and well-being, is one of the greatest blessings of Allah ﷻ that is often taken for granted. One of the ways of expressing gratitude for this immense blessing is by performing different acts of charity or kindness. This charity is not restricted to wealth; it can be any act of kindness as the Prophet ﷺ goes on to explain. The Prophet ﷺ mentions five different acts of kindness that are considered to be a form of charity.

The first is reconciling between two people, "to judge justly between two people is a charity." To bring peace or reconciliation between two people or parties that are arguing, quarreling, or having a dispute is an extremely beautiful and rewarding act of worship. It is one of the best forms of charity that can be done because of the great good it brings about among individuals and in society. Allah ﷻ says in the Quran, "The believers are brothers, so make peace between your two brothers and be mindful of God, so that you may be given mercy."[215] Allah ﷻ also says, "There is no good in most of their secret talk, only in commanding charity, or good, or reconciliation between people. To anyone who does these things, seeking to please God, We shall give a rich

215 49:10 - إِنَّمَا الْمُؤْمِنُونَ إِخْوَةٌ فَأَصْلِحُوا بَيْنَ أَخَوَيْكُمْ ۚ وَاتَّقُوا اللَّهَ لَعَلَّكُمْ تُرْحَمُونَ

reward."[216] The Prophet ﷺ said, "Shall I not inform you of something better than prayer, fasting, and charity?" The Companions said, "Of course." He ﷺ said, "Reconciling between people."[217]

The second act of kindness considered to be a form of charity is "to help a man with his mount, lifting him onto it, or hoisting up his belongings onto it." Physically helping, assisting, aiding, and supporting an individual is a very beautiful act of kindness that develops mutual love and respect between individuals. It is also a sign of one's humility and selflessness. This is a very simple act a person can do to express their gratitude to Allah for granting them health and well-being. This includes giving someone a ride, carrying their groceries, helping someone elderly cross the street or climb the stairs, helping someone load or unload their car, or even jumpstarting someone's car. The Prophet ﷺ said, "Allah continues to assist a servant as long as they continue to assist their brother."[218]

The third act highlighted by the Prophet ﷺ is a good word, "And a good word is charity." What is meant by a good word is anything that brings one closer to Allah, such as the different phrases of praise mentioned in the previous ḥadīth. Other examples of a "good word" are responding to someone's salām, responding to someone who says alḥamdulillah when they sneeze, enjoining good, forbidding evil, giving advice, and speaking in a manner that brings comfort, joy, and happiness to others.

The fourth act mentioned by the Prophet ﷺ is "and every step that you take towards the prayer." Through this statement the Prophet ﷺ is highlighting some of the virtues, rewards, and benefits associated with praying in congregation in the masjid. There are so many aḥādīth that emphasize the importance of Muslims praying together in the masjid. As mentioned earlier, the importance of the masjid in the daily life of a Muslim cannot be overemphasized. Here the Prophet ﷺ is saying that every step a person takes towards prayer is similar to an act of charity in terms of reward.

The last act mentioned by the Prophet ﷺ in this ḥadīth is removing a harmful object from the road. For example, removing thorns, trash, branches, stones, glass, or any other harmful object from the sidewalk or the middle

216 4:114 - لَّا خَيْرَ فِي كَثِيرٍ مِّن نَّجْوَاهُمْ إِلَّا مَنْ أَمَرَ بِصَدَقَةٍ أَوْ مَعْرُوفٍ أَوْ إِصْلَاحٍ بَيْنَ النَّاسِ ۚ وَمَن يَفْعَلْ ذَٰلِكَ ابْتِغَاءَ مَرْضَاتِ اللَّـهِ فَسَوْفَ نُؤْتِيهِ أَجْرًا عَظِيمًا

217 Abū Dāwūd, *k. al-adab, b. fī iṣlāḥ dhāt al-bayn*, 4919

218 Muslim, *k. al-dhikr wa al-duʿā' wa al-tawbah wa al-istighfār, b. faḍl al-ijtimāʿ ʿalā tilāwah al-Quran wa ʿalā al-dhikr*, 2699

of the road. In another ḥadīth, the Prophet ﷺ describes removing a harmful object from the road as one of the several branches of faith.

LESSONS AND BENEFITS

1. THE IMPORTANCE OF GRATITUDE

A believer is a person of deep and genuine gratitude both to their Creator, Allah ﷻ, and to others. The Arabic word for gratitude is shukr, which is to be grateful for the immense and innumerable blessings of Allah ﷻ. Linguistically the word, الشكر, is a verbal noun from the verb شَكَرَ / يَشكُرُ, which means to thank, be thankful, or be grateful. It comes from the root letters ش ك ر that convey the meaning of praising a person for something good that they have favored you with. When a person does الشكر they are praising Allah ﷻ for the blessings that He has favored them with.

Imām al-Munāwi ﵀ says, "Gratitude is of two types; the first is gratitude with the tongue and that is by praising the Giver. The other is gratitude with all of one's limbs and that is by repaying a gift with the value of what it deserves."[219] Ibn al-Qayyim ﵀ writes that gratitude is when the effect of the blessings of Allah ﷻ become apparent on a servant's tongue through praise and acknowledgement, and upon his heart through witnessing and love, and upon his limbs through humility and obedience.[220] Another scholar described it as recognizing blessings with humility.[221] It can be summarized from these descriptions that there are three primary aspects to gratitude:

1. Gratitude of the heart,
2. Gratitude of the tongue, and
3. Gratitude of the limbs

Gratitude is first and foremost recognizing that Allah ﷻ alone is the One who has blessed human beings with numerous blessings that can't be quantified or imagined. This recognition results in them praising Him, increasing their love for Him, and then by using these blessings in a way that is pleasing to Him ﷻ.

219 Munāwī, *al-Tawqīf ʿalā muhimmāt al-Taʿārīf*, 206-207

220 Ibn al-Qayyim, *Madārij al-Sālikīn*, 2:244

221 Fayrūzābādī, *Baṣā'ir dhawi al-Tamyīz fī laṭā'if al-Kitāb al-ʿAzīz*, 3:339

Every single blessing a person enjoys in this world is a gift from Allah ﷻ. Allah ﷻ says, “Whatever blessings you have are from Allah.”[222] A person is constantly being showered with the blessings of Allah ﷻ morning and evening; from the time they wake up in the morning till the time they go back to sleep at night. These blessings are beyond numeration. As Allah ﷻ says, “And if you were to count the blessings of Allah, you would not be able to quantify them. Truly mankind is unjust, ungrateful.”[223] These blessings come in all different shapes and sizes; things that can be seen and touched (by way of material goods: food, clothing, shelter, wealth and the like), as well as things that can’t be seen (such as safety, friendship, love, health and protection from harm and calamity).

2. SETTLING CONFLICTS AND DISPUTES

All relationships go through ups and downs. Having a conflict or dispute between two people whether they are married, friends, colleagues, neighbors, or business partners is natural. However, these disputes and conflicts should not lead towards enmity or hatred and everything possible should be done to reconcile, settle, and resolve the dispute.

3. HELPING AND SERVING PEOPLE

One of the greatest and most rewarding acts a person can do is to help and serve others. That was the quality of the Prophet ﷺ before being selected as a Messenger and remained his quality throughout his mission. The Prophet ﷺ said, “The leader of a nation is their servant.”[224] Real leadership is not about being in a position of power, authority, and control. Real leadership is about responsibility and service. Real leaders don't get served by others, they serve others.

4. GOOD SPEECH

There are several texts from the Quran and Ḥadīth that talk about the importance of controlling one’s speech and being very careful and conscious about what one says and how they say it. The tongue is a very powerful tool. It has the ability to take one to the highest levels of Paradise, and at the same

---

222 16:53 - وَمَا بِكُم مِّن نِّعْمَةٍ فَمِنَ اللَّـهِ

223 14:34 - وَإِن تَعُدُّوا نِعْمَتَ اللَّـهِ لَا تُحْصُوهَا ۗ إِنَّ الْإِنسَانَ لَظَلُومٌ كَفَّارٌ

224 Suyūṭī, *al-Jāmiʿ al-Ṣaghīr*, 4736

time, it has the power to take one to the depths of Hell. The Prophet ﷺ said, "Whoever believes in Allah and the Last Day should say something good or remain silent."[225]

5. PRAYING IN CONGREGATION

The importance of praying in congregation has been mentioned earlier.

6. EXPRESSIONS OF FAITH

Faith expresses itself in many different ways. One of the expressions of faith is to remove anything, big or small, that can cause a person harm.

225 Muslim, *k. al-Īmān, b. al-ḥath ʿalā ikrām al-jār wa al-ḍayf wa luzūm al-ṣamt illa min al-khayr wa kawn dhālika kullihi min al-īmān*, 47

HADITH 27

Righteousness is Good Character

عَنْ النَّوَّاسِ بْنِ سَمْعَانَ رَضِيَ اللَّه عَنْهُ عَنْ النَّبِيِّ صلى اللّٰه عليه و سلم قَالَ: "الْبِرُّ حُسْنُ الْخُلُقِ، وَالْإِثْمُ مَا حَاكَ فِي صَدْرِك، وَكَرِهْت أَنْ يَطَّلِعَ عَلَيْهِ النَّاسُ" رَوَاهُ مُسْلِمٌ. وَعَنْ وَابِصَةَ بْنِ مَعْبَدٍ رَضِيَ الله عَنْهُ قَالَ: أَتَيْتُ رَسُولَ اللَّهِ صلى الله عليه و سلم فَقَالَ: "جِئْتَ تَسْأَلُ عَنْ الْبِرِّ؟ قُلْتُ: نَعَمْ. فقَالَ: اِستَفتِ قلبَكَ، الْبِرُّ مَا اطْمَأَنَّتْ إلَيْهِ النَّفْسُ، وَاطْمَأَنَّ إلَيْهِ الْقَلْبُ، وَالْإِثْمُ مَا حَاكَ فِي النَّفْسِ وَتَرَدَّدَ فِي الصَّدْرِ، وَإِنْ أَفْتَاكَ النَّاسُ وَأَفْتَوْكَ".

حَدِيثٌ حَسَنٌ، رَوَيْنَاهُ فِي مُسْنَدَي الْإِمَامَيْنِ أَحْمَد بْنِ حَنْبَلٍ، وَالدَّارِمِيّ بِإِسْنَادٍ حَسَنٍ.

From al-Nawwās ibn Samʿān ﷺ that the Prophet ﷺ said, "Righteousness is good character, and wrongdoing is that which wavers in your soul, and which you dislike people *finding* out about." Narrated by Muslim. And on the authority of Wābiṣah ibn Maʿbad ﷺ who said: I came to the Messenger of Allah ﷺ and he ﷺ said, "You have come to ask about righteousness." I said, "Yes." He ﷺ said, "Consult your heart. Righteousness is that about which the soul feels at ease and the heart feels tranquil. And wrongdoing is that which wavers in the soul and causes uneasiness in the chest, even though people have repeatedly given their legal opinion [in its favor]."

A good hadīth transmitted from the Musnad of the two imams, Aḥmed ibn Ḥanbal and al-Dārimī, with a good chain of authorities.

THE NARRATOR

The narrator of the first ḥadīth is al-Nawwās ibn Samʿān ibn Khālid ibn ʿAmr al-ʿĀmirī al-Kilābī ﷺ. He is a Companion that is considered to be from among the people of Shām. He came with his father Samʿān to meet the Prophet ﷺ and he supplicated for him. He stayed in Madinah with the Prophet ﷺ for a year to gain a deeper understanding of Islam. He has narrated 17 aḥādīth may Allah ﷻ be pleased with him.

The narrator of the second ḥadīth is Wābiṣah ibn Maʿbad ibn Mālik ibn ʿUbayd al-Asadī ﷺ. He accepted Islam in the ninth year after hijrah when he came to Madinah to see the Prophet ﷺ. He was known to be a very pious person who would cry a lot. He has narrated 11 aḥādīth from the Prophet ﷺ, may Allah ﷻ be pleased with him.

IMPORTANCE

This ḥadīth is also considered to be among the concise yet comprehensive sayings of the Prophet ﷺ. In just a few words the Prophet ﷺ explained the essence of righteousness and sin. Righteousness and sin are polar opposites. al-Birr, or righteousness, is a very comprehensive concept that includes all types of goodness a person can think of. Similarly, sharr, or sin, is also a comprehensive word that includes all types of evil a person can think of.

EXPLANATION

In the first narration the Prophet ﷺ explains righteousness, or birr, as good character; being a person of morality and ethics and one who deals, speaks, and behaves with others in the best way possible. This doesn't mean that all of righteousness is encompassed by good character. It means that good character is a major aspect or part of righteousness. A person can't be considered to be righteous if they don't possess good character. Ibn ʿUmar ﷺ said that righteousness is a simple affair; it is a smiling face and a soft tongue.[226] Ibn Ḥajar mentions that good character is to be fair in one's dealings, to be soft and pleasant in one's speech, to be just in judgment, and to strive hard to do good deeds. He also mentions that good character includes

226 Ibn Rajab, *Jāmiʿ al-ʿUlūm wa al-Ḥikam*, 298

those qualities and characteristics that Allah ﷻ describes the true believers with.[227] Allah ﷻ says, "Righteousness does not consist in turning your face towards East or West. The truly good are those who believe in God and the Last Day, in the Angels, the Scripture, and the Prophets; who give away some of their wealth, however much they cherish it, to their relatives, to orphans, the needy, travelers and beggars, and to liberate those in bondage; those who keep up the prayer and pay the prescribed alms; who keep pledges whenever they make them; who are steadfast in misfortune, adversity, and times of danger. These are the ones who are true, and it is they who are aware of God."[228] There are many other verses where Allah ﷻ describes the characteristics and qualities of true believers. If a person wants to know if they are righteous they should weigh their characteristics against those mentioned in these verses.

In the second narration, the Prophet ﷺ explains righteousness as that with which the soul feels at ease and the heart feels tranquil. Meaning, a person's soul and heart feels content with it. It is not something that a person feels uneasy about or second guesses. True righteousness is part of sound human nature. If a person has a pure and sound heart then righteousness is something natural to them.

The Prophet ﷺ then explains sin as "what causes uneasiness in your heart and what you dislike others to become aware of." In this portion of the ḥadīth the Prophet ﷺ is describing two distinct signs of a sin. The first is that it causes uneasiness in a person's heart; when they are about to engage in something that is sinful there is a hesitation, nervousness, or some sort of inhibition holding them back. The second is that when a person engages in something sinful they would not want others to know about it. They feel a sense of shame and embarrassment.

The Prophet ﷺ concludes by saying, "even though people have repeatedly given their legal opinion [in its favor]." Meaning, there may be a fatwā of a scholar or several scholars that says engaging in something is permissible. However, if a person's heart feels uneasy about it they should still stay away from it for their personal contentment.

---

227 Ibn Ḥajar, *Sharḥ al-Arbaʿīn al-Nawawiyyah*, p.173

228 2:177 - لَّيْسَ الْبِرَّ أَن تُوَلُّوا وُجُوهَكُمْ قِبَلَ الْمَشْرِقِ وَالْمَغْرِبِ وَلَـٰكِنَّ الْبِرَّ مَنْ آمَنَ بِاللَّـهِ وَالْيَوْمِ الْآخِرِ وَالْمَلَائِكَةِ وَالْكِتَابِ وَالنَّبِيِّينَ وَآتَى الْمَالَ عَلَىٰ حُبِّهِ ذَوِي الْقُرْبَىٰ وَالْيَتَامَىٰ وَالْمَسَاكِينَ وَابْنَ السَّبِيلِ وَالسَّائِلِينَ وَفِي الرِّقَابِ وَأَقَامَ الصَّلَاةَ وَآتَى الزَّكَاةَ وَالْمُوفُونَ بِعَهْدِهِمْ إِذَا عَاهَدُوا ۖ وَالصَّابِرِينَ فِي الْبَأْسَاءِ وَالضَّرَّاءِ وَحِينَ الْبَأْسِ ۗ أُولَـٰئِكَ الَّذِينَ صَدَقُوا ۖ وَأُولَـٰئِكَ هُمُ الْمُتَّقُونَ

LESSONS AND BENEFITS

1. IMPORTANCE OF GOOD CHARACTER

True righteousness is not limited to devotional acts of worship such as praying, fasting, giving charity, reciting the Quran, and supplication. True righteousness includes these very important, powerful, profound, and transformative acts of worship along with good character. Good character is an essential part of Muslim identity. The way a person speaks, behaves, and interacts with others should be representative of the faith within their hearts.

2. POWER OF THE HEART

Purification of the heart from spiritual diseases such as disbelief, hypocrisy, pride, envy, greed, enmity, and love of the world is part of īmān. It plays a very significant role in one's relationship with Allah ﷻ and how they see and understand the world. A pure, clean, and sound heart provides one with clarity and allows them to distinguish between what's right and wrong. A sound and pure heart is one of the strongest means of remaining steadfast upon the straight path. It leads towards God-consciousness, steadfastness, patience, reliance, modesty, and humility.

HADITH 28

Holding On to the Sunnah

عَنْ أَبِي نَجِيحٍ الْعِرْبَاضِ بْنِ سَارِيَةَ رَضِيَ اللَّه عَنْهُ قَالَ: "وَعَظَنَا رَسُولُ اللَّهِ صلى الله عليه و سلم مَوْعِظَةً وَجِلَتْ مِنْهَا الْقُلُوبُ، وَذَرَفَتْ مِنْهَا الْعُيُونُ، فَقُلْنَا: يَا رَسُولَ اللَّهِ! كَأَنَّهَا مَوْعِظَةُ مُوَدِّعٍ فَأَوْصِنَا، قَالَ: أُوصِيكُمْ بِتَقْوَى اللَّهِ، وَالسَّمْعِ وَالطَّاعَةِ وَإِنْ تَأَمَّرَ عَلَيْكُمْ عَبْدٌ، فَإِنَّهُ مَنْ يَعِشْ مِنْكُمْ فَسَيَرَى اخْتِلَافًا كَثِيرًا، فَعَلَيْكُمْ بِسُنَّتِي وَسُنَّةِ الْخُلَفَاءِ الرَّاشِدِينَ الْمَهْدِيِّينَ، عَضُّوا عَلَيْهَا بِالنَّوَاجِذِ، وَإِيَّاكُمْ وَمُحْدَثَاتِ الْأُمُورِ؛ فَإِنَّ كُلَّ بِدْعَةٍ ضَلَالَةٌ".

رَوَاهُ أَبُو دَاوُدَ، وَالتِّرْمِذِيُّ وَقَالَ: حَدِيثٌ حَسَنٌ صَحِيحٌ.

From Abū Najīḥ al-ʿIrbāḍ ibn Sāriyah ﵁ who said that the Messenger of Allah ﷺ gave us a sermon by which our hearts were filled with fear and tears came to our eyes. So we said, "O Messenger of Allah! It is as though this is a farewell sermon, so advise us." He ﷺ said, "I advise you to have taqwā (fear) of Allah, and to listen and obey [your leader], even if a slave were to become your leader. Verily he among you who lives long will see great controversy, so you must keep to my Sunnah and to the Sunnah of the Khulafā al-Rāshidīn (the rightly guided caliphs), those who guide to the right way. Cling to it stubbornly [literally: with your molar teeth]. Beware of newly invented matters [in the religion], for verily every bidʿah (innovation) is misguidance."

Narrated by Abū Dāwūd and al-Tirmidhī, who said that it was a good and sound hadīth.

THE NARRATOR

Abū Najīḥ al-ʿIrbāḍ ibn Sāriyah ؓ is a Companion of the Prophet ﷺ from the people of al-Ṣuffah. He wanted to join the Prophet ﷺ for the battle of Tabūk but did not have the necessary provisions to do so. He, along with a group of Companions, came to the Prophet ﷺ asking for provisions but the Prophet ﷺ didn't have anything to give them. Allah ﷻ praises them in Sūrah al-Tawbah saying, "And there is no blame attached to those who came to you [Prophet] for riding animals and to whom you said, 'I cannot find a mount for you': they turned away with their eyes overflowing with tears of grief that they had nothing they could contribute."[229] He passed away in the year 75, may Allah ﷻ be pleased with him.

IMPORTANCE

In this ḥadīth, after giving a powerful, moving, and emotive reminder, the Prophet ﷺ was asked to give some farewell advice. The Prophet ﷺ gave them invaluable advice that would lead to success and happiness both in this life and the next. The Prophet ﷺ advised his companions with four very important topics: God-consciousness, following one's leaders, holding on tight to the teachings of the Prophet ﷺ, and staying away from innovations in religion.

EXPLANATION

The narrator Abū Najīḥ al-ʿIrbāḍ ibn Sāriyah ؓ starts by describing the context of the ḥadīth, "the Messenger of Allah ﷺ gave us a sermon by which our hearts were filled with fear and tears came to our eyes." The Prophet ﷺ gave them an extremely powerful and emotional reminder that had a direct effect upon their hearts. It moved them emotionally bringing them to tears. The power and emotion of the sermon made the Companions feel as if this was the farewell address of the Prophet ﷺ, so they asked him for extra advice and counsel. In response to their request the Prophet ﷺ advised them with four specific things.

229 9:92 - وَلَا عَلَى الَّذِينَ إِذَا مَا أَتَوْكَ لِتَحْمِلَهُمْ قُلْتَ لَا أَجِدُ مَا أَحْمِلُكُمْ عَلَيْهِ تَوَلَّوا وَّأَعْيُنُهُمْ تَفِيضُ مِنَ الدَّمْعِ حَزَنًا أَلَّا يَجِدُوا مَا يُنفِقُونَ

The first piece of advice was to be conscious, mindful, and aware of Allah ﷻ; to be people of taqwā. Oftentimes when the Prophet ﷺ was asked to give advice he would start off with a reminder of taqwā highlighting its importance and significance in a person's life. Taqwā is one of the most essential qualities or traits a Muslim is supposed to nurture and develop within themselves, especially in terms of their relationship with Allah ﷻ. It is the foundation of one's relationship with Allah ﷻ and the source of several other praiseworthy qualities and attributes. It results in one being conscious of Allah ﷻ at all times, in public and in private, leading towards one trying their best to obey Allah's commandments and stay away from His prohibitions.

The second piece of advice given by the Prophet ﷺ is to listen to and obey one's leader, even if they are not qualified or of a lower socioeconomic status. It is important to note that this advice is not absolute; rather it has certain conditions, limits, parameters, and boundaries. For example, the Prophet ﷺ said, "There is no obedience to the creation in the disobedience of the Creator."[230] Maintaining social order, peace, security, safety, and organization is extremely important for building a healthy and vibrant society. The absence of a proper and formal social structure, governance, and hierarchy can lead to chaos and corruption.

The Prophet ﷺ then tells his companions that in the near future they will experience difficulties, hardships, challenges, conflicts, and trials. He advises his Companions during these times to hold on tightly to his Sunnah and the Sunnah of the Rightly Guided Caliphs. He ﷺ says, "Verily he among you who lives long will see great controversy, so you must keep to my Sunnah and to the Sunnah of the Khulafa ar-Rashideen (the rightly guided caliphs), those who guide to the right way. Cling to it stubbornly [literally: with your molar teeth]." He ﷺ is advising his Companions and those that come after them to hold on to his teachings and guidance and those of the Rightly Guided Caliphs - Abū Bakr, ʿUmar, ʿUthmān, and ʿAlī - in terms of beliefs, actions, and statements.

The Prophet ﷺ ends his counsel by advising his Companions to stay away from newly introduced and invented beliefs and practices within the religion. He says, "Beware of newly invented matters [in the religion], for verily every bidʿah (innovation) is misguidance." This is similar to ḥadīth number five where ʿĀ'ishah ؓ narrates that the Prophet ﷺ said, "He who innovates

230 Aḥmad, *Musnad*, 20656

something in this matter of ours [i.e., Islam] that is not of it will have it rejected."

LESSONS AND BENEFITS

1. THE IMPORTANCE OF REMINDERS

The Prophet ﷺ is the best example of a teacher who employed several different methods and styles of teaching to convey his message. He would teach his companions with genuine care, compassion, love, concern, and sincerity. He was a very powerful and effective orator whose words would go straight to the hearts of his audience because of his sincerity, genuineness, and intelligence. He would choose the right times, moments, opportunities, and environments to convey beneficial reminders and lessons to his Companions. He would speak to them regarding topics that were relevant and real for them with wisdom.

2. PURITY OF THE COMPANIONS

The Companions of the Prophet ﷺ were absolutely amazing individuals the likes of whom history had never seen before and will never see again. Allah ﷻ praises them in the Quran when He says, "Allah is pleased with them and they are pleased with Him."[231] The Prophet ﷺ described them as the best generation. Part of what made them so special is the purity of their hearts. This can be seen in how the words of the Prophet ﷺ brought them to tears.

3. IMPORTANCE OF TAQWĀ

Please refer back to ḥadīth #18 above.

4. OBEYING THE LEADER

Islam is a comprehensive way of life that contains guidance for every single aspect of one's life, including politics. There is a whole genre of Islamic literature regarding what is known as al-Siyāsah al-Sharʿīyyah, or Islamic Politics. It discusses rules, regulations, and guidance related to political matters that are derived from the Quran and Sunnah. The objectives of these rules, regulations, and guidance is to build a healthy and vibrant society that

231 98:8 - رَّضِىَ اللَّهُ عَنْهُمْ وَرَضُوا عَنْهُ

is built upon God-consciousness, Quranic morality, ethics, principles, and values. A society that is productive, safe, secure, and peaceful.

5. THE DANGER OF BIDʿAH

Please refer back to ḥadīth #5 above.

HADITH 29

Gates of Goodness and the Path of Guidance

عَنْ مُعَاذِ بْنِ جَبَلٍ رَضِىَ اللَّه عَنْهُ قَالَ: قُلْتُ يَا رَسُولَ اللهِ! أَخْبِرْنِي بِعَمَلٍ يُدْخِلُنِي الْجَنَّةَ وَيُبَاعِدْنِي مِنْ النَّارِ، قَالَ: "لَقَدْ سَأَلْتَ عَنْ عَظِيمٍ، وَإِنَّهُ لَيَسِيرٌ عَلَى مَنْ يَسَّرَهُ اللَّهُ عَلَيْهِ: تَعْبُدُ اللَّهَ لَا تُشْرِكْ بِهِ شَيْئًا، وَتُقِيمُ الصَّلَاةَ، وَتُؤْتِي الزَّكَاةَ، وَتَصُومُ رَمَضَانَ، وَتَحُجُّ الْبَيْتَ، ثُمَّ قَالَ: أَلَا أَدُلُّك عَلَى أَبْوَابِ الْخَيْرِ؟ الصَّوْمُ جُنَّةٌ، وَالصَّدَقَةُ تُطْفِئُ الْخَطِيئَةَ كَمَا يُطْفِئُ الْمَاءُ النَّارَ، وَصَلَاةُ الرَّجُلِ فِي جَوْفِ اللَّيْلِ، ثُمَّ تَلَا: " تَتَجَافَى جُنُوبُهُمْ عَنِ الْمَضَاجِعِ " حَتَّى بَلَغَ "يَعْمَلُونَ"،[32 سورة السجدة / الأيتان : 16 و 17] ثُمَّ قَالَ: أَلَا أُخْبِرُكَ بِرَأْسِ الْأَمْرِ وَعَمُودِهِ وَذُرْوَةِ سَنَامِهِ؟ قُلْتُ: بَلَى يَا رَسُولَ اللَّهِ. قَالَ: رَأْسُ الْأَمْرِ الْإِسْلَامُ، وَعَمُودُهُ الصَّلَاةُ، وَذُرْوَةُ سَنَامِهِ الْجِهَادُ، ثُمَّ قَالَ: أَلَا أُخْبِرُكَ بِمَلَاكِ ذَلِكَ كُلِّهِ؟ فقُلْتُ: بَلَى يَا رَسُولَ اللهِ ! فَأَخَذَ بِلِسَانِهِ وَقَالَ: كُفَّ عَلَيْكَ هَذَا. قُلْتُ: يَا نَبِيَّ اللَّهِ وَإِنَّا لَمُؤَاخَذُونَ بِمَا نَتَكَلَّمُ بِهِ؟ فَقَالَ: ثَكِلَتْكَ أُمُّكَ وَهَلْ يَكُبُّ النَّاسَ عَلَى وُجُوهِهِمْ -أَوْ قَالَ عَلَى مَنَاخِرِهِمْ- إلَّا حَصَائِدُ أَلْسِنَتِهِمْ؟!".

رَوَاهُ التِّرْمِذِيُّ وَقَالَ: حَدِيثٌ حَسَنٌ صَحِيحٌ.

From Muʿādh ibn Jabal ﵁ who said: I said, "O Messenger of Allah, tell me of an act that will take me into Paradise and will keep me away from the Hellfire." He ﷺ said, "You have asked me about a great matter, yet it is easy for him for whom Allah makes it easy: worship Allah, without associating any partners with Him, establish prayer, pay zakāh, fast in Ramaḍān, and perform pilgrimage to the House." Then he ﷺ said, "Shall I not guide you towards the means of goodness? Fasting is a shield, charity wipes away sin as water extinguishes fire, and the praying of a man in the depths of the night." Then he ﷺ recited: "[Those] who forsake their beds, to invoke their Lord in fear and hope, and they spend (charity in Allah's cause) out of what We have bestowed on them. No person knows what is kept hidden for them of joy as a reward for what they used to do." [al-Sajdah, 16-17] Then he ﷺ said, "Shall I not inform you of the head of the matter, its pillar, and its peak?" I said, "Yes, O Messenger of Allah." He ﷺ said, "The head of the matter is Islam, its pillar is the prayer, and its peak is jihād." Then he ﷺ said, "Shall I not tell you of the foundation of all of that?" I said, "Yes, O Messenger of Allah." So he took hold of his tongue and said, "Restrain this." I said, "O Prophet of Allah, will we be taken to account for what we say with it?" He ﷺ said, "May your mother be bereaved of you! Is there anything that throws people into the Hellfire upon their faces — or: on their noses — except the harvests of their tongues?"

Narrated by al-Tirmidhī, who said it was a good and sound ḥadīth.

IMPORTANCE

In this ḥadīth the great Companion Muʿādh ﷺ asked the Prophet ﷺ to tell him about an act that is so great, so virtuous, and so blessed that it would grant him entrance to Paradise and keep him away from the fire. In response, the Prophet ﷺ gave him a complete program to follow and adhere to that would grant him entry into Paradise. The Prophet ﷺ provided him with a roadmap that leads straight to eternal salvation in the life of the Hereafter. The Prophet ﷺ highlights the importance of the five pillars, worship, submission, voluntary deeds, struggling in the path of Allah ﷻ, and controlling one's tongue.

EXPLANATION

The ḥadīth starts with Muʿādh ibn Jabal ﷺ making a very profound, deep, and important request. He says to the Prophet ﷺ, "Tell me about an action that will enter me into Paradise and distance me from the Hellfire." What a beautiful request. This request was made a number of times by several different Companions. The reason why they made this request is because, as believers, they realized that gaining entry into Paradise is one of their main goals in life. In the grand scheme of life this is a question that every believer should be asking themselves, "How can we get to Jannah?" It is said that this question and concern was so great that it would make the Companions uneasy from the inside.

The Prophet ﷺ responded by saying, "You have asked about a very great matter, but it is easy for those whom Allah has made it easy for." Meaning that what you asked about is a great affair, it is something important, significant, and surrounded by difficulties. However, Allah ﷻ has the ability to make it easy. He makes it easy for those people who seek His help and guidance.

The Prophet ﷺ then gives a detailed answer on how to get to Paradise and protect oneself from the Fire starting with faith and worship. "Worship Allah and don't associate anything with Him, establish prayer, pay zakāh, fast Ramaḍān and perform ḥajj." The Prophet ﷺ is telling Muʿādh ﷺ that the key to entering Paradise is performing the five pillars of Islam. That is the bare minimum required to earn Paradise. A person's entire religious practice and submission to Allah ﷻ is built upon these five pillars. In order for a building to be strong and to withstand natural disasters like earthquakes, hurricanes and tornadoes, it has to be built upon a solid foundation. If the foundation is weak, the building will fall apart. The same thing goes for our Islam. If these foundations are weak or unstable, then the entire practice of Islam will be weak and unstable. These are the basics that people have to come back to. In terms of prioritizing what's important in a person's life, these pillars should be on the top of the list. Particular importance should be given to prayer. Out of the five pillars, prayer is the one that has the most frequency.

Then the Prophet ﷺ very beautifully asked Muʿādh, "Shall I not guide you to the gates of goodness?" The pillars of Islam are the obligatory acts that an individual must perform to even have hope of entering Paradise. Now the Prophet ﷺ is telling Muʿādh about voluntary acts (extra credit) that open the doors of goodness.

The first voluntary act mentioned by the Prophet ﷺ is fasting. He says, "Fasting is a shield." One of the most powerful, profound, and transformative acts of worship in Islam is fasting. The Prophet ﷺ described it as a shield; something that protects one from earning the displeasure of Allah ﷻ. Fasting teaches individuals how to control their most instinctive, base, and carnal desires. When a person is fasting, they are in an increased state of consciousness; they are more careful about what they say and more careful about what they do. That is why fasting is related to the quality or characteristic of taqwā. It helps nurture and develop this quality, which serves as a shield of protection.

The second voluntary act highlighted by the Prophet ﷺ is charity. The Prophet ﷺ said, "Charity extinguishes sin just like water extinguishes fire." There are a lot of benefits, rewards, blessings, and virtues associated with generosity and charity. Here the Prophet ﷺ mentions one: charity extinguishes sins just like water extinguishes fire. Being charitable and generous is a way of having one's sins forgiven.

The third voluntary deed mentioned by the Prophet ﷺ is tahajjud, or voluntary prayer in the middle of the night. The Prophet ﷺ says, "And a man's prayer in the middle of the night." Then he recited, "Their sides forsake their beds to invoke their Lord in fear and hope, and they spend out of what We have bestowed on them. No person knows what is kept hidden for them of joy as a reward for what they used to do."[232] Allah ﷻ is describing those individuals who sacrifice their sleep by waking up in the middle of the night to pray. They call upon their Lord in fear of His punishment and in hope of His infinite mercy and grace. Fasting, charity, and tahajjud are all great acts of worship that have immense rewards and benefits associated with them. They are things the Prophet ﷺ was particular about doing himself.

The Prophet ﷺ then continues his answer by saying, "Shall I not tell you about the head of the matter, its pillar, and its highest part?" The Prophet ﷺ began his answer by telling Muʿādh رضي الله عنه the bare minimum it takes to get to paradise. Then he told him what the gates of goodness are; now the Prophet ﷺ is summarizing the answer. "The head of the matter is Islam (submission)." Meaning that the most important factor in attaining paradise is submission to Allah ﷻ, actualizing and internalizing Islam. Without Islam there's no hope of attaining paradise whatsoever. "Its pillar is prayer." The foundation upon which Islam, submission to Allah ﷻ, is built and upon which acceptance into paradise rests is prayer. "Its highest point is jihād." The ultimate expression of submission is to strive and struggle in the path of Allah ﷻ for righteous causes such as helping the weak, poor, and oppressed and establishing justice.

The Prophet ﷺ ends this ḥadīth with priceless advice. "Shall I not inform you of what controls all of this." He took hold of his tongue and said, "Restrain this." Muʿādh رضي الله عنه said, "O Prophet of Allah, will we be held accountable for what we say?" He ﷺ said, "May your mother be bereaved of you! Is there anything that has people thrown on their faces into the fire except that which their tongues reap?" The final piece of advice in this ḥadīth is about self-control; specifically, the ability to control one's tongue.

LESSONS AND BENEFITS

1. ULTIMATE GOAL

One of the main goals and objectives of a believer is to earn eternal salvation and gain entry into Paradise. This should be one of their primary concerns. What can they do to ensure that they are on a path towards eternal bliss and happiness? How can they protect themselves from earning the an-

232 32:16-17 - تَتَجَافَىٰ جُنُوبُهُمْ عَنِ الْمَضَاجِعِ يَدْعُونَ رَبَّهُمْ خَوْفًا وَطَمَعًا وَمِمَّا رَزَقْنَاهُمْ يُنفِقُونَ فَلَا تَعْلَمُ نَفْسٌ مَّا أُخْفِيَ لَهُم مِّن قُرَّةِ أَعْيُنٍ جَزَاءً بِمَا كَانُوا يَعْمَلُونَ

ger and displeasure of their Lord and Creator?

2. STATUS OF THE COMPANIONS

The Companions of the Prophet ﷺ were the best people to walk on the face of this earth after the Prophets and Messengers.

3. IMPORTANCE OF THE FIVE PILLARS

Please refer back to ḥadīth #3 above.

4. VOLUNTARY FASTING

One of the most virtuous and beneficial voluntary deeds a person can practice is fasting. Fasting has a profound effect upon helping one tame their desires and bring them under control. It is a shield that helps protect one's thoughts, tongue, and heart. The Prophet ﷺ would fast on Mondays and Thursdays and would encourage his companions to fast at least three days every month, the white days, which are the 13th, 14th, and 15th.

5. GENEROSITY

One of the defining qualities of a person of faith is selflessness and generosity. There are several verses of the Quran and aḥādīth of the Prophet ﷺ that encourage giving, charity, and generosity. Throughout the Quran, Allah ﷻ provides detailed descriptions of the characteristics and qualities of the people of īmān. One of those characteristics and qualities is generosity. Generosity in Islam is not limited to the amount of money one gives. It is related to the willingness to give.

6. THE NIGHT PRAYER

One of the most virtuous voluntary prayers in terms of sincerity and reward is tahajjud, which can be referred to as the night prayer. Tahajjud is the voluntary prayer one performs at night between ʿishā'a and fajr after going to sleep. The Prophet ﷺ said, "The most virtuous prayer after the obligatory prayers is the prayer of the night."[233] The Prophet ﷺ also said, "I advise you to perform the night prayer. It is the habit of the righteous before you. Truly the night prayer is a means of getting close to Allah, prevents one from sin,

233 Muslim, *k. al-Ṣiyāml, b. Faḍl ṣawm al-muḥarram*, 1163

expiates sins, and repels illness from the body."[234]

7. CONTROLLING THE TONGUE

In this ḥadīth, the Prophet ﷺ describes controlling the tongue as the foundation of self-restraint and self-control. Please refer back to ḥadīth #15 above for a discussion on the importance of controlling one's tongue.

234 al-Tirmidhī, *k. al-daʿwāt ʿan Rasūlillah* ﷺ, b., 3549

HADITH 30

The Limits and Boundaries of Allah

عَنْ أَبِي ثَعْلَبَةَ الْخُشَنِيِّ جُرْثُومِ بن نَاشِر رَضِيَ اللَّه عَنْهُ عَنْ رَسُولِ اللَّهِ صلى اللَّه عليه و سلم قَال: "إنَّ اللَّهَ تَعَالَى فَرَضَ فَرَإِضَ فَلَا تُضَيِّعُوهَا، وَحَدَّ حُدُودًا فَلَا تَعْتَدُوهَا، وَحَرَّمَ أَشْيَاءَ فَلَا تَنْتَهِكُوهَا، وَسَكَتَ عَنْ أَشْيَاءَ رَحْمَةً لَكُمْ غَيْرَ نِسْيَانٍ فَلَا تَبْحَثُوا عَنْهَا".

حَدِيثٌ حَسَنٌ، رَوَاهُ الدَّارَقُطْنِيّ "فِي سننه، وَغَيْرُهُ.

From Abū Thaʿlabah al-Khushanī — Jurthūm ibn Nāshir ﵁ — that the Messenger of Allah ﷺ said, "Verily Allah has prescribed the obligatory deeds, so do not neglect them. He has set limits; so do not go beyond them. He has forbidden things so do not violate them. And He has been silent about some things, out of mercy upon you and not out of forgetfulness, so do not seek after them."

A ḥasan ḥadīth narrated by al-Dāraquṭnī and others.

THE NARRATOR

His name is Jurthūm ibn Nāshir and he is more well-known as Abū Thaʿlabah al-Khushanī ﷺ. He is among the Companions that pledged allegiance to the Prophet ﷺ under the tree in al-Ḥudaybiyyah. The Prophet ﷺ sent him to his people, Khushaynah, and they accepted Islam at his hands. He has narrated 40 aḥādīth from the Prophet ﷺ and passed away in the year 75, may Allah ﷻ be pleased with him.

IMPORTANCE

This ḥadīth is also considered to be among the concise and comprehensive statements of the Prophet ﷺ that are few in words but extremely deep in meaning. In this ḥadīth the Prophet ﷺ explains the categories of rulings within the Sharīʿah. The Prophet ﷺ divides rulings into four categories:

1. Obligatory Acts
2. Prohibited Acts
3. Limits, and
4. Acts about which nothing has been said

It is said that anyone who acts upon this ḥadīth has gathered all the reward and is safe from punishment. A person who does these things has fulfilled the rights of the religion.

EXPLANATION

The Prophet ﷺ starts by highlighting the importance of fulfilling and performing acts and deeds that Allah ﷻ has made obligatory. He ﷺ says, "Verily Allah has prescribed the obligatory deeds, so do not neglect them." An obligatory deed or action is defined as an act the Lawgiver commands a person who is legally responsible to do in certain and binding terms. Examples of acts that are considered to be farḍ are the five daily prayers, fasting, ḥajj, zakāh, and fulfilling one's contracts. When something is farḍ it has to be done. The one who does it will be rewarded and the one who chooses not to is liable and deserving of punishment.

The Prophet ﷺ then mentions the limits and boundaries of Allah ﷻ that should not be crossed or broken. He ﷺ says, "He has set limits; so do not go beyond them." Most commentators mention that this is referring to the specific set of laws found in the Quran and Sunnah that determine the punishment for very specific crimes. The term al-ḥudūd is often translated as the fixed punishments or the divinely ordained punishments. The word ḥadd literally means a boundary or limit that separates and prevents one thing from intruding on another. Technically, within the Sharīʿah, it refers to a quantitatively fixed punishment that is imposed for a violation of the right of Allah ﷻ. In simpler terms they are fixed punishments that are prescribed by the Qur'ān and Sunnah. There are five divinely ordained punishments:

1. Ḥadd al-Zina (adultery/fornication),
2. Ḥadd al-Qadhf (accusing someone of adultery/fornication),
3. Ḥadd al-Sariqah (specific theft)
4. Ḥadd Shurb al-Khamr (consuming wine), and
5. Ḥadd al-Ḥirābah (highway robbery)

Each of these terms is referring to a very specific crime within the scope of the Shari'ah. They have been ascribed fixed punishments because they are considered to be extremely heinous crimes that are harmful to both the individual and society.

The Prophet ﷺ then reminds his Companions to stay away from those things that are prohibited. He ﷺ says, "He has forbidden things so do not violate them." A prohibition is defined as an act that has been prohibited by the Lawgiver in certain and binding terms. For example, murder, theft, consuming intoxicants, and false accusations are all ḥarām. An individual who does something that is prohibited is liable and deserving of blame and sin, but at the same time, will be rewarded for not committing those actions.

The Prophet ﷺ ends the ḥadīth by showing one of the aspects of Allah's infinite and limitless mercy. He ﷺ says, "And He has been silent about some things, out of mercy upon you and not out of forgetfulness, so do not seek after them." There are certain things that Allah ﷻ has not mentioned intentionally in order to facilitate ease and prevent unnecessary hardship and difficulty.

LESSONS AND BENEFITS

1. LEGAL RULINGS

Within the Sharīʿah, with respect to legal rulings, human conduct and behavior can be divided into five well-known categories:

1. Farḍ / Wājib (Obligatory)
2. Sunnah / Mustḥab / Mandūb (Recommended)
3. Ḥarām (Forbidden)
4. Makrūh (Disliked), and
5. Mubāḥ / Ḥalāl (Permissible)

The Ḥanafīs divide it into seven categories:

1. Farḍ (Obligatory)
2. Wājib (Mandatory)
3. Mandūb (Recommended)
4. Makrūh Tanzīhan (Slightly Disliked)
5. Makrūh Taḥrīman (Prohibitively Disliked)
6. Ḥarām (Prohibited) and
7. Mubāḥ (Permissible)

Knowing what is permissible and what is impermissible is essential for a person's practice of Islam. There is a base level of knowledge and literacy that every single Muslim should have that allows them to practice their faith and religion properly in a manner that is pleasing to Allah ﷻ. Seeking this base level of literacy is an obligation upon each and every single Muslim. As the Prophet ﷺ said, "Seeking knowledge is an obligation upon every single Muslim."[235] This does not mean that everyone has to become a scholar; rather, everyone has to learn enough knowledge that will allow them to worship their Creator properly with understanding.

2. CRIME AND PUNISHMENT

Please refer back to ḥadīth #8 above.

---

235 Ibn Mājah, *k. al-muqaddimah*, 229

3. DON'T ASK UNNECESSARY QUESTIONS

The Sharīʿah encourages asking intelligent, useful, well-thought-out, and practical questions. Good questions are described as being half of knowledge. What is discouraged is asking unnecessary questions, questions for the sake of showing off, or questions for the sake of debate and argumentation. Allah ﷻ discourages these types of questions in the Quran as well. He ﷻ says, "You who believe, do not ask about matters which, if made known to you, might make things difficult for you- if you ask about them while the Quran is being revealed, they will be made known to you- for God has kept silent about them: God is most forgiving and forbearing."[236]

---

236 يَا أَيُّهَا الَّذِينَ آمَنُوا لاَ تَسْأَلُوا عَنْ أَشْيَاءَ إِن تُبْدَ لَكُمْ تَسُؤْكُمْ وَإِن تَسْأَلُوا عَنْهَا حِينَ يُنَزَّلُ الْقُرْآنُ تُبْدَ لَكُمْ عَفَا اللَّهُ عَنْهَا ۗ وَاللَّهُ غَفُورٌ حَلِيمٌ - 5:101

HADITH 31

Zuhd

عَنْ أَبِي الْعَبَّاسِ سَهْلِ بْنِ سَعْدٍ السَّاعِدِيّ رَضِيَ اللَّه عَنْهُ قَالَ: جَاءَ رَجُلٌ إلَى النَّبِيِّ صلى اللَّه عليه و سلم فَقَالَ: يَا رَسُولَ اللَّه! دُلَّنِي عَلَى عَمَلٍ إذَا عَمِلْتُهُ أَحَبَّنِي اللهُ وَأَحَبَّنِي النَّاسُ؛ فَقَالَ: "ازْهَدْ فِي الدُّنْيَا يُحِبَّك اللهُ، وَازْهَدْ فِيمَا عِنْدَ النَّاسِ يُحِبَّك النَّاسُ".

حديث حسن، رَوَاهُ ابْنُ مَاجَهْ وَغَيْرُهُ بِأَسَانِيدَ حَسَنَةٍ.

From Abū al-ʿAbbās Sahl ibn Saʿd al-Sāʿidī ﷺ who said: A man came to the Prophet ﷺ and said, "O Messenger of Allah, direct me to an act which, if I do it, [will cause] Allah to love me and the people to love me." So he ﷺ said, "Renounce the world and Allah will love you, and renounce what the people possess and the people will love you."

A ḥasan ḥadīth narrated by ibn Mājah and others with good chains of authority.

THE NARRATOR

The narrator of this ḥadīth is Sahl ibn Saʿd al-Sāʿidī al-Anṣārī al-Khazrajī ﵁. Both him and his father were noble Companions of the Prophet ﷺ. During the days of ignorance his name was Ḥuzn, which translates as sorrow, so the Prophet ﷺ changed his name to Sahl, which means easygoing. He was only 15 years old when the Prophet ﷺ left this world and lived for a long time after that passing the age of 100. He has narrated 88 aḥādīth and passed away in the year 88, may Allah ﷻ be pleased with him.

IMPORTANCE

Ibn Ḥajr al-Haytamī writes that all of Islam revolves around four aḥādīth and this ḥadīth is one of them.[237] In this narration the Prophet ﷺ explains how to earn the love of Allah ﷻ and the love of people. The Prophet ﷺ talks about the concept of zuhd, which is usually translated as asceticism.

EXPLANATION

Sahl ﵁ asked the Prophet ﷺ to tell him about an act or deed, something he could do, so that both Allah ﷻ and people would love him. He said, "O Messenger of Allah, direct me to an act which, if I do it, [will cause] Allah to love me and the people to love me." It is natural for a person to desire to be loved by Allah ﷻ and to be liked and loved by people. Nobody wants to be someone who is disliked.

The Prophet ﷺ responded, "Be indifferent to the world, Allah will love you." The Prophet ﷺ told him that if he wants to be loved by Allah ﷻ then he should be indifferent to the world; he should have zuhd towards the dunyā. Zuhd or asceticism is to leave what a person doesn't need in this world and to be content and pleased with having what is necessary to get by. Imām al-Nawawī ﵀ defines it as leaving what is not needed in this world and doing with the necessities, piety, and leaving doubtful matters. Zuhd is an extremely important concept and an ideal that a person is supposed to work towards. Oftentimes zuhd is associated with being poor, or choosing to live a life of extreme simplicity, or choosing poverty. For instance, some people

237 Bughā and Mistū, *al-Wāfī fī Sharḥ al-Arbaʿīn al-Nawawiyyah*, p.230

think it's a sign of zuhd to wear old and used clothes or to drive an old car even though they can afford a new one. In reality zuhd is not related to how much money a person has or what material things they possess. Zuhd is related to the heart; it's not being attached to the material things of this world. Zuhd is not being in love with money, and not being obsessed with having the nicest car, clothes, watch, or shoes. Zuhd in this world is not being concerned with what has been lost and not being extremely happy with what you have been given. It all comes down to recognizing the reality of this world. The life of this world is temporary, finite, limited, and will come to an end. The life of the hereafter is a life of eternity.

The Prophet ﷺ then teaches Sahl ؓ how to become beloved to people, "and renounce what the people possess and the people will love you." Meaning, don't be covetous or desirous of other people's possessions. Don't be a person who is greedy, jealous, and envious. If a person is not concerned about people and their material possessions they will be more inclined towards them by interacting with them and conversing with them without any unfound suspicions or doubts.

LESSONS AND BENEFITS

1. THE IMPORTANCE OF ZUHD

As mentioned above, zuhd has been defined and explained by scholars in several different ways. The reality and essence of each of these definitions and explanations is that zuhd is detaching one's heart from the love of the material world and attaching one's heart to Allah ﷻ and the hereafter. Imām Aḥmad ؒ narrated from Abū Idrīs al-Khawlānī ؒ that he said, "Zuhd in this world is not to deem the permissible impermissible or by avoiding material wealth. Real zuhd is having more certainty in what is with Allah than what is in your hands and when you are afflicted with a difficulty you have more hope and concern in receiving its reward and benefits than the actual difficulty itself."[238] From this explanation it is understood that zuhd is an action of the heart. The origin of zuhd is certainty in the existence, oneness, might, power, glory, wisdom, and magnificence of Allah ﷻ that then expresses itself through one's behavior and attitude towards the life of this world. Because of this certainty in Allah ﷻ a person is not fazed or negatively affected

238 Bughā and Mistū, *al-Wāfī fī Sharḥ al-Arbaʿīn al-Nawawiyyah*, p.230

by the hardships, difficulties, and losses they experience in life. A unique way of expressing zuhd is that one's possessions are in their hands, not in their hearts. If they receive more blessings from Allah ﷻ they are grateful and if they experience any loss they are patient.

2. EARNING THE LOVE OF ALLAH ﷻ

If a person is loved by Allah ﷻ they don't need anything else in this world. Allah ﷻ will take care of them and their needs by helping, assisting, and supporting them. He will look after them by providing for them and showering them with His infinite mercy, blessings, and grace. In this ḥadīth, the Prophet ﷺ teaches one avenue or one way of earning Allah's love; by being a person of zuhd in the life of this world. Another way is by following the way of the Prophet ﷺ and internalizing his teachings. Allah ﷻ says in Sūrah Āl ʿImrān, "Say, 'If you love God, follow me, and God will love you and forgive you your sins; God is most forgiving, most merciful.'"[239]

3. EARNING THE LOVE OF OTHERS

Once Allah ﷻ loves an individual, love for them naturally enters into the hearts of others. Allah ﷻ says in Sūrah Maryam, "Truly the Lord of Mercy will give love to those who believe and do righteous deeds."[240] Those who believe in Allah ﷻ, the Messengers, life after death, perform righteous deeds, do what is pleasing to Allah ﷻ, and are steadfast in their faith, then Allah ﷻ plants love and affection for them in the hearts of others. Allah ﷻ creates an environment of mutual love and goodwill around them.

Abū Hurairah رضي الله عنه narrated that the Prophet ﷺ said, "Verily, whenever Allah loves a servant of His, He calls Jibrīl and says, "O Jibrīl, verily I love so-and-so, so love him." Thus, Jibrīl will love him. Then, he (Jibrīl) will call out to the dwellers of the heavens, "Verily, Allah loves so-and-so, so you too must love him." Then the dwellers of the heavens love him and he will be given acceptance in the earth. Whenever Allah hates a servant of His, He calls Jibrīl and says, "O Jibrīl, verily I hate so-and-so, so hate him." Thus, Jibrīl will hate him. Then, he (Jibrīl) will call out amongst the dwellers of the heavens, "Verily, Allah hates so-and-so, so you too must hate him." Then the dwellers of

---

239 3:31 - قُلْ إِن كُنتُمْ تُحِبُّونَ اللَّهَ فَاتَّبِعُونِي يُحْبِبْكُمُ اللَّهُ وَيَغْفِرْ لَكُمْ ذُنُوبَكُمْ ۗ وَاللَّهُ غَفُورٌ رَّحِيمٌ

240 19:96 - إِنَّ الَّذِينَ آمَنُوا وَعَمِلُوا الصَّالِحَاتِ سَيَجْعَلُ لَهُمُ الرَّحْمَٰنُ وُدًّا

the heavens hate him and hatred for him will be placed in the earth."[241] This is something that is experienced.

---

241 Muslim, k. *al-birr wa al-ṣilah wa al-ādāb*, b. *Idhā aḥabba Allah ʿabdan ḥabbabahu ilā ʿibādihi*, 2637

HADITH 32

No Harm

عَنْ أَبِي سَعِيدٍ سَعْدِ بْنِ مَالِكِ بْنِ سِنَانٍ الْخُدْرِيّ رَضِيَ اللَّه عَنْهُ أَنَّ رَسُولَ اللَّهِ صلى الله عليه و سلم قَالَ:"لَا ضَرَرَ وَلَا ضِرَارَ".

حَدِيثٌ حَسَنٌ، رَوَاهُ ابْنُ مَاجَهْ، وَالدَّارَقُطْنِيّ، وَغَيْرُهُمَا مُسْنَدًا. وَرَوَاهُ مَالِكٌ فِي "الْمُوَطَّإِ" عَنْ عَمْرِو بْنِ يَحْيَى عَنْ أَبِيهِ عَنْ النَّبِيِّ صلى الله عليه و سلم مُرْسَلًا، فَأَسْقَطَ أَبَا سَعِيدٍ، وَلَهُ طُرُقٌ يُقَوِّي بَعْضُهَا بَعْضًا.

From Abū Saʿīd al-Khudrī ﷺ that the Messenger of Allah ﷺ said: "There should be neither harming (ḍarar) nor reciprocating harm (ḍirār)."

A ḥasan ḥadīth narrated by ibn Mājah, al-Dāraquṭni and others as a musnad ḥadīth. It was also narrated by Mālik in al-Muwaṭṭa in mursal form from ʿAmr ibn Yaḥya, from his father from the Prophet ﷺ, but leaving Abū Saʿīd from the chain. And it has other chains of narrations that strengthen one another.

IMPORTANCE

This ḥadīth is also from the concise comprehensive sayings of the Prophet ﷺ that are few in words and extremely vast in meaning. Through these words the Prophet ﷺ establishes one of the most well-known maxims of Islamic Law, which is "there is to be no harm". Imām Abū Dāwūd ؒ mentioned that this is one of the aḥādīth around which fiqh revolves.

EXPLANATION

The Prophet ﷺ, through a few simple words, established the basis of many legal rulings within the Sharīʿah. He ﷺ said, "There should be neither harming nor reciprocating harm." The Scholars of ḥadīth have given many different explanations for the two words used by the Prophet ﷺ. Some scholars held that they both mean the same thing, which is harm. The Prophet ﷺ mentioned them together for emphasis. However, there is a principle in the Arabic language that to understand a new meaning from a word or sentence is better than understanding it as simply providing emphasis. Imam al-Nawawī ؒ mentions that ḍarar means to harm someone else and ḍirār means to reciprocate harm. That is why most translators of the ḥadīth translate it as, "There should be neither harming nor reciprocating harm." According to the commentators of this ḥadīth, harm is referring to harm that is unlawful and unjustified.

Causing any type of harm to anybody, Muslim or non-Muslim, living or non-living, animate or inanimate, plant or animal is absolutely prohibited. The reason is because causing harm is considered to be a type of oppression and as mentioned in a previous ḥadīth ẓulm is prohibited. As a matter of fact, if something is beneficial for an individual but causes harm to another it should be avoided. One of the conclusions drawn from this ḥadīth is that Allah ﷻ has not ordered or commanded anything that is harmful for human beings. Everything that has been legislated in the Sharīʿah has divine wisdom behind it and is designed to either bring benefit to mankind or prevent harm.

This narration also serves as the basis for one of the major maxims of fiqh (al-qawāʿid al-fiqhiyyah). A maxim is a general rule that applies to all of its related particulars. It is a theoretical extraction in the form of a short statement that expresses in a few words the goals and objectives of the Sharīʿah. It is a principle derived from the detailed reading of rulings of fiqh on various matters. The wordings of these maxims are usually extracted from the Quran and ḥadīth. The four schools of thought generally agree upon the main legal maxims. The purpose of legal maxims is to facilitate a better understanding of the Sharīʿah, not necessarily to derive rulings.

The legal maxim derived from this ḥadīth is that harm may neither be inflicted nor reciprocated in Islam. There are a number of other maxims that are derived from this such as:

1. Harm is eliminated to the extent that it is possible, and
2. A greater harm is eliminated by means of a lesser harm.

LESSONS AND BENEFITS

1. DON'T CAUSE HARM

An individual should try their absolute best to not be a source of harm or inconvenience to others. This is a sign that Islam has truly entered the heart of an individual. The Prophet ﷺ said, "A Muslim is one from whose tongue and hand other Muslims are safe."[242]

2. ISLAM IS A RELIGION OF EASE

Allah ﷻ, in His infinite and divine wisdom, has made Islam easy for human beings to follow, implement, and practice in their daily lives. Every single command within the Sharīʿah is designed to benefit humanity in some way and every single prohibition is designed to prevent some sort of harm. The Prophet ﷺ said, "The religion is easy."[243] Ease is a relative term. What is easy for one person may be difficult for another and what is difficult for a person may be very easy for another. What is meant by the religion being easy is that every single human being has the ability to practice it. Allah ﷻ says, "God does not burden any soul with more than it can bear."[244]

3. HARM SHOULD BE REMOVED

---

242 Bukhārī, *k. al-Riqāq, b. Al-intihā ʿan al-maʿāṣī*, 6484

243 Bukhārī, *k. al-īmān, b. Al-dīn yusr*, 39

244 لاَ يُكَلِّفُ اللَّـهُ نَفْسًا إِلاَّ وُسْعَهَا - 2:286

Another legal maxim derived from this particular ḥadīth is that harm should be removed.

HADITH 33

Burden of Proof and Court Procedure

عَنْ ابْنِ عَبَّاسٍ رَضِيَ اللَّهُ عَنْهُمَا أَنَّ رَسُولَ اللَّهِ صلى الله عليه وسلم قَالَ: "لَوْ يُعْطَى النَّاسُ بِدَعْوَاهُمْ لَادَّعَى رِجَالٌ أَمْوَالَ قَوْمٍ وَدِمَاءَهُمْ، لَكِنَّ الْبَيِّنَةَ عَلَى الْمُدَّعِي، وَالْيَمِينَ عَلَى مَنْ أَنْكَرَ".

حَدِيثٌ حَسَنٌ، رَوَاهُ الْبَيْهَقِيُّ، وَغَيْرُهُ هَكَذَا، وَبَعْضُهُ فِي "الصَّحِيحَيْنِ".

From ibn ʿAbbās ﵄ that the Messenger of Allah ﷺ said, "Were people to be given everything that they claimed, men would [unjustly] claim the wealth and lives of [other] people. But, the burden of proof is upon the claimant, and the taking of an oath is upon the one who denies."

A ḥasan ḥadīth narrated by al-Bayhaqī and others in this form, and part of it is in the two Ṣaḥīḥs.

IMPORTANCE

Regarding this ḥadīth Imām al-Nawawī ﵀ says, "This ḥadīth is a major principle from the principles of legal rulings."[1] In this narration the Prophet ﷺ gives a description of the judicial process in Islam, particularly court cases in which a claim is made against another party. The Prophet ﷺ mentions that the burden of proof is upon the claimant or the plaintiff and that swearing an oath is the responsibility of the defendant.

EXPLANATION

The Prophet ﷺ starts this narration by highlighting a certain aspect of human nature. He ﷺ says, "Were people to be given everything that they claimed, men would [unjustly] claim the wealth and lives of [other] people." By nature, human beings are drawn and attracted towards material wealth and possessions. They are greedy, jealous, and covetous by nature. If there was no system or procedure to determine the truthfulness of a person's claims, then they would falsely claim the wealth and lives of people simply to get what they want and to fulfill their desires. A claim by itself is not sufficient for a right to be recognized until it is supported with adequate proof.

The Prophet ﷺ then explains what the proper procedure is for proving the truthfulness of one's claim. He ﷺ says, "But, the burden of proof is upon the claimant, and the taking of an oath is upon him who denies." When it comes to disputes and arguments that are brought before a judge to be settled, the claimant or the plaintiff has to bring proof to corroborate their claim. In the vast majority of cases the proof has to be in the form of two male eyewitnesses or one male and two female eyewitnesses. If the claimant does not have any proof or is unable to produce any proof, then the defendant is asked to take an oath saying that what they are accused of is false. If they take the oath then the case will be decided in their favor.

LESSONS AND BENEFITS

1. JUDICIAL PROCESS IN ISLAM

As mentioned previously, Islam is a complete way of life that provides

1 Ibn Ḥajar, *Sharḥ al-Arbaʿīn al-Nawawiyyah*, 193

guidance for every sphere of human activity. Part of that guidance is the proper procedure and process for settling conflicts and disputes. In this ḥadīth, the Prophet ﷺ provides a basic outline for the judicial process in Islam. The process is fairly simple and straightforward. A person will start the process of litigation by bringing their claim to court in front of a judge. The judge will then ask the defendant if the claim is true. If they deny the claim the plaintiff will be asked to produce evidence. When a person makes a claim against someone or an allegation and the other party denies it, they are required to produce evidence. In the vast majority of cases, that evidence is in the form of eyewitnesses. If the claimant produces two male witnesses or one male and two female witnesses, then the case will be decided in their favor.

If the claimant is unable to produce witnesses, then the defendant is asked by the judge to take an oath saying that the claim is wrong or what they are accused of is false. If they take the oath, then the case will be decided in their favor. However, if the defendant refuses to take the oath then the case will be decided in the claimants favor. The reason being that if the charges weren't true there would be no reason for the defendant to refuse.

A claim in itself is not sufficient for a right to be recognized unless it is accompanied by adequate proof. The accused or defendant is also considered to be innocent until proven guilty. The Sharīʿah has also given clear definitions of who is considered the plaintiff and who is considered the defendant. The plaintiff is defined as the person who is claiming something other than what is apparent or what has not been established in the past. That is why the burden of proof is placed on them; they are claiming something that is contrary to the status quo that is subject to doubt. There are many more details to this that are beyond the scope of this short book and can be found in the larger works of Islamic Jurisprudence.

2. *OBJECTIVES OF THE SHARĪʿAH*

Please refer back to ḥadīth #8 above.

HADITH 34

Objecting to Evil

عَنْ أَبِي سَعِيدٍ الْخُدْرِيّ رَضِيَ اللَّه عَنْهُ قَالَ سَمِعْتُ رَسُولَ اللهِ صلى اللَّه عليه و سلم يَقُولُ: "مَنْ رَأَى مِنْكُمْ مُنْكَرًا فَلْيُغَيِّرْهُ بِيَدِهِ، فَإِنْ لَمْ يَسْتَطِعْ فَبِلِسَانِهِ، فَإِنْ لَمْ يَسْتَطِعْ فَبِقَلْبِهِ، وَذَلِكَ أَضْعَفُ الْإِيمَانِ".
رَوَاهُ مُسْلِمٌ.

From Abū Saʿīd al-Khudrī ﷺ who said that I heard the Messenger of Allah ﷺ say, "Whosoever of you sees an evil, let him change it with his hand; and if he is not able to do so, then [let him change it] with his tongue; and if he is not able to do so, then with his heart — and that is the weakest of faith."

Narrated by Muslim.

IMPORTANCE

This ḥadīth deals with the extremely important concept and ideal of enjoining good and forbidding evil. Enjoining good and forbidding evil is one of the defining qualities of the Muslim Ummah. The community of Muslims is considered to be the best of communities because of this particular quality or attribute. Allah ﷻ praises the Muslims saying, "[Believers], you are the best community singled out for people: you order what is right, forbid what is wrong, and believe in God."[245] Depending on the situation and circumstance, it is either a personal obligation or a communal obligation. Allah ﷻ says, "There has to be a group of people from among you who call towards good, and enjoin good and forbid evil. And it is those who are successful."[246] Even though this is such an important and virtuous act, there are a lot of rules and regulations regarding it.

EXPLANATION

In this ḥadīth, the Prophet ﷺ explains three different levels or ways of changing what is wrong depending on one's capabilities, abilities, and opportunities. The first is changing something evil or wrong physically through action. The Prophet ﷺ says, "Whoever sees an evil should change it with their hand." The word the Prophet ﷺ uses to describe what's wrong or evil is munkar. Munkar is defined as anything that is objectionable from the viewpoint of the Sharīʿah, not just sins or acts of disobedience. The opposite of munkar is maʿrūf, which is translated as good. It is any act of obedience, goodness, or righteousness that is encouraged by the Sharīʿah.

Now the question is, who is this statement addressed to? Most scholars explain that this statement is general and is addressed to all Muslims. Any Muslim who has the authority, ability, and influence to prevent evil physically is obligated to do so. Sometimes this obligation is individual and sometimes it's communal.

If a person is unable to prevent or change evil with their hands then they should speak out against it with their tongues. The Prophet ﷺ says, "If he is not able to then with his tongue." Words and speech are extremely power-

245 3:110 - كُنتُمْ خَيْرَ أُمَّةٍ أُخْرِجَتْ لِلنَّاسِ تَأْمُرُونَ بِالْمَعْرُوفِ وَتَنْهَوْنَ عَنِ الْمُنكَرِ وَتُؤْمِنُونَ بِاللَّهِ

246 3:104 - وَلْتَكُن مِّنكُمْ أُمَّةٌ يَدْعُونَ إِلَى الْخَيْرِ وَيَأْمُرُونَ بِالْمَعْرُوفِ وَيَنْهَوْنَ عَنِ الْمُنكَرِ ۚ وَأُولَٰئِكَ هُمُ الْمُفْلِحُونَ

ful and have the ability to change a person's heart and mind. As a matter of fact, there may be times when speech is more effective than action. Speaking truth to power is considered to be a very praiseworthy quality. The Prophet ﷺ said, "The best form of jihād is speaking the truth in front of a tyrant."[247] While correcting and changing through speech, it is extremely important to remember the proper etiquette and manners of doing so. A person should try their best to be wise, gentle, caring, sincere, compassionate, forbearing, forgiving, and patient. They should not be the cause of driving people further away from Allah ﷻ and religion. Rather, they should be the means of bringing people closer to Allah ﷻ. That is one of the reasons why the Prophet ﷺ taught his Companions, "Give glad tidings and don't push people away. Make things easy and don't make things difficult."[248] They should not be harsh, abrasive, rude, and impatient thus becoming a means for people to be pushed away.

There may be instances and circumstances where a person is unable to speak up for the truth and prevent or stop evil. There may be a legitimate fear of causing more harm than good or even a fear of personal harm or injury. In such circumstances it is a part of one's faith to still have a deep dislike for the evil or wrong in their heart. The Prophet ﷺ says, "If he is not able to, then with his heart and that is the weakest of faith." A person should never become desensitised or apathetic towards evil. Munkar is never something that is acceptable to a believer. Although they may be unable to do something about it physically or verbally, they still dislike it and disapprove of it with their hearts. If they had the ability to change it physically or verbally, they would.

A very similar ḥadīth is narrated by ibn Masʿūd رضي الله عنه that the Prophet ﷺ said, "There is no Prophet that was sent to a nation before me except that he had from his nation helpers and companions. They would follow his way and implement his orders. Then came afterwards generations that would say what they did not do and do what they did not say. Whoever struggled against them with his hand is a believer. Whoever struggled against them with his tongue is a believer. Whoever struggled against him with his heart is a believer. Beyond that there is no faith, even equivalent to the amount of

247 Abū Dāwūd, *k. al-malāḥim, b. al-amr wa al-nahy*, 4344

248 Muslim, *k. al-jihād wa al-siyar, b. fī al-amr bi al-taysīr wa tark al-tanfīr*, 1732

a mustard seed."[249]

LESSONS AND BENEFITS

1. ENJOINING GOOD AND FORBIDDING EVIL

One of the defining qualities of the Muslim Ummah is its general concern for the health, well-being, safety, security, protection, and prosperity of the community. Islam is not an individualistic religion; it has a very strong social and communal aspect to it. One of the ways in which the community works towards creating a healthy society built on the values and ideals of the Quran and the teachings of the Prophet ﷺ is through enjoining good and forbidding evil. Reminding one another of their obligations and responsibilities towards Allah ﷻ and those around them. Stopping people from engaging in destructive behavior that can negatively affect an individual and others physically, emotionally, or spiritually. This can be both a communal as well as an individual responsibility.

2. INVITING TOWARDS ALLAH WITH WISDOM AND GENTLENESS

Allah ﷻ says in Sūrah al-Naḥl, "[Prophet], call [people] to the way of your Lord with wisdom and good teaching. Argue with them in the most courteous way, for your Lord knows best who has strayed from His way and who is rightly guided."[250] In this verse Allah ﷻ reminds the Prophet ﷺ about three very important components of inviting and reminding others; wisdom, good teaching, and courtesy. This includes being sincere, having genuine concern, gentleness, compassion, and leniency. However, there are circumstances and situations that require one to be a little more stern and sometimes even harsh. Sufyān al-Thawrī said, "No one should enjoin good and forbid evil until they have three qualities; they are gentle with what they enjoin and forbid, they are just with what they enjoin and forbid, and they have knowledge of what they enjoin and forbid."

---

249 Muslim, *k. al-īmān, b. Bayān kawn al-nahy ʿan al-munkar min al-īmān...*, 50

250 ادْعُ إِلَىٰ سَبِيلِ رَبِّكَ بِالْحِكْمَةِ وَالْمَوْعِظَةِ الْحَسَنَةِ ۖ وَجَادِلْهُم بِالَّتِي هِيَ أَحْسَنُ ۚ إِنَّ رَبَّكَ هُوَ أَعْلَمُ بِمَن ضَلَّ عَن سَبِيلِهِ ۖ وَهُوَ أَعْلَمُ بِالْمُهْتَدِينَ - 16:125

3. DANGER OF NOT PREVENTING EVIL

Islam places a lot of importance upon the health, well-being, and morality of society as a whole. If evil is allowed to continue unabated without any opposition it will lead to the moral decay of society. The people of faith and righteousness will shoulder some of the blame for that moral decay because they didn't try to stop it. Allah ﷻ says, "Those Children of Israel who defied [God] were rejected through the words of David, and Jesus, son of Mary, because they disobeyed, they persistently overstepped the limits, and they did not forbid each other to do wrong. How vile their deeds were!"[251] There are also several aḥādīth that convey the same message. The Prophet ﷺ said, "If any man is among a people in whose midst he does acts of disobedience, and, though they are able to make him change (his acts), they do not, Allah will smite them with punishment before they die."[252] The Prophet ﷺ also gave a beautiful example of how the actions of community members affect each other. He ﷺ said, "The example of the person abiding by Allah's order and restrictions in comparison to those who violate them is like the example of those persons who drew lots for their seats in a boat. Some of them got seats in the upper part, and the others in the lower. When the latter needed water, they had to go up to bring water (and that troubled the others), so they said, 'Let us make a hole in our share of the ship (and get water) saving those who are above us from troubling them.' So, if the people in the upper part left the others to do what they had suggested, all the people of the ship would be destroyed, but if they prevented them, both parties would be safe."[253]

4. KNOWLEDGE

It is extremely important for a believer's actions to be based on knowledge and understanding. This is especially true when teaching or advising others. In order for a person to enjoin good and forbid evil they have to know and understand what is considered to be good and evil within the scope of the Sharīʿah.

---

251 78-79 : 5 لُعِنَ الَّذِينَ كَفَرُوا مِن بَنِي إِسْرَائِيلَ عَلَىٰ لِسَانِ دَاوُودَ وَعِيسَى ابْنِ مَرْيَمَ ۚ ذَٰلِكَ بِمَا عَصَوا وَّكَانُوا يَعْتَدُونَ كَانُوا لَا يَتَنَاهَوْنَ عَن مُّنكَرٍ فَعَلُوهُ ۚ لَبِئْسَ مَا كَانُوا يَفْعَلُونَ

252 Abū Dāwūd, *k. al-malāḥim, b. al-amr wa al-nahy*, 4339

253 Bukhārī, *k. al-sharikah, b.hal yuqraʿ fī al-qismah wa al-istihām fīhi*, 2493

5. DEALING WITH VALID DIFFERENCES OF OPINION

No one should be rebuked, reprimanded, scolded, corrected, advised, or yelled at for following a valid difference of opinion. The Shāfiʿī's developed a beautiful saying, "Issues of ijtihād are not rejected with force, and it is not allowed for anyone to force people to follow their opinion regarding them. Rather they should discuss them using scholarly proofs. If one opinion appears correct to a person, he should follow it, and whoever follows the opposite opinion then there's no blame on him." When it comes to these types of issues people should be left to practice what they've learned as long as it's a valid opinion. Sufyān al-Thawrī ﷺ said, "If you see someone doing something that's disagreed upon and you have another opinion, don't stop him." Imām Mālik ﷺ remarked, "If you try to change them from what they are familiar with to something they're not familiar with, they will consider that disbelief." Another important principle is "censuring a matter that is not impermissible is impermissible itself."[254]

254 All of the statements regarding accepting valid differences of opinion are taken from ʿAwwamah's *Adab al-Ikhtilāf*.

HADITH 35

Brotherhood

عَنْ أَبِي هُرَيْرَةَ رَضِيَ اللَّه عَنْهُ قَالَ: قَالَ رَسُولُ اللَّهِ صلى الله عليه و سلم " لَا تَحَاسَدُوا، وَلَا تَنَاجَشُوا، وَلَا تَبَاغَضُوا، وَلَا تَدَابَرُوا، وَلَا يَبِعْ بَعْضُكُمْ عَلَى بَيْعِ بَعْضٍ، وَكُونُوا عِبَادَ اللَّهِ إخْوَانًا، الْمُسْلِمُ أَخُو الْمُسْلِمِ، لَا يَظْلِمُهُ، وَلَا يَخْذُلُهُ، وَلَا يَكْذِبُهُ، وَلَا يَحْقِرُهُ، التَّقْوَى هَاهُنَا، وَيُشِيرُ إلَى صَدْرِهِ ثَلَاثَ مَرَّاتٍ، بِحَسْبِ امْرِئٍ مِنْ الشَّرِّ أَنْ يَحْقِرَ أَخَاهُ الْمُسْلِمَ، كُلُّ الْمُسْلِمِ عَلَى الْمُسْلِمِ حَرَامٌ: دَمُهُ وَمَالُهُ وَعِرْضُهُ".

رَوَاهُ مُسْلِمٌ.

From Abū Hurairah ﷺ who said that the Messenger of Allah ﷺ said, "Do not envy one another, and do not inflate prices for one another, and do not hate one another, and do not turn away from one another, and do not undercut one another in trade, but [rather] be slaves of Allah and brothers [amongst yourselves]. A Muslim is the brother of a Muslim: he does not oppress him, nor does he fail him, nor does he lie to him, nor does he hold him in contempt. Taqwā (piety) is right here [and he pointed to his chest three times]. It is evil enough for a man to hold his Muslim brother in contempt. The whole of a Muslim is inviolable for another Muslim: his blood, his property, and his honor."

Narrated by Muslim.

IMPORTANCE

This is an extremely important and practical ḥadīth that explains how believers are supposed to behave and interact with one another. It is an extremely deep and beautiful saying of the Prophet ﷺ that provides practical steps on how to attain true brotherhood and sisterhood. If Muslims follow this advice of the Prophet ﷺ, they will truly find their love, respect, appreciation, and honor increase for one another. The Prophet ﷺ has repeatedly mentioned that Islam is not just a set of beliefs and rituals. It includes morals and manners. True faith and taqwā are expressed through how people deal with one another. Brotherhood and Sisterhood in Islam aren't just ideals, rather they are practical goals that the community has to work towards attaining.

EXPLANATION

In this narration, the Prophet ﷺ informs his blessed Companions of nine things they should completely avoid when dealing with one another; actions that lead towards ill-will, hard feelings, and disunity. The Prophet ﷺ emphasizes that the relationship between believers is like the relationship of blood and kinship; they are all part of one big family.

The first thing the Prophet ﷺ advises is not to have ḥasad, envy or jealousy, towards one another. Ḥasad is usually translated as envy or jealousy. It is one of the major diseases of the heart. As a matter of fact, some scholars consider it to be the root of all spiritual diseases. Most scholars agree that it is the first manifestation of wrongdoing and the first cause of disobedience against Allah ﷻ. It is one of the first sins ever committed. It is the reason why Satan refused to prostrate to Adam. It is what drove Satan to become Satan.

Ḥasad is when a person hates to see anyone better off than them. Some scholars define it as hoping or wishing that someone's blessings are taken away from them; to dislike a blessing that someone else has received and hoping that they lose it. It is such a dangerous sin that it eats up good deeds. The Prophet ﷺ said, "Beware of ḥasad. Ḥasad eats good deeds like fire eats wood."[255] Not only is it spiritually harmful, but it is extremely harmful to

255 Abū Dāwūd, *k. al-adab, b. fī al-ḥasad*, 4903

relationships. It can be the root cause of conflicts between spouses, siblings, friends, and families.

The second thing the Prophet ﷺ prohibits is najash, which is translated as artificially raising prices against one another. Najash is a type of interference in a sale where a third party who is not interested in purchasing the product offers a higher price to drive up the price of the product. For example, Bakr owns a cellphone store and he has one of his friends, Aḥmad, offer a higher price whenever a customer comes in. ʿUmar walks into the store and Bakr offers to sell him a cellphone for $100. Before he can accept the offer, Aḥmed interferes and says he will pay $150 for it. If ʿUmar really wants it he will offer to match that price or pay even more. The intention behind this scheme is to benefit the seller or harm the buyer. It is prohibited because it is dishonest, unethical, and a form of cheating and deceiving the buyer. Not only is it causing financial harm to the customer but it can also lead towards conflict and dispute.

The Prophet ﷺ then mentions a general prohibition against having hatred for one another. "And do not hate one another." It is not permissible for believers to have hatred or dislike for one another in any way, shape, or form. The believers are a single community or a single family that is supposed to interact with each other with mutual love, respect, honor, and kindness. Allah ﷻ says, "The believers are brothers, so make peace between your two brothers and be mindful of God, so that you may be given mercy."[256] Having love for one another is an expression of one's īmān. The Prophet ﷺ said, "By the One in whose Hand is my soul, none of you will enter Paradise until you believe. And you will not truly believe until you love one another. Shall I not guide you towards an affair that if you do it you will love one another? Spread salām among each other."[257] This is one of the reasons why it is so important to avoid things that will lead towards hatred and ill-will such as backbiting and gossip.

The Prophet ﷺ then says, "And don't turn your backs to one another." This is referring to boycotting, ignoring, or cutting off relations completely from another Muslim because of a conflict or dispute. It is prohibited to avoid a person for more than three days, especially if they are avoiding them because of some personal reason. The Prophet ﷺ said, "It is not permissible

256 49:10 - إِنَّمَا الْمُؤْمِنُونَ إِخْوَةٌ فَأَصْلِحُوا بَيْنَ أَخَوَيْكُمْ ۚ وَاتَّقُوا اللَّهَ لَعَلَّكُمْ تُرْحَمُونَ

257 Abū Dāwūd, *k. al-adab, b. fī ifshā al-salām*, 5193

for a man to boycott his brother for more than three nights."[258]

The fifth prohibition mentioned by the Prophet ﷺ is, "Do not interfere in one another's transactions." This is referring to interfering in another person's business transactions. For example, someone purchases a book for ten dollars. Then during the time in which they are allowed to return the book, another individual comes and offers to sell the same book to them for five dollars. Another example is if the price has been agreed upon between the buyer and seller yet the transaction hasn't taken place. Then another person comes and interferes saying that they will sell them the same product or better for cheaper. The Prophet ﷺ is emphasizing the importance of ethics in business. In Islam business is conducted in a manner that is both fair and ethical.

The Prophet ﷺ then clarifies the main purpose or objective behind these five specific prohibitions. He ﷺ says, "And be Servants of Allah as brothers." Avoiding envy, hatred, and unethical business practices leads towards creating an environment of mutual love, respect, and honor. The Prophet ﷺ is reminding the believers that they are all servants of Allah ﷻ and part of that servitude is to treat each other as family. "A Muslim is the brother of a Muslim." This is a very powerful and profound statement. The bond that ties believers together is stronger and deeper than blood. It is the bond of faith; belief in Allah ﷻ and His Messenger ﷺ.

Since the believers are like family they have rights upon each other and responsibilities towards one another. That is why there are so many aḥadīth that encourage engaging in actions and behaviors that strengthen this bond of brotherhood and sisterhood such as spreading salām, exchanging gifts, inviting each other, and sharing in times of happiness and sorrow. Similarly, there are several aḥādīth that highlight actions and behaviors that should be avoided because they lead towards enmity and conflict.

In this ḥadīth, the Prophet ﷺ highlights four severe matters that lead towards conflict, dislike, and disunity: wronging another person (ẓulm), betrayal (khadhlān), lying (kidhb), and belittling (iḥtiqār). The Prophet ﷺ says, "He doesn't wrong him. He doesn't fail him in times of need. He doesn't lie to him. He doesn't belittle him." Ẓulm is translated as injustice, oppression, or wrongdoing. Here it refers to wronging someone else in any way, shape, or form. For a more detailed discussion on ẓulm please see ḥadīth #24.

---

258 Bukhārī, *k. al-adab, b. al-hijrah*, 6076

Kadhlān refers to betraying or abandoning someone in worldly or religious affairs. For example, not helping someone who is being wronged despite having the ability to do so. Another example is not advising someone who is engaging in something wrong despite having the ability to do so. This shows that a person has no care or concern for another person's well-being, safety, protection, and happiness in this world or the next.

Lying is considered to be one of the major sins of the tongue. It is impermissible to lie and fabricate stories in order to fool or deceive someone. Honesty and integrity are hallmarks of a true believer. The Prophet ﷺ describes lying as one of the hallmarks and signs of a hypocrite. The Prophet ﷺ also says, "It is great treachery that you should tell your brother something and have him believe you when you are lying."[259]

Belittling others, mocking, ridiculing, and making fun of them is a major sign of arrogance, pride, and conceit. It is a sign that a person believes that they are somehow better than the person they are belittling. The Prophet ﷺ said, "It is enough evil for a person to belittle their Muslim brother." The Prophet ﷺ also said, "Pride is rejecting the truth and disdaining people."[260]

The Prophet ﷺ then very beautifully highlights the basis, foundation, or catalyst behind staying away from all of these prohibitions; taqwā, being mindful, conscious, and aware of Allah ﷻ. If a person is mindful and conscious of Allah in their social interactions they will find it easy to follow this counsel and guidance from the Prophet ﷺ. The Prophet ﷺ points to his heart three times saying "taqwā is here" to clarify that it is an action of the heart; it is not something that someone wears on their sleeve. It is not possible to know if a person has taqwā simply from their outer appearance. Taqwā is born from having deep conviction in the existence and oneness of Allah ﷻ and recognizing and internalizing that He is the All-Knowing, the All-Hearing, and the All-Seeing. By being conscious and aware that everything a person says and does is being recorded and that on the Day of Judgment they will stand before Allah ﷻ and be held accountable. This consciousness and awareness then drives a person to try their best to obey the commands of Allah ﷻ and stay away from His prohibitions.

The ḥadīth ends with the Prophet ﷺ declaring the sanctity of a Muslim's life, wealth, and honor. "The entire Muslim is inviolable to another; his

---

259 Abū Dāwūd, *k. al-adab, b. fī al-maʿārīḍ*, 4971

260 Muslim, *k. al-īmān, b. taḥrīm al-kibr wa bayānihi*, 91

blood, wealth, and honor." As mentioned previously, the life, wealth, and honor of a Muslim are considered to be sacred inviolable rights. The Prophet ﷺ highlighted this throughout his various sermons during the farewell pilgrimage.

LESSONS AND BENEFITS

1. UNITY AND MUTUAL LOVE

Please see ḥadīth #13 above.

2. AVOIDING ENVY AND JEALOUSY

Please see ḥadīth #13 above.

3. ETHICAL BUSINESS PRACTICES

Economic activity - buying, selling, leasing, hiring, renting, loans, partnerships, general financial contract, debt - is a very important and crucial part of human life. Economic activity is also governed by divine guidance through the Quran and Sunnah. Sometimes the guidance is very specific and detailed and sometimes it is more general. Within a general economy, Islam recognizes the concepts of private ownership, profit motive, and market forces such as supply and demand. However, it has placed certain restrictions such as the prohibition of interest, gambling, hoarding, dealing in unlawful goods or services, short sales, speculative transactions, cheating, and deception. These rules and regulations are designed to fulfill higher objectives such as maintaining economic balance in society, justice, fairness, safeguarding against deception and harm, and the distribution of wealth. Business practices should be fair and ethical.

4. TAQWA

Please refer back to ḥadīth #18 above.

5. SANCTITY OF A MUSLIM

Please refer back to ḥadīth #8 and 14 above.

HADITH 36

Helping Others and Seeking Knowledge

عَنْ أَبِي هُرَيْرَةَ رَضِيَ اللَّه عَنْهُ عَنْ النَّبِيِّ صلى اللَّه عليه و سلم قَالَ: "مَنْ نَفَّسَ عَنْ مُؤْمِنٍ كُرْبَةً مِنْ كُرَبِ الدُّنْيَا نَفَّسَ اللَّهُ عَنْهُ كُرْبَةً مِنْ كُرَبِ يَوْمِ الْقِيَامَةِ، وَمَنْ يَسَّرَ عَلَى مُعْسِرٍ، يَسَّرَ اللَّهُ عَلَيْهِ فِي الدُّنْيَا وَالْآخِرَةِ، وَمَنْ سَتَرَ مُسْلِمًا سَتَرَهُ اللهُ فِي الدُّنْيَا وَالْآخِرَةِ ، وَاَللَّه فِي عَوْنِ الْعَبْدِ مَا كَانَ الْعَبْدُ فِي عَوْنِ أَخِيهِ، وَمَنْ سَلَكَ طَرِيقًا يَلْتَمِسُ فِيهِ عِلْمًا سَهَّلَ اللَّهُ لَهُ بِهِ طَرِيقًا إلَى الْجَنَّةِ، وَمَا اجْتَمَعَ قَوْمٌ فِي بَيْتٍ مِنْ بُيُوتِ اللَّهِ يَتْلُونَ كِتَابَ اللَّهِ، وَيَتَدَارَسُونَهُ فِيمَا بَيْنَهُمْ؛ إلَّا نَزَلَتْ عَلَيْهِمْ السَّكِينَةُ، وَغَشِيَتْهُمْ الرَّحْمَةُ، وَ حَفَّتْهُمْ المَلاَئِكَة، وَذَكَرَهُمْ اللَّهُ فِيمَنْ عِنْدَهُ، وَمَنْ أَبطَأَ بِهِ عَمَلُهُ لَمْ يُسْرِعْ بِهِ نَسَبُهُ".

رَوَاهُ مُسْلِمٌ بهذا اللفظ.

From Abū Hurayrah ﵁ that the Prophet ﷺ said: "Whoever relieves the distress/difficulty of a believer from the difficulties of this world, then Allah will remove a difficulty from the difficulties of the Day of Judgment for him. And whoever alleviates the need of a needy person, Allah will alleviate his needs in this world and the Hereafter. Whoever conceals the faults of a Muslim, Allah will conceal his faults in this life and the next. And Allah will aid His slave so long as he aids his brother. And whoever follows a path to seek knowledge therein, Allah will make easy for him a path to Paradise. No people gather together in one of the Houses of Allah, reciting the Book of Allah and studying it among themselves, except that tranquility descends upon them, mercy envelops them, the angels surround them, and Allah mentions them amongst those who are with Him. And whoever is slowed down by his actions, will not be hastened forward by his lineage."

Narrated by Muslim in these words.

IMPORTANCE

This is a very beautiful and eloquent ḥadīth that discusses the virtues, rewards, and blessings of three very important deeds: helping others, seeking knowledge, and studying the Quran. Imām al-Nawawī ﷺ says, "This is an extremely important ḥadīth that brings together several branches of knowledge, principles, and manners." Ibn ʿAlān adds "and virtues, benefits, and rulings." The Prophet ﷺ also mentions important acts that strengthen the bonds of brotherhood and sisterhood. The previous ḥadīth mentioned the prohibition of all kinds of harm and abuse and this one encourages aid, protection, and support of others.

EXPLANATION

The ḥadīth starts with the Prophet ﷺ describing the amazing reward in store for those who are selfless and try their best to help others. The Prophet ﷺ says, "Whoever relieves the distress/difficulty of a believer from the difficulties of this world, then Allah will remove a difficulty from the difficulties of the Day of Judgment for him. And whoever alleviates the need of a needy person, Allah will alleviate his needs in this world and the Hereafter. Whoever conceals the faults of a Muslim, Allah will conceal his faults in this life and the next. And Allah will aid His slave so long as he aids his brother." The Prophet ﷺ mentions three ways in which a person can help and assist someone else; relieving distress, alleviating needs, and concealing faults.

Relieving distress or difficulty is referring to any type of difficulty or hardship that a person faces in their daily life. A difficulty or hardship can be physical, financial, psychological, emotional, or spiritual. If a person helps ease the difficulties and hardships of others in this life, then Allah ﷻ will remove the difficulties and hardships of the Day of Judgment. Obviously those difficulties are infinitely more difficult than the hardships of this world.

Alleviating the needs of a needy person refers to helping them monetarily by providing them with money, food, clothes, or shelter. It also refers to helping a person who is in debt. The reward for doing so is that Allah ﷻ alleviates that person's needs both in this world and the next.

Every human being has their own personal faults, shortcomings, and weaknesses. Making mistakes, sinning, and slipping up are part of human nature. When a person commits a sin in private, that is between them and Allah ﷻ. It is something between them and their Creator and they are encouraged to seek forgiveness and repent. That is why believers are encouraged to not publicize their sins or faults. They are also taught not to search for people's faults and encouraged to conceal others' sins, faults, and private affairs as well. If a person conceals the private and non-harmful faults of others, Allah ﷻ will conceal their faults in this world and on the Day of Judgment.

The Prophet ﷺ then highlights one of the many blessings and virtues associated with seeking knowledge. "Whoever travels a path seeking knowledge, Allah will make the path to Paradise easy for them." According to ḥadīth scholars the knowledge being referred to in this narration is knowledge that brings one closer to Allah ﷻ and increases their love for the Prophet ﷺ. This would include studying the Islamic disciplines such as Tafsīr (Quranic Exegesis), ʿUlūm al-Quran (Quran Studies), Ḥadīth Studies, Fiqh (Jurisprudence), Uṣūl al-Fiqh (Principles of Islamic Jurisprudence), ʿAqīdah (Theology), Sīrah (Prophetic Biography), and Tazkiyah (Purification of the Soul). It could also include the study of Biology, Chemistry, Physics or any other subject that increases one's love for Allah ﷻ and His Messenger ﷺ. Whoever travels a path seeking this knowledge, Allah ﷻ makes the path to Paradise easy for that person. One of the reasons for that is because a person who learns this knowledge refines their character, manners, behavior, and understanding. If they act upon their knowledge they are on the path to becoming among the people of Allah ﷻ; people of taqwā, patience, forbearance, gratitude, humility, and generosity. It also helps one obey the commands of Allah ﷻ and stay away from His prohibitions because that knowledge allows them to know what is right and wrong, required, recommended, permissible, discouraged, and impermissible.

The Prophet ﷺ concludes this ḥadīth by highlighting four distinct virtues or rewards for reciting and studying the Quran together in the masjid: tranquility, mercy, being surrounded by Angels, and honorific mention.

Nuzūl al-Sakīnah means calmness, peace, tranquility, contentment, and ease descends upon the gathering. This is something that can be experienced and felt. Oftentimes life is very hectic, busy, and stressful. Several things happen throughout the day that create anxiety, stress, and worry which cause hearts and minds to be preoccupied and distracted. When a person comes to the masjid, the house of Allah ﷻ, the most beloved of places to Allah ﷻ, and they sit down and connect their heart to His words, they feel a sense of relief. They find solace, peace, contentment, tranquility, comfort, and reassurance in the words of Allah ﷻ. Allah ﷻ describes the Quran as a cure and healing for what is inside our hearts.

The second blessing described is that mercy covers them. This is referring to the divine infinite mercy of Allah ﷻ. The mercy of Allah ﷻ is something that is absolutely unique and amazing. It is infinite, never-ending, and limitless as opposed to human mercy, which is limited and finite. It encompasses every single thing in this universe, and it is the key to entering Paradise. The Prophet ﷺ said, "Your deeds alone will never enter you into Paradise." The Companions asked, "Not even you O Messenger of Allah?" He said, "Not even me, unless Allah ﷻ covers me with His mercy."[261]

The third blessing described for reciting and studying the Quran together in the masjid is that Angels surround that gathering. Other narrations mention that they fill up all of the empty space and when there's no space left they continue to gather on top of each other until they reach the heavens. The Prophet ﷺ is describing a phenomenon from the world of the unseen; something human beings are unable to see but experience.

The fourth blessing mentioned is that Allah ﷻ mentions each of the individuals in that gathering by name. This is a great and amazing honor. Allah ﷻ, the Lord of the Heavens and the Earth, acknowledges their efforts and mentions them by name. There is absolutely nothing better to do than spending time learning the Quran and attaching one's heart to it.

LESSONS AND BENEFITS

1. SERVING AND BENEFITING OTHERS

As mentioned before, Islam is a religion of community. It provides teaching, guidance, counsel, manners, etiquettes, morals, principles, and values that are designed to create a healthy, vibrant, and wholesome community and society. A community or society can't be healthy and wholesome unless it is built upon the foundations of mutual love, cooperation, togetherness, service, and unity. There should be this willingness and desire to help

261 Bukhārī, *k. al-marḍā, b. Tamannī al-marīḍ al-mawt*, 5673

and serve others physically, financially, emotionally, and spiritually. Allah ﷻ says, "help one another to do what is right and good; do not help one another towards sin and hostility. Be mindful of God, for His punishment is severe."[262] The Prophet ﷺ said, "Truly the believer for another believer is like a building; they provide strength to one another."[263]

One of the greatest and most virtuous acts a person can engage in is serving and helping others. The Prophet ﷺ said, "Among the best of deeds is to make a believer happy; to clothe them if they are unclothed, to feed them if they are hungry, and to fulfill their needs."[264] The reward for doing so as mentioned in the ḥadīth is receiving the help, assistance, and support of Allah ﷻ.

2. THE IMPORTANCE OF KNOWLEDGE

The importance of seeking knowledge, learning, and understanding within Islam cannot be emphasized enough. The first words revealed to the Prophet ﷺ were, "Read with the name of your Lord who created." Since the beginning of revelation, the practice of Islam has always been built upon knowledge. There is no way to know and recognize Allah ﷻ, to love the Prophet ﷺ, and to understand this way of life without learning. That is one of the reasons why the Prophet ﷺ described seeking knowledge as the path to Paradise. Allah ﷻ praises the people of knowledge in the Quran saying, "God will raise up, by many degrees, those of you who believe and those who have been given knowledge: He is fully aware of what you do."[265] Allah ﷻ also says, "It is those of His servants who have knowledge who stand in true awe of God. God is almighty, most forgiving."[266]

In another version of this ḥadīth the Prophet ﷺ says, "Whoever follows a path in the pursuit of knowledge, Allah will make easy for him a path to Paradise. The angels lower their wings in approval of the seeker of knowledge, and everyone in the heavens and on earth prays for forgiveness for the seeker of knowledge, even the fish in the sea. The superiority of the scholar over the worshipper is like the superiority of the moon above all other heav-

262 5:2 - وَتَعَاوَنُوا عَلَى الْبِرِّ وَالتَّقْوَىٰ ۖ وَلَا تَعَاوَنُوا عَلَى الْإِثْمِ وَالْعُدْوَانِ ۚ وَاتَّقُوا اللَّهَ ۖ إِنَّ اللَّهَ شَدِيدُ الْعِقَابِ

263 Bukhārī, *k. al-ṣalāh, b. Tashbīk al-aṣābiʿ fī al-masjid wa ghayrihi*, 481

264 al-Mundhirī, *al-Targhīb wa al-Tarhīb*, 3:346

265 58:11 - يَرْفَعِ اللَّهُ الَّذِينَ آمَنُوا مِنكُمْ وَالَّذِينَ أُوتُوا الْعِلْمَ دَرَجَاتٍ ۚ وَاللَّهُ بِمَا تَعْمَلُونَ خَبِيرٌ

266 35:28 - إِنَّمَا يَخْشَى اللَّهَ مِنْ عِبَادِهِ الْعُلَمَاءُ ۗ إِنَّ اللَّهَ عَزِيزٌ غَفُورٌ

enly bodies. The scholars are the heirs of the Prophets, for the Prophets did not leave behind dinars or dirhams, rather they left behind knowledge, so whoever takes it has taken a great share."[267] The Prophet ﷺ describes the scholars as the heirs of the Prophets.

There are several aḥādīth that describe the virtues, rewards, and blessings associated with seeking knowledge. These narrations are designed to create a sense of zeal, motivation, and enthusiasm for spending time, energy, and effort in the pursuit of knowledge. The Prophet ﷺ teaches that seeking knowledge is an obligation. He ﷺ says, "Seeking knowledge is an obligation upon every Muslim."[268] This doesn't mean that everyone has to become a scholar; rather, everyone has to learn enough knowledge that will allow them to worship their Creator properly with understanding.

3. *STUDYING THE QURAN*

One of the words used by Allāh ﷻ to describe the Qur'ān is mubārak, or blessed. This one-word description of the Qur'ān is actually very comprehensive. Every single aspect of the Qur'ān is blessed: its words, meanings, style, stories, commands, and prohibitions. Its recitation, memorization, interpretation, learning, and teaching are all acts of worship that bring huge amounts of rewards and blessings.

Part of its blessings is that those who learn it and teach it to others are considered to be the best of people. The Prophet ﷺ said, "The best amongst you are those who learn the Qur'ān and teach it." For every single letter of the Qur'ān that is recited, a person is rewarded with a good deed that is multiplied by ten. "Whoever recites a letter from the book of Allāh, then for them is a good deed, and a good deed is multiplied by ten. I am not saying that Alif lām mīm is one letter, but alif is a letter, lām is a letter, and mīm is a letter." The Qur'ān will intercede for its companion on the Day of Judgment. "Recite the Qur'ān because it will come as an intercessor for its companion on the Day of Judgment." Through the Qur'ān, some nations are elevated while others are lowered.

There are several other narrations that mention the virtues, blessings, and rewards for reciting the words of Allah ﷻ. It is clear from these narrations that reading the Quran is not like reading any other book. That is be-

267 Ibn Mājah, *al-Muqaddimah*, 223

268 Ibn Mājah, *al-Muqaddimah*, 224

cause the Quran is not simply a book; it is the divine speech of Allah ﷻ -- His words revealed to the Prophet ﷺ. It is the last and final revelation sent for the guidance of humanity for all times and all places. It is the primary source of beliefs, rituals, ethics, morals, and laws in Islam. Our entire lives as Muslims revolve around the teachings of the Quran. The primary objective of the Quran is for us to think, ponder, and reflect over its meanings. As Allah ﷻ tells us, "[This is] a blessed Book which We have revealed to you, [O Muḥammad], that they might reflect upon its verses and that those of understanding would be reminded."[269]

The Quran is first and foremost a book of guidance. It contains guidance for every single aspect of human life. It contains a detailed explanation of what humanity needs in terms of guidance, success both in this life and the next and salvation. Allah ﷻ says, "This revelation is no fabrication: it is a confirmation of the truth of what was sent before it; an explanation of everything; a guide and a blessing for those who believe."[270] It should be treated as a personal guidebook: a roadmap towards faith, practice, morality, ethics, God-consciousness, obedience, worship, paradise, and essentially the Divine. One should take the time to read, reflect and ponder over the meanings of the verses and then internalize their message through practice. "We have made it easy to learn lessons from the Quran: will anyone take heed?"[271]

4. IMPORTANCE OF THE MASJID

The masjid is not just simply a place for performing prayer together in congregation; that is definitely one of its functions, but not the only. It is a community space that should also be used for education, counselling, social services, and building relationships all with the intention of remembering Allah ﷻ. The masjid is the most beloved place to Allah ﷻ on the face of this Earth.

In Sūrah al-Nūr, Allah ﷻ tells us, "In houses that Allah has commanded to be raised, and where His name is remembered and His purity is pronounced, in the morning and evening."[272] This verse is speaking about those who have been guided to and by the light of Allah ﷻ; the people of knowl-

---

269 38:29 - كِتَابٌ أَنزَلْنَاهُ إِلَيْكَ مُبَارَكٌ لِّيَدَّبَّرُوا آيَاتِهِ وَلِيَتَذَكَّرَ أُولُو الْأَلْبَابِ

270 12:111 - مَا كَانَ حَدِيثًا يُفْتَرَىٰ وَلَـٰكِن تَصْدِيقَ الَّذِى بَيْنَ يَدَيْهِ وَتَفْصِيلَ كُلِّ شَىْءٍ وَهُدًى وَرَحْمَةً لِّقَوْمٍ يُؤْمِنُونَ

271 54:17 - وَلَقَدْ يَسَّرْنَا الْقُرْآنَ لِلذِّكْرِ فَهَلْ مِن مُّدَّكِرٍ

272 24:36 - فِي بُيُوتٍ أَذِنَ اللَّـهُ أَن تُرْفَعَ وَيُذْكَرَ فِيهَا اسْمُهُ يُسَبِّحُ لَهُ فِيهَا بِالْغُدُوِّ وَالْآصَالِ

edge and guidance, al-Muhtadūn. Allah ﷻ mentions in the previous verse, "Allah guides to His light whom He wills."[273] The commentators of the Quran mention that the word "houses" in this verse is referring to masājid. Ibn 'Abbas says, "The 'houses' are those masājid that are dedicated to the worship of Allah. And verily, the masājid light up the earth for the inhabitants of the heavens, just as stars light up the heavens for the inhabitants of the earth." Allah ﷻ has commanded the believers to build and establish centers of worship. The word adhina comes from idhn, which means to allow or give permission. However, here it means commanded and ordered. Ibn Kathīr mentions that it means Allah ﷻ has ordered believers to establish masājid; build them, honor them, fill them, and take care of them. It is a direct command to establish, build, attend, and honor the masājid. That is one of the reasons why the reward for helping build a masjid is so great. The Prophet ﷺ said, "Whoever builds a masjid seeking the pleasure of Allah, Allah will build him a house in paradise."[274] The word turfaʿ in the verse carries two meanings; building and honoring.

The last part of the verse explains the primary role of the masājid, "And where His name is remembered and His purity is pronounced, in the morning and evening." The masjid is a place where the name of Allah ﷻ is mentioned. This includes all types of remembrance; praying, recitation of the Quran, teaching and learning about our religion, fiqh, ḥadīth, tafsīr, sermons, and lectures. "And His purity is pronounced in the morning and evening." Meaning, the masjid is a place of prayer and worship. Through this verse we learn that the primary purpose, the primary role of a masjid is to serve as a place for the remembrance and worship of Allah ﷻ.

---

273 24:35 - يَهْدِى اللَّهُ لِنُورِهِ مَن يَشَاءُ

274 Ibn Mājah, *k. al-masājid wa al-jamāʿāt, b. man banā lillāhi masjidan*, 736

HADITH 37

Allah's Grace and Justice

عَنْ ابْنِ عَبَّاسٍ رَضِيَ اللَّهُ عَنْهُمَا عَنْ رَسُولِ اللَّهِ صلى الله عليه
و سلم فِيمَا يَرْوِيهِ عَنْ رَبِّهِ تَبَارَكَ وَتَعَالَى، قَالَ: "إِنَّ اللَّهَ كَتَبَ
الْحَسَنَاتِ وَالسَّيِّئَاتِ، ثُمَّ بَيَّنَ ذَلِكَ، فَمَنْ هَمَّ بِحَسَنَةٍ فَلَمْ يَعْمَلْهَا
كَتَبَهَا اللَّهُ عِنْدَهُ حَسَنَةً كَامِلَةً، وَإِنْ هَمَّ بِهَا فَعَمِلَهَا كَتَبَهَا اللَّهُ عِنْدَهُ
عَشْرَ حَسَنَاتٍ إِلَى سَبْعِمِائَةِ ضِعْفٍ إِلَى أَضْعَافٍ كَثِيرَةٍ، وَإِنْ هَمَّ
بِسَيِّئَةٍ فَلَمْ يَعْمَلْهَا كَتَبَهَا اللَّهُ عِنْدَهُ حَسَنَةً كَامِلَةً، وَإِنْ هَمَّ بِهَا
فَعَمِلَهَا كَتَبَهَا اللَّهُ سَيِّئَةً وَاحِدَةً".

رَوَاهُ الْبُخَارِيُّ، وَمُسْلِمٌ فِي "صحيحيهما" بهذه الحروف.

From ibn 'Abbās ☙, from the Messenger of Allah ﷺ, from what he has related from his Lord: "Verily Allah the Most High has written down the good deeds and the evil deeds, and then explained it (by saying): 'Whosoever intended to perform a good deed, but did not do it, then Allah writes it down with Himself as a complete good deed. And if he intended to perform it and then did perform it, then Allah writes it down with Himself as ten good deeds up to seven hundred times, up to many times multiplied. And if he intended to perform an evil deed, but did not do it, then Allah writes it down with Himself as a complete good deed. And if he intended it (i.e., the evil deed) and then performed it, then Allah writes it down as one evil deed.'"

Narrated by al-Bukhārī and Muslim in their two Ṣaḥīḥ collections in these words.

IMPORTANCE

This is a very beautiful, eloquent, and profound ḥadīth qudsī that highlights the infinite grace and mercy of Allah ﷻ along with His ultimate justice. It provides a general principle for the scale that Allah ﷻ uses for reward and punishment. Allah ﷻ categorizes deeds into four broad categories: good deeds, bad deeds, firm resolve to do a good deed, and firm resolve to do a bad deed.

EXPLANATION

The narration starts by Allah ﷻ explaining that He has already decreed and decided the reward for good deeds and the punishment for bad deeds, "Verily Allah the Most High has written down the good deeds and the evil deeds." Allah ﷻ then clarifies and explains what that decree and decision is.

"Whosoever intended to perform a good deed, but did not do it, then Allah writes it down with Himself as a complete good deed." If a person makes a firm intention to perform a good deed, but for some reason or another they are unable to do so, Allah ﷻ from His infinite mercy and grace will still give them the reward of one good deed.

If a person actually performs the good deed the reward for it will automatically be multiplied by ten. Allah ﷻ says, "Whoever has done a good deed will have it ten times to his credit."[275] That is the bare minimum. The reward can be doubled and multiplied up to 700 times more and beyond. "And if he intended to perform it and then did perform it, then Allah writes it down with Himself as from ten good deeds up to seven hundred times, up to many times multiplied."

If a person intends to perform an evil deed and then they decide not to do it out of the fear of Allah ﷻ it gets recorded as one good deed. "And if he intended to perform an evil deed, but did not do it, then Allah writes it down with Himself as a complete good deed." Allah ﷻ says, "And whoever has done a bad deed will be repaid only with its equivalent- they will not be wronged."[276] Again, this is from the infinite and limitless mercy and grace of Allah ﷻ. If a person does an evil deed it gets recorded as one single evil deed, and this

---

275 6:160 - مَن جَاءَ بِالْحَسَنَةِ فَلَهُ عَشْرُ أَمْثَالِهَا

276 6:160 - وَمَن جَاءَ بِالسَّيِّئَةِ فَلاَ يُجْزَى إِلاَّ مِثْلَهَا وَهُمْ لاَ يُظْلَمُونَ

is from the ultimate and infinite justice of Allah ﷻ. "And if he intended it [i.e., the evil deed] and then performed it, then Allah writes it down as one evil deed."

LESSONS AND BENEFITS

1. INFINITE GRACE AND MERCY OF ALLAH

The system of reward and punishment instituted by Allah ﷻ is an expression of His infinite mercy and grace.

2. ULTIMATE JUSTICE AND FAIRNESS OF ALLAH

Reward and punishment are a reality; they are part of belief in the hereafter. Allah ﷻ will reward the righteous believers through His infinite and limitless mercy and grace and will hold others accountable through His infinite justice.

3. POWER OF INTENTION

Please refer back to ḥadīth #1.

4. CLASSIFICATION OF THOUGHTS

Scholars have classified the thoughts that come to a person's heart and mind into five types:

1. al-Hājis
2. al-Khāṭir
3. Ḥadīth al-Nafs
4. al-Hamm
5. al-ʿAzm

al-Hājis is defined as a fleeting thought that comes to a person's mind involuntarily and then immediately leaves. It is not given much thought and it leaves their mind quickly. al-Khāṭir is described as a thought that comes to the mind by itself and stays for a short period of time; however, it doesn't reach the level of the person thinking about doing it or not. It stays for a few moments then leaves. Ḥadīth al-Nafs is a thought that comes to a person's mind, stays, and leads to the individual contemplating and weighing whether they should do it or not. However, both sides are equal. These three levels of thought come to a person involuntarily; they have no control over it. That is why there is no reward or punishment associated with them. Reward and punishment are only associated with things that a person controls and does by choice.

al-Hamm is when a person thinks about doing a deed and makes the decision to do it. However, the decision isn't very strong. In this case a person is rewarded for thinking about it, even if they don't do it. In the case of a bad deed, they are rewarded for not acting upon it. al-ʿAzm is a firm resolve and decision to actually act or not act upon the thought.

HADITH 38

Getting Close to Allah ﷻ

عَنْ أَبِي هُرَيْرَة رَضِيَ اللَّه عَنْهُ قَالَ: قَالَ رَسُول اللَّهِ صلى الله عليه و سلم إنَّ اللَّهَ تَعَالَى قَالَ: "مَنْ عَادَى لِي وَلِيًّا فَقْد آذَنْتُهُ بِالْحَرْبِ، وَمَا تَقَرَّبَ إلَيَّ عَبْدِي بِشَيْءٍ أَحَبَّ إلَيَّ مِمَّا افْتَرَضْتُهُ عَلَيْهِ، وَلَا يَزَالُ عَبْدِي يَتَقَرَّبُ إلَيَّ بِالنَّوَافِلِ حَتَّى أُحِبَّهُ، فَإِذَا أَحْبَبْتُهُ كُنْتُ سَمْعَهُ الَّذِي يَسْمَعُ بِهِ، وَبَصَرَهُ الَّذِي يُبْصِرُ بِهِ، وَيَدَهُ الَّتِي يَبْطِشُ بِهَا، وَرِجْلَهُ الَّتِي يَمْشِي بِهَا، وَلَئِنْ سَأَلَنِي لَأُعْطِيَنَّهُ، وَلَئِنْ اسْتَعَاذَنِي لَأُعِيذَنَّهُ".
رَوَاهُ الْبُخَارِيُّ.

From Abū Hurairah ﵁ who said that the Messenger of Allah ﷺ said, "Verily Allah the Most High has said: 'Whosoever shows enmity to a walī (close servant) of Mine, then I have declared war against him. And My servant does not draw near to Me with anything more beloved to Me than the religious duties I have obligated upon him. And My servant continues to draw near to me with voluntary deeds until I love him. When I love him, I am his hearing with which he hears, and his sight with which he sees, and his hand with which he strikes, and his foot with which he walks. Were he to ask [something] of Me, I would surely give it to him; and were he to seek refuge with Me, I would surely grant him refuge.'"

Narrated by al-Bukhārī.

IMPORTANCE

This narration is also classified as a ḥadīth qudsī; the words are those of the Prophet ﷺ and the meanings are inspired directly from Allah ﷻ. This ḥadīth explains how an individual can draw near to Allah ﷻ and become among those whom He loves. It provides a roadmap for how to become a walī; a close intimate servant of Allah ﷻ. It also explains some of the great rewards and benefits associated with being among the close servants of Allah ﷻ. Imām al-Shawkānī رحمه الله says this ḥadīth contains several benefits for those who truly understand it and contemplate its meanings properly.[277] al-Ṭūkhī says that this ḥadīth is the foundation for journeying to Allah ﷻ, recognizing Him, and loving Him.[278] It provides guidance on how to internalize īmān, act upon Islam, and reach iḥsān.

EXPLANATION

Allah ﷻ starts off this statement with a severe warning to those people who have enmity and hatred towards His awliyā, or His close and intimate servants. "Whosoever shows enmity to a wali (close friend) of Mine, then I have declared war against him." What is meant by a walī in this ḥadīth is a true and sincere believer, a person who has faith and taqwā. That is how Allah ﷻ Himself defines a walī in the Quran. He ﷻ says, "Listen! The friends of Allah shall have no fear, nor shall they grieve. Those who have believed and have been conscious of Allah."[279] Allah ﷻ is announcing that whoever harms, has enmity or hatred towards a walī, then He is at war with them. When Allah ﷻ is at war with someone He completely and utterly destroys them. Allah ﷻ then tells His servants how they can become His special servants.

"My servant has not come near to Me with anything more beloved to Me than what I have made obligatory upon him." Meaning that the best way to get closer to Allah ﷻ and to increase one's love for Allah ﷻ is by fulfilling those things He has made obligatory. Fulfilling one's obligations towards Allah ﷻ and others, whether it is praying, fasting, giving charity, or being kind

277 al-Bughā and Mistū, *al-Wāfī fī Sharḥ al-Arbaʿīn al-Nawawiyyah*, 335

278 al-Bughā and Mistū, *al-Wāfī fī Sharḥ al-Arbaʿīn al-Nawawiyyah*, 335

279 10 :62-63 - أَلَاَ إِنَّ أَوْلِيَاءَ اللَّهِ لاَ خَوْفٌ عَلَيْهِمْ وَلاَ هُمْ يَحْزَنُونَ الَّذِينَ آمَنُوا وَكَانُوا يَتَّقُونَ

to our parents is the absolute most important thing to do. If a person wants to be loved by Allah ﷻ, if they want to earn His love and mercy then they have to do what He has commanded them to do. In terms of prioritizing what actions are most important for a person to do, then the obligations top the list. Allah ﷻ is the One who decided that His servants must perform these deeds, and He is the One that is telling them that He is most pleased by these deeds. Part of this is staying away from what Allah ﷻ has prohibited. ʿUmar ؓ said, "The most virtuous deed is to perform the deeds Allah has made obligatory and to stay away from what Allah has forbidden."

Allah ﷻ then continues to explain how a servant can get even closer to Him, so much so that He begins to love them. "And my servant continues drawing near to Me with voluntary deeds until I love him." Not only does a walī fulfill their obligations to Allah ﷻ, but they also continue to do a lot of voluntary deeds. They try to get as much extra credit as they can. Performing extra deeds is proof of a person's sincerity and their willingness to draw closer to Allah ﷻ. In general, a person becomes closer to another by doing more than the minimum, more than what was simply required. This is what gains them their love and gaining the love of Allah ﷻ is one of the most important goals of a Muslim. The goal of a Muslim in everything they do is to earn the love, mercy, pleasure, and forgiveness of Allah ﷻ.

Once a person gains the love of Allah ﷻ then they are set both in this world and the next. "If I love him, then I am his hearing with which he hears, his seeing with which he sees, his hand with which he touches, and his leg with which he walks." Once Allah ﷻ loves a person then He makes him busy with his remembrance, obedience, and protects him from Shaytan. He uses his limbs for obedience. What this means is that Allah ﷻ protects his sight, his hearing, his hands and feet from being used for acts of disobedience. A person will not listen to what Allah ﷻ has not allowed them to listen to, they will not look at what they're not supposed to look at, they won't use their hands for what they're not supposed to, and they will not use their legs except for what Allah ﷻ has allowed. Once a person reaches this level they truly become a walī of Allah ﷻ. Their whole being, internal and external, becomes obedient to Allah ﷻ.

Allah ﷻ then mentions some of the rewards of the individuals who reach this level. "And if he asks Me, then I will indeed give him. If he were to seek refuge with Me, I will surely give him refuge." Allah ﷻ highlights two distinct virtues: their supplications will be answered and they will be protected by Allah ﷻ.

LESSONS AND BENEFITS

1. STRIVING FOR EXCELLENCE

A person should never be complacent with their current level of knowledge, understanding, faith, and practice. There should always be a desire to advance and improve one's relationship with Allah ﷻ. A person should have lofty goals and actively work towards reaching them. One of those goals is to become a close intimate servant of Allah ﷻ as highlighted in this ḥadīth.

2. PRIORITIES

It is important for a person to recognize and set priorities when it comes to religious practices and one's relationship with Allah ﷻ. The absolute most important thing for a person to take care of is their obligations towards Allah ﷻ and towards others.

3. VOLUNTARY DEEDS

One of the best ways of drawing near to Allah ﷻ is through voluntary deeds. This can include extra prayers throughout the night and day, fasting on Mondays and Thursdays, regular charity, seeking knowledge, and serving humanity.

HADITH 39

Excused

عَنْ ابْنِ عَبَّاسٍ رَضِيَ اللَّهُ عَنْهُمَا أَنَّ رَسُولَ اللَّهِ صلى الله عليه و سلم قَالَ: "إنَّ اللَّهَ تَجَاوَزَ لِي عَنْ أُمَّتِي الْخَطَأَ وَالنِّسْيَانَ وَمَا اسْتُكْرِهُوا عَلَيْهِ".

حَدِيثٌ حَسَنٌ، رَوَاهُ ابْنُ مَاجَهْ، وَالْبَيْهَقِيّ.

From ibn ʿAbbās ﵄ that the Messenger of Allah ﷺ said, "Indeed Allah on my behalf has pardoned my nation for mistakes, forgetfulness, and what they are forced to do."

A ḥasan hadīth narrated by ibn Mājah, and al-Bayhaqī and others.

IMPORTANCE

This is an important ḥadīth that deals with a specific rule or principle that plays a major role in legal rulings. It deals with the topic of personal responsibility; is a person responsible and accountable for something they do mistakenly, out of forgetfulness, or are forced to do? It demonstrates one of the ways in which Allah ﷻ has removed hardship from people. Imām al-Nawawī رحمه الله says regarding this ḥadīth that it is inclusive of several benefits and important matters. If all of them were to be gathered a book could be compiled.[280]

EXPLANATION

In this ḥadīth the Prophet ﷺ says that Allah ﷻ through His infinite mercy and grace, as a favor and blessing upon the Prophet ﷺ, has overlooked and excused what believers do by mistake, forgetfulness, and coercion. Meaning, if someone involuntarily does something wrong because of a mistake, forgetfulness, or coercion they will not be deserving of blame in this world and they will not be held accountable in the world to come.

This same message is highlighted by Allah ﷻ Himself in the Quran. Allah ﷻ says in Sūrah al-Baqarah, "God does not burden any soul with more than it can bear: each gains whatever good it has done, and suffers its bad- 'Lord, do not take us to task if we forget or make mistakes. Lord, do not burden us as You burdened those before us. Lord, do not burden us with more than we have strength to bear. Pardon us, forgive us, and have mercy on us. You are our Protector, so help us against the disbelievers.'"[281] Allah ﷻ also says in Sūrah al-Aḥzāb, "You will not be blamed if you make a mistake, only for what your hearts deliberately intend; God is most forgiving and merciful."[282]

It is important to note that what is overlooked and forgiven is the sin of the action and being held accountable for it in the life of the hereafter. As for the consequence of the action in this world, then it may still be applicable.

---

280 al-Bughā and Mistū, *al-Wāfī fī Sharḥ al-Arbaʿīn al-Nawawiyyah*, 335

281 2:286 - لَا يُكَلِّفُ اللَّهُ نَفْسًا إِلَّا وُسْعَهَا ۚ لَهَا مَا كَسَبَتْ وَعَلَيْهَا مَا اكْتَسَبَتْ ۗ رَبَّنَا لَا تُؤَاخِذْنَا إِن نَّسِينَا أَوْ أَخْطَأْنَا ۚ رَبَّنَا وَلَا تَحْمِلْ عَلَيْنَا إِصْرًا كَمَا حَمَلْتَهُ عَلَى الَّذِينَ مِن قَبْلِنَا ۚ رَبَّنَا وَلَا تُحَمِّلْنَا مَا لَا طَاقَةَ لَنَا بِهِ ۖ وَاعْفُ عَنَّا وَاغْفِرْ لَنَا وَارْحَمْنَا ۚ أَنتَ مَوْلَانَا فَانصُرْنَا عَلَى الْقَوْمِ الْكَافِرِينَ

282 33:5 - وَلَيْسَ عَلَيْكُمْ جُنَاحٌ فِيمَا أَخْطَأْتُم بِهِ وَلَٰكِن مَّا تَعَمَّدَتْ قُلُوبُكُمْ ۚ وَكَانَ اللَّهُ غَفُورًا رَّحِيمًا

For example, if someone misses a prayer unintentionally either because they forgot or by mistake, they will not be sinful. However, they will still have to make the prayer up. The Prophet ﷺ said, "He who forgets the prayer should perform it when they remember it. There is no expiation for it, except this." [283]This will especially be the case if someone was wronged or some property was damaged.

LESSONS AND BENEFITS

1. ACCOUNTABILITY

Every sane adult is known as a mukallaf; an individual that is legally responsible in front of Allah ﷻ. Meaning, their actions and statements are being recorded and they will be held accountable for them on the Day of Judgment. A person will be held accountable for whatever they do voluntarily. They will not be held accountable in the life of the hereafter for what they do by mistake, forgetfulness, or coercion.

2. INFINITE MERCY AND GRACE OF ALLAH ﷻ

Refer back to ḥadīth #37 above.

283 Muslim, *k. al-masājid wa mawāḍiʿ al-ṣalāh, b. Qaḍā al-ṣalāh al- fā'itah wa istiḥbāb taʿjīlihā,* 684

HADITH 40

Be a Stranger in This World

عَنْ ابْن عُمَرَ رَضِىَ اللَّهُ عَنْهُمَا قَالَ: أَخَذَ رَسُولُ اللَّهِ صلى الله عليه و سلم بِمَنْكِبِي، وَقَالَ: "كُنْ فِي الدُّنْيَا كَأَنَّك غَرِيبٌ أَوْ عَابِرُ سَبِيلٍ". وَكَانَ ابْنُ عُمَرَ رَضِىَ اللَّهُ عَنْهُمَا يَقُولُ: إذَا أَمْسَيْت فَلَا تَنْتَظِرْ الصَّبَاحَ، وَإِذَا أَصْبَحْتَ فَلَا تَنْتَظِرْ الْمَسَاءَ، وَخُذْ مِنْ صِحَّتِك لِمَرَضِكَ، وَمِنْ حَيَاتِك لِمَوْتِكَ.

رَوَاهُ الْبُخَارِيُّ.

From ʿAbdullah ibn ʿUmar ﷺ who said that the Messenger of Allah ﷺ took me by the shoulder and said, "Be in this world as if you are a stranger or a traveler." Ibn ʿUmar ﷺ used to say, "In the evening do not expect [to live until] the morning, and in the morning do not expect [to live until] the evening. Take [advantage of] your health before times of sickness, and [take advantage of] your life before your death."

Narrated by al-Bukhārī.

IMPORTANCE

This ḥadīth is also among the concise yet comprehensive sayings of the Prophet ﷺ that convey extremely deep and profound meanings. The Prophet ﷺ is describing how the believers are supposed to view life in this world. It is a very powerful reminder that the life of this world is short, temporary, and fleeting and that the life of the hereafter is eternal. It is a powerful and eloquent reminder to prepare for the Day that neither wealth nor family will benefit except for one who comes with a pure heart. It is described as a very noble ḥadīth, great in status, full of lessons, reminders, and morals.

EXPLANATION

Ibn 'Umar ﵁ mentions that the Prophet ﷺ took him by the shoulder and told him, "Be in this world as if you are a stranger or a traveler." During this time ibn 'Umar was a young adolescent child and the Prophet ﷺ taking him by the shoulder was a sign of love, genuine care, and concern. The Prophet ﷺ did so to make sure that he felt comfortable and was paying very careful attention.

The Prophet ﷺ then gave Ibn 'Umar ﵁ advice on how to understand and view the temporary and finite life of this world. He told him to live in this world as a stranger or a traveler. A stranger is described as a person whom one does not know or with whom one is not familiar. A believer is a stranger in the life of this world; they are uncomfortable, uneasy, and unfamiliar with their surroundings. They feel as if they are in a place where they don't belong far away from their friends and family. That is because their real home, their place of permanent residence, is in the life of the hereafter in Paradise.

A traveler is a person who is on a temporary journey with the ultimate goal of returning home. Since their journey is temporary they try their best to pack as lightly as possible not taking too many things with them that will slow them down. They also try their best to reach their destination as quickly as possible and return home without any stops or delays. The same is the attitude or mindset of the believer in the life of this world. They are simply travelers in the life of this world on a journey to the life of the hereafter. Just as a traveler prepares for their journey, a believer prepares for their journey to the hereafter.

The Prophet ﷺ is essentially advising ibn 'Umar ؓ to not attach his heart to the life of this world; that he is not a permanent resident here and that this world and everything it contains will eventually come to an end. The real life is the life of the Hereafter. That is why this particular ḥadīth is so deep and profound. If a person reflects over its meanings and tries their best to act upon it they will be successful in this world and the next. If a person implements this ḥadīth in their daily life it will transform them into a slave of Allah ﷻ instead of a slave of this world.

Ibn 'Umar ؓ understood this advice of the Prophet ﷺ extremely well. He had internalized its meanings and tried his best to live by it. That is why after narrating this ḥadīth he would say, "In the evening do not expect [to live until] the morning, and in the morning do not expect [to live until] the evening. Take [advantage of] your health before times of sickness, and [take advantage of] your life before your death." Ibn 'Umar ؓ is encouraging people to take advantage of their time, good health, and life. A person shouldn't take their time and good health in this world for granted. Time and good health are very precious, valuable, and limited commodities and no one knows how much of it they have. Death can literally call upon them at any time, unexpectedly.

LESSONS AND BENEFITS

1. LOVE OF THE WORLD

One of the most powerful and constant reminders throughout the Quran is that the life of this world is temporary. In several places throughout the Quran Allah ﷻ reminds mankind about the reality of the life of this world and the next. They are made to realize that this world is temporary, fleeting, and will eventually come to an end. And that the life to come, the life of the hereafter, is a life of eternity. Allah ﷻ says, "My people, the life of this world is only a brief enjoyment; it is the Hereafter that is the lasting home."[284] "Say, The enjoyment of this world is little, and the Hereafter is better for he who fears Allah."[285] "But you prefer the worldly life, while the Hereafter is better and more enduring."[286] "And this worldly life is not but diversion and amuse-

---

284   40:39 - يَا قَوْمِ إِنَّمَا هَـٰذِهِ الْحَيَاةُ الدُّنْيَا مَتَاعٌ وَإِنَّ الْآخِرَةَ هِيَ دَارُ الْقَرَارِ

285   4:77 - قُلْ مَتَاعُ الدُّنْيَا قَلِيلٌ وَالْآخِرَةُ خَيْرٌ لِمَنِ اتَّقَى

286   17:16-17 : 87 - بَلْ تُؤْثِرُونَ الْحَيَاةَ الدُّنْيَا وَالْآخِرَةُ خَيْرٌ وَأَبْقَى

ment. And indeed, the home of the Hereafter - that is the [eternal] life, if only they knew."[287] "And the worldly life is not but amusement and diversion; but the home of the Hereafter is best for those who fear Allah, so will you not reason?"

The Quran constantly reminds humanity to not be fooled, tricked, and deceived by the life of this world. "And what is the life of this world except the enjoyment of delusion?"[288] "O mankind, indeed the promise of Allah is truth, so let not the worldly life delude you and be not deceived about Allah by the Deceiver."[289]

One of the most consuming and powerful diseases of the heart is love of the world. Ḥasan al-Baṣrī ﵀ said, "Love of the world is the origin of every sin."[290] If a person were to get to the root cause of every single sin they will find that it is the love of this world. It is the reason for that one glance, the reason for cheating on that one exam, the reason behind backbiting, or the reason for missing fajr yesterday.

The word "dunyā" literally translates as "the world". It shares the same root letters as the verb danā/yadnū, which means to be near or to be close. It can also mean to be low or lowly. This world is called the dunya because of its nearness or because of its lowliness. It signifies the enjoyments, blessings or good of the present world or life; worldly blessings or prosperity. The term is used to refer to temporal things or possessions; earthly things or concerns. It is not just the world and everything it contains. Rather, it is everything that pleases the self and does not lead to merit in the life to come. This can include wealth, property, material possessions, clothes, shoes, jewelry, televisions, cell phones, tablets, watches, cars, homes, food and drink, the opposite gender, sports, and anything else that may take a person away from remembrance of the life to come. Anything in this world that distracts a person from their true purpose in life can be classified as dunya.

It is important to note that the world, the dunyā, is not something that is inherently evil. The Prophet ﷺ prohibited vilification of the world. He ﷺ said, "Do not curse the world, for Allah created the world, and the world is a means to reaching the knowledge of Allah." The world is just like any other

---

287 29:64 - وَمَا هَـٰذِهِ الْحَيَاةُ الدُّنْيَا إِلَّا لَهْوٌ وَلَعِبٌ ۚ وَإِنَّ الدَّارَ الْآخِرَةَ لَهِيَ الْحَيَوَانُ ۚ لَوْ كَانُوا يَعْلَمُونَ

288 3:185 - وَمَا الْحَيَاةُ الدُّنْيَا إِلَّا مَتَاعُ الْغُرُورِ

289 35:5 - يَا أَيُّهَا النَّاسُ إِنَّ وَعْدَ اللَّـهِ حَقٌّ ۖ فَلَا تَغُرَّنَّكُمُ الْحَيَاةُ الدُّنْيَا ۖ وَلَا يَغُرَّنَّكُم بِاللَّـهِ الْغَرُورُ

290 Suyūṭī, *al-Jāmiʿ al-Ṣaghīr*, 3646

tool; it can be used for both good and bad. This world and everything that it contains is a means to reach our goal or destination. It is not the goal or destination itself.

Love of this world blinds a person and makes them forget that their goal is salvation in the life of the hereafter. Since people become so blind to this reality they end up making the means the goal. An Islamic tradition attributed to ʿIsā ﷺ states, "The world is a bridge; so pass over it to the next world, but do not try to build on it." The world and all of its enjoyments, pleasures and distractions have been made to look attractive. The reality is that what Allah ﷻ has reserved for His servants in the hereafter is much better.

2. *TAKE ADVANTAGE OF HEALTH AND TIME*

As mentioned above, two of the most valuable and precious blessings Allah ﷻ has given to any human being are health and time. Oftentimes these two blessings are taken for granted and end up being under-utilized or even wasted. The Prophet ﷺ said, "There are two blessings that most people are deceived by; good health and free time."[291] The Prophet ﷺ also advised his companions, "Take advantage of five before five; youth before old age, health before illness, wealth before poverty, free time before becoming occupied, and life before death."[292]

3. *THE PROPHET ﷺ AS A TEACHER AND MENTOR*

Not only is the Prophet ﷺ the best example of a teacher, but he is also the best example of a mentor. He taught his companions using several different methods of teaching and nurtured them into God-conscious, moral, upright, ethical, principled, and courageous individuals. Within a period of 23 years the Prophet ﷺ produced the best generation of people to walk on the face of this earth. He ﷺ said, "The best of generations is my generation, then the one after it, and then the one after it."[293] The Prophet ﷺ nurtured, trained, and educated amazing individuals, both men and women, the likes of whom history had never seen before, and will perhaps never see again. The Prophet ﷺ didn't write or produce books; rather, he produced men and women who completely transformed themselves and the society around them.

291 Bukhārī, *k. al-Riqāq, b. Mā jā'a fī al-riqāq wa an lā ʿaysh illah ʿaysh al-ākhirah*, 6412

292 al-Bayhaqī, *Shuʿab al-Īmān*, 7:3319

293 Bukhārī, *k. al-aymān wa al-nudhūr, b. Ithm man lā yafī bi al-nadhr*, 6695

HADITH 41

In the Footsteps of the Prophet ﷺ

عَنْ أَبِي مُحَمَّدٍ عَبْدِ اللَّهِ بْنِ عَمْرِو بْنِ الْعَاصِ رَضِيَ اللَّهُ عَنْهُمَا، قَالَ: قَالَ رَسُولُ اللَّهِ صلى الله عليه و سلم "لَا يُؤْمِنُ أَحَدُكُمْ حَتَّى يَكُونَ هَوَاهُ تَبَعًا لِمَا جِئْتُ بِهِ".

حَدِيثٌ حَسَنٌ صَحِيحٌ، رَوَيْنَاهُ فِي كِتَابِ "الْحُجَّةِ" بِإِسْنَادٍ صَحِيحٍ.

From Abū Muḥammad ʿAbdullah ibn ʿAmr bin al-ʿĀṣ ﷺ who said that the Messenger of Allah ﷺ said, "None of you [truly] believes until his desires are subservient to that which I have brought."

We have related it in Kitāb al-Ḥujjah with an authentic chain of narrators.

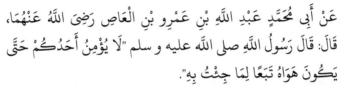

IMPORTANCE

In this ḥadīth the Prophet ﷺ is clarifying an extremely important aspect of one's īmān. In order for a person to be a true and complete believer their desires have to become subservient to revelation as taught by the Prophet ﷺ. In just a few words the Prophet ﷺ encompassed the meanings of true submission, devotion, and obedience; what it truly means to submit to the will of Allah ﷻ.

EXPLANATION

The Prophet ﷺ is explaining that in order for a person to be a complete believer, their ambitions, desires, and goals have to match with what is pleasing to Allah ﷻ and His Messenger ﷺ. Desires are a very powerful force that can lead and pull an individual in several directions. Part of faith is to learn how to control those desires and act upon them within the boundaries and limits set by Allah ﷻ and the Prophet ﷺ. A person's desires must be subservient to the rules and regulations of Allah ﷻ and His Messenger ﷺ. The way to reach this state is by subduing one's lower self from acting upon impulses that are in violation of Allah's rules and to patiently persevere in fulfilling the commands of Allah ﷻ and staying away from His prohibitions.

Imām al-Nawawī رحمه الله said that this means that a person must measure their deeds against the Quran and Sunnah, oppose their own desires, and follow everything that the Prophet ﷺ conveyed. A true believer is happy to obey Allah ﷻ and careful about doing it the right way. Anyone who claims to love Allah ﷻ and the Prophet ﷺ, yet doesn't obey Allah ﷻ or follow the Sunnah of the Prophet ﷺ, is not only telling a lie, but also exposing the weakness of their faith.

LESSONS AND BENEFITS

1. COMPLETE BELIEVER

Islam is not simply a slogan or a claim. When a person enters into the fold of Islam their entire being - heart, tongue, limbs, intellect, internal, and external - submits to Allah ﷻ in devotion, obedience, and servitude. There has to be congruence between a person's internal and external state.

2. *CONTROLLING DESIRES*

Allah has created human beings with certain innate and natural desires; the two most powerful being the desires associated with food and drink and intimacy. That is one of the reasons why the Prophet said, "Whoever can guarantee (the chastity of) what is between his two jaw-bones and what is between his two legs (i.e. his tongue and his private parts), I guarantee Paradise for him."[294] Islam doesn't require one to completely surpress their desires; rather, it provides guidance on how to control them and fulfill them withing the bounds of the Sharīʿah. Allah says, "Do not follow your desires, lest they divert you from God's path: those who wander from His path will have a painful torment because they ignore the Day of Reckoning."[295] The Prophet said, "The clever person is the one who subjugates his soul, and works for what is after death. And the incapable is the one who follows his desires and merely hopes in Allah."[296]

That is why it is so important to strive and struggle against one's soul, avoid temptations, and subjugate one's desires. The Prophet described one who struggles against their soul as a mujāhid. Allah praises them saying, "As for the one who feared standing before their Lord and restrained their soul from following desire, then, truly Paradise will be their home."[297]

3. *LOVE OF ALLAH AND HIS MESSENGER*

A very important aspect of one's faith is to love Allah and His Messenger. As a matter of fact, Allah and His Messenger should be more beloved to a person than anyone or anything else in this world. The basis and foundation of one's relationship with their Lord and the Prophet is love. Allah says in Sūrah al-Tawbah, "Say [Prophet], 'If your fathers, sons, brothers, wives, tribes, the wealth you have acquired, the trade which you fear will decline, and the dwellings you love are dearer to you than God and His Messenger and the struggle in His cause, then wait until God brings about His punishment.' God does not guide those who break away."[298]

---

294 Bukhārī, *k. al-Riqāq, b. Hifẓ al-lisān*, 6474

295 38:26 - وَلَا تَتَّبِعِ الْهَوَىٰ فَيُضِلَّكَ عَن سَبِيلِ اللَّهِ ۚ إِنَّ الَّذِينَ يَضِلُّونَ عَن سَبِيلِ اللَّهِ لَهُمْ عَذَابٌ شَدِيدٌ بِمَا نَسُوا يَوْمَ الْحِسَابِ

296 Tirmidhī, *k. Ṣifah al-qiyāmah wa al-riqāq wa al-warʿ ʿan rasūlillah*, 2459

297 79: 41-42 - وَأَمَّا مَنْ خَافَ مَقَامَ رَبِّهِ وَنَهَى النَّفْسَ عَنِ الْهَوَىٰ فَإِنَّ الْجَنَّةَ هِيَ الْمَأْوَىٰ

298 9:24 - قُلْ إِن كَانَ آبَاؤُكُمْ وَأَبْنَاؤُكُمْ وَإِخْوَانُكُمْ وَأَزْوَاجُكُمْ وَعَشِيرَتُكُمْ وَأَمْوَالٌ اقْتَرَفْتُمُوهَا وَتِجَارَةٌ تَخْشَوْنَ كَسَادَهَا وَمَسَاكِنُ تَرْضَوْنَهَا أَحَبَّ إِلَيْكُم مِّنَ اللَّهِ وَرَسُولِهِ وَجِهَادٍ فِي سَبِيلِهِ فَتَرَبَّصُوا حَتَّىٰ يَأْتِيَ اللَّهُ بِأَمْرِهِ ۗ وَاللَّهُ لَا يَهْدِي الْقَوْمَ الْفَاسِقِينَ

This particular verse of Sūrah al-Tawbah was revealed about those people who didn't migrate from Makkah to Madinah when it was made mandatory upon them. When migration was made mandatory, it wasn't a simple matter of obligation; rather it was a hallmark and symbol of being a Muslim. Anyone who didn't migrate at that time, even though they had the ability to do so, wasn't considered a Muslim. Their love for their family, wealth, property and fear stopped them from fulfilling this difficult obligation. Allah ﷻ asked His Prophet ﷺ to tell them that if all of these relationships and all of these material things are worth more to them, are more beloved to them, are more dear to them than Allah ﷻ and His Messenger ﷺ, more specifically obeying Allah ﷻ and His Messenger ﷺ, then they should wait for the command of Allah ﷻ to come. This verse was a direct warning to these people that the love of other things, particularly material things, should never come between them and their obedience of Allah ﷻ and His Messenger ﷺ.

Having love for all of these things, particularly the eight mentioned in this verse, is natural. It's natural to love one's parents, children, siblings, spouses, clan, wealth (it's the result of our hard work and effort), business, and homes. However, there is a limit or an extent to how much one should love these things. Although a person's love for these things is so strong and natural, something that Allah ﷻ made intrinsic within humans, He still commands them to love Him and His Messenger ﷺ even more. Allah ﷻ is the One who has given humanity all of these things. He is the One who bestowed all of these blessings upon them. He is the ultimate source of every single blessing and favor in this universe.

As for the Prophet ﷺ, he is a mercy for the entire world. Through the grace of Allah ﷻ he saved humanity at large from misguidance, brought them from darkness to light, from disbelief to belief. He is the best example for all of humanity in every single thing that he said or did. He is the best person to ever set foot on the face of this earth. He is the most beloved and closest to Allah ﷻ. He is the leader of the Prophets and the last and final Messenger. When love for these things compete with a person's relationship with Allah ﷻ and His Messenger ﷺ, then their relationship with Allah ﷻ and His Messenger ﷺ has to be given precedence.

There is a principle of tafsīr that states, "that which is given consideration is the generality of the wording not the specificity of the cause."[299]

---

299 al-Suyūṭī, Jalāl al-Dīn, *al-Itqān fī 'Ulūm al-Quran.*

Meaning, that although this verse was revealed to a specific group of people, the rulings, morals, and lessons are applicable to every single Muslim. This verse is conveying the obligatory nature of loving Allah ﷻ and the Prophet ﷺ.

Not only is it obligatory but it is also a part of faith. The Prophet ﷺ said, "Whoever possesses three characteristics has found the sweetness of īmān."[300] The first thing he mentioned is that Allah ﷻ and His Messenger ﷺ are more beloved to a person than anything else in this world. In another narration the Prophet ﷺ said, "None of you truly believes until I am more beloved to him than his father, child, and all of humanity."[301] Meaning in order for a person to be a true believer, in order for their faith to be complete, they have to love the Prophet ﷺ more than anything else in this world.

300 Bukhārī, *k. al-īmān, b. Ḥalāwah al-īmān*, 16

301 Muslim, *k. al-īmān, b. Wujūb maḥabbah rasūlillah akthara min al-ahl wa al-walad wa al-wālid wa al-nās ajmaʿīn*, 44

HADITH 42

Forgiveness

عَنْ أَنَسِ بْنِ مَالِكٍ رَضِيَ اللَّهُ عَنْهُ قَالَ: سَمِعْتُ رَسُولَ اللَّهِ صلى الله عليه و سلم يَقُولُ: قَالَ اللَّهُ تَعَالَى: "يَا ابْنَ آدَمَ! إِنَّكَ مَا دَعَوْتَنِي وَرَجَوْتَنِي غَفَرْتُ لَكَ عَلَى مَا كَانَ مِنْكَ وَلَا أُبَالِي، يَا ابْنَ آدَمَ! لَوْ بَلَغَتْ ذُنُوبُكَ عَنَانَ السَّمَاءِ ثُمَّ اسْتَغْفَرْتَنِي غَفَرْتُ لَكَ، يَا ابْنَ آدَمَ! إِنَّكَ لَوْ أَتَيْتَنِي بِقُرَابِ الْأَرْضِ خَطَايَا ثُمَّ لَقِيتَنِي لَا تُشْرِكُ بِي شَيْئًا لَأَتَيْتُكَ بِقُرَابِهَا مَغْفِرَةً".

رَوَاهُ التِّرْمِذِيُّ، وَقَالَ: حَدِيثٌ حَسَنٌ صَحِيحٌ.

From Anas ﷺ who said that I heard the Messenger of Allah ﷺ say, "Allah the Almighty has said: 'O Son of Adam, as long as you invoke Me and ask of Me, I shall forgive you for what you have done, and I shall not mind. O Son of Adam, were your sins to reach the clouds of the sky and you then asked forgiveness from Me, I would forgive you. O Son of Adam, were you to come to Me with sins nearly as great as the Earth, and were you then to face Me, ascribing no partner to Me, I would bring you forgiveness nearly as great as it [too].'"

It was related by al-Tirmidhī, who said that it was a ḥasan ḥadīth.

IMPORTANCE

This particular ḥadīth is also classified as a ḥadīth qudsī. The words are the words of the Prophet ﷺ, but the meaning is inspired directly from Allah ﷻ. This particular ḥadīth is extremely beautiful and profound. It has a very powerful impact on a person's relationship with Allah ﷻ. It helps them understand the magnitude of the mercy, forgiveness, and grace of Allah ﷻ; it creates an immense sense of hope. It helps them understand that no matter how much they've sinned before, no matter what they've done in the past, no matter how bad or ugly their actions were, they can still earn forgiveness from Allah ﷻ, the Most Merciful of those who are merciful. It helps them recognize and internalize the verse of Allah, "Say (on My behalf), "O servants of Mine who have acted recklessly against their own selves, do not despair of Allah's mercy. Surely, Allah will forgive all sins. Surely, He is the One who is the Most-Forgiving, the Very-Merciful."[302]

EXPLANATION

The narration starts by Allah ﷻ addressing each and every single human being directly, "O son of Adam!" This is done in order to ensure that everyone is listening carefully and attentively. Allah ﷻ then describes three separate scenarios and situations, all which result in mercy and forgiveness.

The first is, "As long as you call upon Me and put your hope in Me, I shall forgive you for what you have done, and I shall not mind." Allah ﷻ is telling His servants that one of the ways of earning His forgiveness is through supplication and hope; duʿā and rajā.

Duʿā, supplication, calling upon Allah ﷻ, is one of the absolute most powerful tools that a believer has. The Prophet ﷺ said, "Dua is the weapon of the believer."[303] It is a direct line of communication between a believer and their Lord and Creator. It is considered to be the essence or epitome of worship. When a person raises their hands in supplication to Allah ﷻ it shows that they recognize the reality of their relationship with Him. They recognize that they are His servants and that He is their Lord and Creator. They acknowledge and admit that they don't have the power, ability, or capability to do anything without the help and assistance of Allah ﷻ. By supplicating to Allah ﷻ they are fulfilling their obligation of calling upon Him. And the beautiful thing is that when they call upon Him, He answers. Allah ﷻ says, "And your Lord says call upon me and I will respond to you."[304] Similarly, in Surah al-Baqarah Allah ﷻ says, "[Prophet], if My servants ask you about Me, I am near. I respond to those who call Me, so let them respond to Me, and believe in Me, so that they may be guided."[305] When a person frequently calls upon Allah ﷻ it shows that they have firm faith and a strong relationship with their Lord and Creator.

Hope means that a person has a positive attitude in terms of their relationship with Allah ﷻ; that they are optimistic. They have hope in His infinite forgiveness, mercy, grace, bounty, and reward. At the same time they balance that hope with a sense of fear; they fear His anger, displeasure, and his punishment. This balance between hope and fear is the reality of īmān. It is also how one expresses their love for Allah ﷻ. If a person maintains these two things, supplication and hope, then Allah ﷻ says, "I shall forgive you for what you have done, and I shall not mind."

The second scenario described in this ḥadīth is one in which a person has sinned so much that if they were to be piled up they would reach the clouds. "O Son of Adam, were your sins to reach the clouds of the sky and you then asked forgiveness from Me, I would forgive you." No matter how great or how many sins a person has committed, they can never be greater than the forgiveness and mercy of al-Raḥmān, al-Raḥīm, and al-Ghafūr. A person simply has to turn back to Allah ﷻ and ask for His forgiveness. They have to humble themselves, acknowledge their faults, confess their sins to Allah ﷻ, and simply ask Him for forgiveness. Allah ﷻ says in Sūrah al-Nisā, "Whoever acts evil or wrongs himself, then seeks forgiveness from Allah, shall find Allah Most-Forgiving, Very-Merciful."[306] Similarly, Allah ﷻ tells His servants to ask for His forgiveness: "And seek Allah's forgiveness. Truly Allah is forgiving merciful."

Seeking forgiveness, actually turning to Allah ﷻ, and asking Him to forgive sins is a very humbling and empowering experience. It requires one to humble themselves, acknowledge their mistakes, and actually ask for forgiveness. This simple, yet powerful act, can have a profound impact on a person's mindset and attitude. Perhaps that is one of the reasons why the Proph-

---

304 40:60 - وَقَالَ رَبُّكُمُ ادْعُونِي أَسْتَجِبْ لَكُمْ

305 2:186 - وَإِذَا سَأَلَكَ عِبَادِي عَنِّي فَإِنِّي قَرِيبٌ ۖ أُجِيبُ دَعْوَةَ الدَّاعِ إِذَا دَعَانِ ۖ فَلْيَسْتَجِيبُوا لِي وَلْيُؤْمِنُوا بِي لَعَلَّهُمْ يَرْشُدُونَ

306 4:110 - وَمَن يَعْمَلْ سُوءًا أَوْ يَظْلِمْ نَفْسَهُ ثُمَّ يَسْتَغْفِرِ اللَّهَ يَجِدِ اللَّهَ غَفُورًا رَّحِيمًا

et ﷺ taught his followers to seek forgiveness from Allah ﷻ 100 times a day.

The third scenario described in this ḥadīth is that a person comes to Allah ﷻ with an earthful of sins. Meaning, they have sinned so much that the amount of their sins would fill the entire earth. Allah says, "O Son of Adam, if you were to come to Me with sins that are close to filling the Earth, and then you were to meet Me without associating any partners with Me, I would bring you forgiveness nearly as great as it [too]." Meaning, if a person meets Allah ﷻ with pure tawḥīd on the Day of Judgment, Allah ﷻ through His infinite grace and mercy will forgive their sins.

LESSONS AND BENEFITS

1. IMPORTANCE OF TAWBAH

Every single human being is in great need of the mercy and forgiveness of Allah ﷻ. Everyone is guilty of some sort of mistake, sin, poor choice, or act of disobedience. There is no such thing as a perfect human being. Everyone has their own faults, shortcomings, and weaknesses. The pull of the world, the dunya, temptations, desires, and wants is extremely powerful. The struggle is real. The Prophet ﷺ even said, "Every single son of Adam is a profuse wrongdoer. And the best of profuse wrongdoers are those who repent frequently."[307] Meaning, not only do people sin, but they sin a lot. People sin publicly and privately, knowingly and unknowingly, big and small.

Although a person may not initially recognize it, these sins have a huge effect upon one's heart. The Messenger of Allah ﷺ said: "Verily, when the slave (of Allah) commits a sin, a black spot appears on his heart. When he refrains from it, seeks forgiveness and repents, his heart is polished clean. But if he returns, it increases until it covers his entire heart. And that is the 'Rān' which Allah mentioned: 'Nay, but on their hearts is the Rān which they used to earn.'"[308]

Allah ﷻ says, "O you who have believed, repent to Allah with sincere repentance. Perhaps your Lord will remove from you your misdeeds and admit you into gardens beneath which rivers flow [on] the Day when Allah will not disgrace the Prophet and those who believed with him. Their light will

---

307 Tirmidhī, *k. ṣifah al-qiyāmah wa al-riqāq wa al-war' ʿan rasūlillah*, 2499

308 Tirmidhī, *k. tafsīr al-Quran ʿan rasūlillah*, 3334

proceed before them and on their right; they will say, 'Our Lord, perfect for us our light and forgive us. Indeed, You are over all things competent.'"[309] Allah ﷻ loves those who turn to Him in repentance. "Indeed, Allah loves those who are constantly repentant and loves those who purify themselves."[310] Repentance is extremely powerful; it removes one's sins. The Prophet ﷺ said, "One who repents from sin is like one who has no sin at all."[311]

---

309 66:8 - يا أَيُّهَا الَّذِينَ آمَنُوا تُوبُوا إِلَى اللَّهِ تَوْبَةً نَّصُوحًا عَسَىٰ رَبُّكُمْ أَن يُكَفِّرَ عَنكُمْ سَيِّئَاتِكُمْ وَيُدْخِلَكُمْ جَنَّاتٍ تَجْرِي مِن تَحْتِهَا الْأَنْهَارُ يَوْمَ لَا يُخْزِي اللَّهُ النَّبِيَّ وَالَّذِينَ آمَنُوا مَعَهُ ۖ نُورُهُمْ يَسْعَىٰ بَيْنَ أَيْدِيهِمْ وَبِأَيْمَانِهِمْ يَقُولُونَ رَبَّنَا أَتْمِمْ لَنَا نُورَنَا وَاغْفِرْ لَنَا ۖ إِنَّكَ عَلَىٰ كُلِّ شَيْءٍ قَدِيرٌ

310 2:222 - إِنَّ اللَّهَ يُحِبُّ التَّوَّابِينَ وَيُحِبُّ الْمُتَطَهِّرِينَ

311 al-Bayhaqī, *Shuʿab al-Īmān*, 6780

Concluding Remarks

Through the grace and mercy of Allah ﷻ, we have journeyed through 42 extremely important narrations from the Prophet ﷺ benefitting from his knowledge, wisdom, guidance, counsel, advice, and light. As mentioned in the introduction, Imām al-Nawawī ؒ selected these narrations because he felt that they covered the most fundamental aspects of our belief and practice. Through these narrations, we learned about our most important beliefs, devotional practices, morals, values, ethics, principles, manners, and etiquettes. He writes in the introduction of his blessed collection, "Everyone who desires and looks forward to the Hereafter must be familiar with these aḥādīth because they cover the most important aspects of the religion and offer direction to all forms of obedience of Allah ﷻ. This is clear to anyone who ponders these aḥādīth."

Now that we have read and understood these amazing narrations it is our responsibility to put them into practice. Knowledge is meant to be transformative. Within our tradition, learning is not simply an academic endeavor; it is not done simply to acquire information. The purpose of knowledge is to internalize it and act upon it so that we can draw nearer to our Lord and Creator. Beneficial knowledge is knowledge that translates into action, increasing one's love for Allah ﷻ and His Messenger ﷺ.

May Allah ﷻ grant all of us the ability to act upon what we learn and allow us to follow in the footsteps of our beloved Prophet and Messenger, the Leader of all Prophets and Messengers, the Seal of Prophethood, the Mercy for the worlds, Muḥammad ﷺ.

Bibliography

- al-ʿAsqalānī, ibn Ḥajar. Sharḥ al-Arbaʿīn al-Nawawiyyah. Jordan: Dār al-Fatḥ, 2015
- al-Bayhaqī, Aḥmad ibn Ḥusain. Shuʿab al-Īmān. Beirut: Dār al-Kutub al-ʿIlmiyyah, 2008
- al-Bughā, Muṣṭafā and Mistū, Muḥy al-Dīn. al-Wāfī fī Sharḥ al-Arbaʿīn al-Nawawiyyah. Beirut: Dār ibn Kathīr, 2007
- al-Bukhārī, Muḥammad b. Ismāʿīl. al-Jāmiʿ al-Ṣaḥīḥ. Cited by chapter, subchapter system.
- al-Fayrūzābādī, Muḥammad ibn Yaʿqūb. Baṣā'ir dhawi al-Tamyīz fī Laṭā'if al-Kitāb al-ʿAzīz. Cairo: Wizārah al-Awqāf, 1996
- al-Ḥākim, Muḥammad b. ʿAbdallah al-Naysāburi. al-Mustadrak ʿalā al-Ṣaḥiḥayn. Beirut: Dār al-Kutub al-ʿIlmiyyah, 1990
- al-Haythamī, ʾAlī ibn Abī Bakr. Majmaʿ al-Zawā'id. Beirut: Dār al-Minhāj, 2015
- al-Jawziyyah, ibn al-Qayyim. Madārij al-Sālikīn. KSA: Dār al-Ṣumayʿī, 2017
- al-Muḥāsibī, al-Ḥārith ibn Asad. Risālah al-Mustarshidīn. Beirut: Dār al-Bashā'ir al-Islāmiyyah, 2005
- al-Munāwī, ʿAbd al-Ra'ūf. al-Tawqīf ʿalā Muhimmāt al-Taʿārīf. Cairo: ʿĀlam al-Kutub, 1990
- al-Mundhirī, ʿAbd al-ʿAẓīm. al-Targhīb wa al-Tarhīb. Dār ibn Rajab, 2003

- al-Nasā'ī, Ahmad b. Shu'ayb. Sunan. Cited by chapter, subchapter system.
- al-Qārī, Mullā ʿAlī. Mirqāt al-Mafātīḥ. Beirut: Dār al-Kutub al-ʿIlmiyyah, 2001
- al-Qārī, Mullā ʿAlī. al-Mubīn al-Muʿīn li fahm al-Arbaʿīn al-Nawawiyyah. KSA: Dār al-ʿĀṣima, 2014
- al-Sijistāni, Abū Dāwūd. Al-Sunan. Cited by chapter, subchapter system.
- al-Suyūṭī, Jalāl al-Dīn. Al-Itqān fī 'ulūm al-Qurʾān. Beirut: Al-Maktabah Al- 'Asriyyah, 2006
- al-Tirmidhī, Muḥammad b. 'īsā. Al-Jāmi'. Cited by chapter, subchapter system.
- al-ʿUthaymīn, Muḥammad ibn Ṣāliḥ. Sharḥ al-Arbaʿīn al-Nawawiyyah. KSA: Dār al-Thurayyā, 2003
- Brown, Jonathan. Hadith: Muhammad's Legacy in the Medieval and Modern World. Oneworld Academic, 2018
- ibn al-Ḥajjāj, Muslim. Ṣaḥīḥ Muslim. Cited by chapter, subchapter system.
- Ibn Kathīr, Abū al-Fidā'a. al-Bidāyah wa al-Nihāyah. Beirut: Dār al-Kutub al-ʿIlmiyyah, 1994
- ibn Rajab, ʿAbd al-Raḥmān ibn Aḥmad. Jāmiʿ al-ʿUlūm wa al-Ḥikam. Beirut: Dār al-Kitāb al-ʿArabī, 2004
- Kamali, Hashim. Qawa'id al-Fiqh: The Legal Maxims of Islamic Law. The Association of Muslim Lawyers
- Zarabozo, Jamaal al-Din. Commentary on the Forty Hadith of al-Nawawi. al-Basheer Company for Publications and Translations, 1999

ABOUT THE AUTHOR

Shaykh Furhan Zubairi was born in 1983 in Indianapolis, IN. Shortly thereafter, he moved and spent most of his youth in Southern California, graduating from high school in Irvine in 2001. He began his pursuit of Islamic knowledge and spirituality at the Institute of Knowledge (IOK) in 1998 where he started the memorization of the Quran and studied the primary books in the Islamic sciences and Arabic language. After starting college, he took a break and went to Karachi, Pakistan for 9 months to complete the memorization of the Quran at Jamiʿah Binoria. He returned home and completed his B.S. in Biological Sciences from the University of California, Irvine in 2005. He then traveled to Egypt to further his studies of the Arabic language. Thereafter, his pursuit of Islamic knowledge led him back to Pakistan where he completed a formal 'Alamiyyah degree (Masters in Arabic and Islamic Studies) at the famous Jami'ah Darul-Uloom in Karachi, where he studied with prominent scholars. He has obtained numerous ijaazaat (traditional licenses) in the six authentic books of hadith Siha Sittah as well as the Muwattas of Imam Malik and Imam Muhammad and has also received certification in the field of Islamic Finance. Shaykh Furhan Zubairi serves as the Dean of the Seminary Program (IOKseminary.com) at the Institute of Knowledge in Diamond Bar, CA. He regularly delivers khutbahs and lectures at various Islamic Centers and events in Southern California.

The Institute of Knowledge Seminary Curriculum Series is a collection of books designed to build literacy amongst the Muslim community in the major branches of Islamic Studies including ʿAqīdah, Quran, Ḥadīth, Fiqh, Uṣūl al-Fiqh, Sīrah and Tazkiyah. The books go hand in hand with the with the courses offered through the IOK Seminary Program, which provides educational courses, programs and seminars to the wider local and international community.

Visit **IOKseminary.com** to learn more, view the full catalog and attend classes on-site, online and on-demand.

OTHER AVILABLE WORKS:

- An Introduction to the Sciences of the Qur'an
- Introduction to Ḥadīth Studies
- Introduction to Uṣūl al-Fiqh
- Hajj and Umrah: A Brief Guide

FORTHCOMING WORKS:

- Tafsīr of Surah al-Kahf
- A Brief Introduction to Tajwīd
- Tafsīr of Juz ʿAmma
- An Introduction to the Ḥanafī Madhab

Made in the USA
Las Vegas, NV
13 August 2024

93769594R00206